EXTRATERRITORIALITY:
Its Rise and Its Decline

STUDIES IN HISTORY, ECONOMICS AND PUBLIC LAW

EDITED BY THE FACULTY OF POLITICAL SCIENCE OF COLUMBIA UNIVERSITY

Volume CXVIII]   [Number 2

Whole Number 263

EXTRATERRITORIALITY:

Its Rise and Its Decline

BY

SHIH SHUN LIU

AMS PRESS
NEW YORK

COLUMBIA UNIVERSITY
STUDIES IN THE
SOCIAL SCIENCES

263

This Series was formerly known as
Studies in History, Economics and Public Law.

Reprinted with the permission of Columbia University Press
From the edition of 1925, New York
First AMS EDITION published 1969
Manufactured in the United States of America

Library of Congress Catalogue Card Number: 72-82238

AMS PRESS, INC.
NEW YORK, N. Y. 10003

PREFACE

THE present thesis is not an exhaustive treatise on the vastly complicated subject of extraterritoriality. It does not pretend to deal with the legal intricacies of this peculiar institution, on which numerous works of unsurpassable value and insight are in existence. All it attempts to do is to present briefly the historical development of the system of consular jurisdiction as a whole, to show how it arose, how it later grew in importance, and how finally it has in recent years declined. It is the author's firm conviction that most aspects of international law have or ought to have their *raison d'être* somewhere in the cumulative experience of centuries gone by, and his belief seems to be borne out by the history of extraterritoriality. Though the latter is an institution essentially incompatible with modern conceptions of territorial sovereignty, on which the science of international law is founded, the story of its rise and decline will nevertheless serve to demonstrate the continuity of legal development.

In making this study, the attitude adopted by the author is one of impartial investigation. His sole obligation is to bring to the light of day all the salient facts connected with the rise and decline of extraterritoriality, and to draw such conclusions as the facts warrant. He advocates nothing, and suggests nothing. He presents no practical solution of the as yet unsettled problems arising out of the existence of extraterritoriality, but he has sought to furnish the background of historical fact, which is the first condition to a philosophical as well as a practical approach to these problems.

287]

As to the material used, the author has relied chiefly upon the treaties, diplomatic correspondence and other state papers published from the archives of the leading countries of the world. Secondary works have been employed only as clues to the sources, and many of them have been of unusual assistance to the author. Such works as Miltitz's *Manuel des consuls* and Martens's *Das Consularwesen und die Consularjurisdiction im Orient* are indispensable aids to every student of the development of the consular office. The author's indebtedness to them can hardly be measured by the references made in the body of the thesis.

This monograph was written under a Fellowship awarded by the Carnegie Endowment for International Peace. Part of the manuscript was submitted to the criticism of Professor John Bassett Moore, whose example and inspiration have not infrequently kept the author from faltering in the face of the innumerable obstacles confronting a research student at every step. Professor Moore's retirement from Columbia University left the author to finish his work with Dr. Julius Goebel, Jr., to whom he is under the heaviest obligations. Dr. Goebel has not only read and re-read the manuscript with the care of a discerning scholar, but has suggested many alterations and emendations, which have added much to the work. Acknowledgment should also be made of the assistance rendered by Mr. Edward R. Hardy in reading some difficult mediaeval documents. To Dr. Edward M. Earle, of the Department of History, who read the sections on the Near East, the author is indebted for a number of helpful hints and suggestions. Finally, thanks are due to Chang Wei Chiu, a fellow student as well as a close friend, for assistance in proofreading.

Shih Shun Liu

Columbia University
New York City
March, 1925.

CONTENTS

CHAPTER II

In the Levant Prior to 1453

CHAPTER III

In the Levant and Africa After 1453

CHAPTER IV

In the Far East

PART II

THE DECLINE OF EXTRATERRITORIALITY

CHAPTER V

ANNEXATION

CHAPTER VI

TRANSFER OF JURISDICTION

CHAPTER VII

CHAPTER VIII

PROTECTION

CHAPTER IX

UNILATERAL CANCELLATION

CHAPTER X

Diplomatic Negotiation

INTRODUCTION

IT is a recognized principle of modern international law that every independent and sovereign State possesses absolute and exclusive jurisdiction over all persons and things within its own territorial limits. This jurisdiction is not qualified by differences of nationality, and extends to the persons and property of subjects and foreigners alike.[1] Nowhere is this principle of territorial jurisdiction more effectively pronounced than in the case of *The Schooner Exchange* v. *M'Faddon & Others,* where Chief Justice Marshall gave his opinion in this oft quoted passage:

The jurisdiction of the nation within its own territory is necessarily exclusive and absolute. It is susceptible of no limitation not imposed by itself. Any restriction upon it, deriving validity from an external source, would imply a diminution of its own sovereignty to the extent of the restriction, and an investment of that sovereignty to the same extent in that power which could impose such restrictions. All exceptions, therefore, to the full and complete power of a nation within its own territories, must be traced up to the consent of the nation itself. They can flow from no other legitimate source.[2]

In this passage due allowance is made for the limitations upon the main principle; and in practice there are a number of well-known exceptions to the general rule.[3] One of the

---

[1] Hall, *A Treatise on International Law* (7th ed., Oxford, 1917), p. 49; Phillimore, *Commentaries upon International Law* (3rd ed., London, 1879-89), vol. i, p. 443.

[2] 7 Cranch 116, 136.

[3] For the immunities of foreign sovereigns, diplomatic agents, military

most important of these exceptions is the system of extra-territoriality.

The word " extraterritoriality " is often used interchange-ably with the word " exterritoriality " to denote the special status of foreign ambassadors, who enjoy the right of ex-emption from the local jurisdiction. By a confusion of ideas, the persons to whom this immunity is attached are deemed to be legally removed from the territory in which they actually reside,[1] and consequently, it has been main-tained by some writers, foreign ambassadors may exercise civil and criminal jurisdiction over their suite.[2] This theory is now found to be inconsistent with the facts and is dis-carded by the most competent writers on international law. After discussing the extent and nature of the immunities

forces and public vessels, see Hall, *op. cit.,* pp. 179-209; Phillimore, *op. cit.,* vol. i, pp. 475-481, vol. ii, pp. 139, 140, 141; *The Schooner Exchange,* 7 Cranch 116. The whole system of private international law is an important exception to the exercise of territorial jurisdiction, but being founded in international comity and constituting, in fact, a part of municipal law, it does not fall within the province of public interna-tional law. See Phillimore, *op. cit.,* vol. iv, pp. 1 *et seq.;* Westlake, *A Treatise on Private International Law* (6th. ed., London, 1922), p. 1.

[1] Under the section " the rights of *exterritoriality* and inviolability," Lorimer says: " An English ambassador, with his family and his suite, whilst abroad in the public service, is domiciled in England, and his house is English ground." *Institutes of the Law of Nations* (Edinburgh & London, 1883-84), vol. i, p. 248. *Cf.* Wheaton, *Elements of Interna-tional Law* (Dana's edition, Boston, 1866), p. 300, where the American jurist says: " To give a more lively idea of this complete exemption from the local jurisdiction, the fiction of *extraterritoriality* has been invented, by which the minister, though actually in a foreign country, is supposed still to remain within the territory of his own sovereign."

[2] " It follows from the principle of the extra-territorality of the min-ister, his family, and other persons attached to the legation, or belong-ing to his suite, and their exemption from the local laws and jurisdic-tion of the country where they reside, that the civil and criminal juris-diction over these persons rests with the minister, to be exercised according to the laws and usages of his own country." Wheaton, *ibid.,* p. 302.

enjoyed by foreign ambassadors, etc., Hall declares that " it is clear that the fiction of exterritoriality is not needed to explain them, and even that its use is inconvenient." [1] For this reason, he has avoided the expression throughout his discussion of the subject. Today, the term " extraterritoriality " is generally employed to describe the condition of law existing in certain Oriental countries, under which foreigners are exempt from the local jurisdiction and are subject to their national authorities, by virtue of well-established usage or treaty arrangement.[2] In the present treatise, an attempt is made to examine into the rise and decline of the system of extraterritoriality in all the countries in which it has existed or still exists.

[1] *Op. cit.*, p. 210. *Cf.* Moore, *A Digest of International Law* (Washington, 1906), vol. ii, pp. 774-779.

[2] *Cf.* Moore, *ibid.*, p. 593: " Owing to diversities in law, custom, and social habits, the citizens and subjects of nations possessing European civilization enjoy in countries of non-European civilization, chiefly in the East, an extensive exemption from the operation of the local law. This exemption is termed ' extraterritoriality.' "

PART I
THE RISE OF EXTRATERRITORIALITY

CHAPTER I

In Europe

I. RELIGIOUS BASIS OF EARLY LAW

THE principle of territorial sovereignty as stated in the epoch-making opinion of Chief Justice Marshall in the case of *The Schooner Exchange* mentioned above was unknown in the ancient world. In fact, during a large part of what we usually term modern history, no such conception was ever entertained.[1] In the earlier stages of human development, race or nationality rather than territory formed the basis of a community of law. An identity of religious worship seems to have been during this period a necessary condition of a common system of legal rights and obligations. The barbarian was outside the pale of religion, and therefore incapable of amenability to the same jurisdiction to which the natives were subjected.[2] For this reason, we find that in the ancient world foreigners were either placed under a special jurisdiction or completely exempted from the local jurisdiction. In these arrangements for the safeguarding of foreign interests we find the earliest traces of extra-territoriality.

Under the reign of King Proteus of Egypt, in the thirteenth century, B. C., Phoenician merchants from the city of Tyre were allowed to dwell around a special precinct in Memphis known as the " camp of the Tyrians," and to have

[1] Maine, *Ancient Law* (3d Am. ed., New York, 1888), p. 99. *Cf.* Moore, *op. cit.*, vol. ii, p. 761.

[2] *Cf.* Twiss, *Law of Nations* (2d ed., Oxford, 1884), vol. i, p. 444.

a temple for their own worship.[1]   Seven centuries later,
King Amasis (570-526, B. C.) permitted the Greeks to establish a factory at Naucratis, where they might live as a
distinct community under their own laws and worshipping
their own gods.[2]   In his work on *The International Law
and Custom of Ancient Greece and Rome,* Dr. Coleman
Phillipson says: " The Egyptians often allowed foreign merchants to avail themselves of local judges of their own
nationality in order to regulate questions and settle differences arising out of mercantile transactions, in accordance
with their foreign laws and customs;—the Greeks especially
enjoyed these privileges on Egyptian territory." [3]

In Athens and in other Greek cities, the institution of
proxenia existed, the *proxenus* being appointed either by the
foreign government which he represented or by the State
in which he resided.[4]   The choice was made from among
the citizens of the latter State, and had to be approved by
them.[5]   The office of the *proxenus* was similar to the
modern consulate and is even regarded by some as its earliest
prototype.[6]   It is said that nearly all the Greek republics
had *proxenoi* in Egypt.[7]

[1] Herodotus, bk. ii, ch. 112. Sir Travers Twiss also mentions " that
the merchants of Tyre who were strangers to the religion of Egypt,
were nevertheless permitted in the Twelfth Century before Christ to
establish trading factories in three different cities on the Tanitic branch
of the Nile, where they were allowed the privilege of living under their
own laws, and of worshipping according to their own religious rites."
Op. cit., vol. i, p. 444.

[2] Herodotus, bk. ii, ch. 178.   *Cf.* Twiss, *op. cit.,* vol. i, p. 445;
Pardessus, *Collection de lois maritimes antérieures au XXVIIIe siècle*
(Paris, 1828-45), vol. i, p. 21.

[3] Vol. i, p. 193.

[4] Phillipson, *op. cit.,* vol. i, p. 150. The earliest evidence of the existence of *proxenoi* dates from the middle of the fifth century, *ibid.,* p. 148.

[5] Pardessus, *op. cit.,* vol. i, p. 52; Hautefeuille, *Histoire du droit maritime international* (2d ed., Paris, 1869), p. 96, n. 1.

[6] Phillipson, *op. cit.,* vol. i, p. 149; Miltitz, *Manuel des consuls* (London
and Berlin, 1837-41), vol. i, p. 11.

[7] Hautefeuille, *ibid.*

Of more interest to us is the special system of jurisdiction for foreigners, which, in ancient Greece and Rome, received its most remarkable development. On this, Dr. Phillipson says:

In Greece special magistrates ξενοδίκαι (a general term, for which special names were substituted in different localities), were instituted for trying questions in which foreigners were involved. Sometimes such magistrates were appointed on the initiative of the particular national government in question, sometimes provisions were arranged to that effect by means of special conventions between States. In some cases these judges exercised full judicial power in pronouncing decisions as to the matters in dispute, in others they appear to have merely investigated the points at issue, and submitted their results to the ordinary magistrates who were to deliver the final verdict.[1]

The writer goes on to enumerate instances of such special judges, all of which go to prove the immiscibility of the alien in the ancient world, so far as his judicial status was concerned.

Somewhat like the *xenodikai* in Greece was the Roman magistrate, *prætor peregrinus,* whose influence on the development of international law is universally recognized. The name of this officer, as it appears in the present form, is, according to Mommsen, an incorrect one, deriving its popularity from mere usage. The full title of the Roman magistrate designated by the abbreviated form *prætor peregrinus* was, under the Republic, *prætor qui inter peregrinos jus dicit,* and under the Empire, *prætor qui inter cives et peregrinos jus dicit.*[2] The office was established about 242 B. C., in addition to that of the *prætor urbanus,* which was already in existence. The competence of the peregrine

---

[1] *Op. cit.,* p. 192.

[2] Mommsen et Marquardt, *Manuel des antiquités romaines* (Paris, 1888-1907), vol. iii (Mommsen, *Le Droit public romain,* vol. iii), p. 225.

prætor, as his full title suggests, extended to disputes between peregrines and between them and Roman citizens.[1] The connotation of the word *peregrini* is described by Girard as follows :

The peregrines, *peregrini,* formerly *hostes,* were not, in developed Roman law, true foreigners. The most ancient of them were certainly foreigners bound to Rome by treaties. But the development of the Roman power made them, like the others, members of the Roman State. They were subjects of Rome, the free inhabitants of the empire, who were neither citizens nor Latins.[2]

Outside of the peregrines, the foreigners who did not maintain treaty relations with Rome enjoyed no legal protection and were not amenable to Roman justice.[3] It was the peregrines who were placed under the jurisdiction of the *prætor peregrinus,* and it was to them that he administered the *jus gentium,* for even the foreigners of allied nationality, who later became subjects of the Roman State, were not amenable to the *jus civile,* which was applicable to a very restricted number of Roman citizens and Latins.[4] With the extension of Roman citizenship to all the provincials of the Empire under Caracalla, in 212 A. D., however, the office of the *prætor peregrinus* disappeared from the judicial system of Rome.[5]

It is true that the *prætor peregrinus* of Roman times was merely a Roman officer administering the *jus gentium,* which

[1] *Ibid.,* p. 252.

[2] Girard, *Manuel élémentaire de droit romain* (6th ed., Paris, 1918), p. 113.

[3] Mommsen et Marquardt, *op. cit.,* vol. vi, pt. ii (Mommsen, *op. cit.,* vol. vi, pt. ii), p. 216.

[4] For the jurisdiction of the *prætor urbanus* over the Latins, see Mommsen, *op. cit.,* vol. vi, pt. ii, p. 221 ; Girard, *op. cit.,* p. 112.

[5] Mommsen et Marquardt, *op. cit.,* vol. iii, p. 260, n. 3.

was municipal law, to foreigners resident in Rome, and that his competence bears little or no resemblance to the modern system of extraterritoriality, under which the consul or other authority invested with the exercise of the jurisdiction, is appointed by the State which he represents and administers his national law. But the fact that the Romans made a discrimination against the subjects of non-treaty Powers and that even those of the treaty Powers were subjected to a special jurisdiction serves to show the extralegal status of the foreigner in ancient times, out of which most probably extraterritoriality drew its impetus in its early development.

The germs of extraterritoriality were, however, not entirely absent in the Roman Empire. In the first century of the Christian era, Emperor Claudius (41-54, A. D.) accorded to the merchants of Cadiz the privilege of choosing magistrates, who were given the jurisdiction of the tribunals established by Caesar in Baetice.[1] Under the rule of Justinian (483-565, A. D.), the Armenians were granted the benefit of the same laws on certain subjects as those by which the Romans were ruled; but questions of marriage, succession to property, and personal status generally, were left to be settled either by the Armenians themselves or by a magistrate named by the Emperor to administer Armenian law.[2]

II. THE MEDIAEVAL THEORY OF THE PERSONALITY OF LAWS

In the absence of any views of territorial sovereignty, there developed in mediaeval Europe a complete system of personal jurisdiction, which has left in its wake many interesting survivals extending to modern times, and which has undoubtedly exercised an immense influence upon the development of extraterritoriality. In the days which fol-

[1] Miltitz, *op. cit.*, vol. i, p. 15.
[2] Pears, *Fall of Constantinople* (New York, 1886), p. 148.

lowed the downfall of the Roman Empire, as in the days of
ancient Greece and Rome, but in a much more marked degree, racial consanguinity was treated as the sole basis of
amenability to law. Thus, in the same country—and even
in the same city at times—the Lombards lived under Lombard law, and the Romans under Roman law. This differ-
entiation of laws extended even to the various branches of
the Germanic invaders; the Goths, the Franks, the Burgun-
dians, each submitted to their own laws while resident in
the same country. Indeed, the system was so general that
in one of the tracts of the Bishop Agobard, it is said: " It
often happens that five men, each under a different law,
would be found walking or sitting together." [1]

As an example of the prevalence in mediaeval Europe of
the theory of the personality of laws, we may cite the retention of Roman law in the old provinces of Rome. Savigny
shows that in the Burgundian laws and in the Constitution
of Chlotar, the validity of Roman law in cases involving
Romans was fully recognized.[2]

In the same way, the principle of the personality of laws
was applied and carried out by the invaders themselves in
their relations with one another. The laws of the Visigoths
contain the remarkable provision that " when foreign merchants have disputes with one another, none of our judges
shall take cognizance, but they shall be decided by officers
of their nation and according to their laws." [3] Theodoric
the Great (493-525), the first of the Ostrogothic rulers,

---

[1] Savigny, *Geschichte des Römischen Rechts im Mittelalter* (Heidel-
berg, 1834-51), vol. i, p. 116.

[2] *Ibid.*, p. 126. *Cf.* Jenks, *Law and Politics in the Middle Ages* (London, 1913), p. 14.

[3] " *Dum transmarini negotiatores inter se causam habuerint, nullus de
sedibus nostris eos audire presumat, nisi tantummodo suis legibus
audiantur apud telonarios suos." Leges Visigoth.*, lib. xi, tit. iii, cap. ii,
Pardessus, *op. cit.*, vol. i, p. 152.

instituted special judges or courts (*comtes*) to decide litigations between Goths and, with the assistance of a Roman
jurisconsult, to decide cases between Goths and Romans.[1]
In the first half of the eighth century, the Lombards in
France were tried according to Lombard law and at least
partly by judges who were Alamanns, the latter having once
been Lombards and lived under Lombard law.[2]   The oldest
part of the *Lex Ribuaria* (tit. 31) is found to contain a
passage which ensures to the Frank, Burgundian, Alamann
or any other, the benefit of his own law.[3]   In the Capitu-
laries of Charlemagne and of Louis I, recognition was given
to the applicability of Roman and other foreign laws to
cases involving the respective foreign subjects.[4]

It is noteworthy that under the régime of personal jurisdiction, the law applied was that of the defendant, except
in cases of serious crime, in which the law of the injured
party or plaintiff prevailed.[5]   A connection might be established between this rule and the principle *actor sequitur
forum rei,* one of the basic formulae of modern extraterritorial jurisdiction, under which the plaintiff follows the
defendant into his court.

III. EARLY MARITIME CODES OF EUROPE

In the maritime codes of the European cities in the Middle
Ages, the influence of the principle of the personality of
laws was clearly discernible.   It is said that one of the
cardinal principles of the celebrated Hanseatic League was
the absolute independence of its members of all foreign
jurisdiction wherever they resided and traded.[6]   In the

[1] Miltitz, *op. cit.,* vol. i, p. 24.

[2] Savigny, *op. cit.,* vol. i, p. 124.

[3] Jenks, *op. cit.,* p. 16.

[4] Savigny, *op. cit.,* vol. i, p. 127.

[5] *Ibid.,* pp. 167-8.

[6] Pardessus, *op. cit.,* vol. ii, p. cxxvij.

twelfth century, Lübeck enjoyed such exemption in Wisby, and acquired the right to transfer the privilege to other cities.[1] From about the same time, the German merchants and other inhabitants of Wisby on the island of Gothland in the Baltic enjoyed similar privileges in the Republic of Novgorod in Russia.[2]

In the Statute of Gaeta, M. Pardessus finds a chapter on foreign consuls, which he dates back to the thirteenth century, where it is laid down that foreign consuls had sole jurisdiction over their nationals in all civil cases, and that their competence in such cases could not be transferred to any other authority.[3]

That the Amalfitan Tables provided for extraterritorial jurisdiction is evidenced by the fact that as early as 1190 the city of Amalfi was permitted to maintain consuls in the neighboring town of Naples to decide disputes between Amalfitan merchants.[4] Even in the fourteenth century, the maritime statute of Ancona, which bore the date of 1397, required all merchants of Ancona trading abroad to elect their own consuls and to submit to them their disputes, the penalty for resorting to any other tribunal being a fine of fifty pounds.[5]

Finally, in 1402, a Florentine consul resided at London. The statutes of that consulate, collected and approved in 1513, provided that the consul, assisted by two counsellors, should decide all contests between the subjects of the republic resident in England; those who resorted to any other court were liable to a pecuniary fine, and in order to bring those who were not subjects of the republic under its juris-

---

[1] *Ibid.*, pp. lxxxix, cxxvij.

[2] Miltitz, *op. cit.*, vol. i, pp. 401-408.

[3] Pardessus, *op. cit.*, vol. v, p. 230.

[4] *Ibid.*, vol. i, p. 144. The text of the Diploma of 1190 is reproduced in Miltitz, *op. cit.*, vol. ii, pt. i, p. 502.

[5] *Rubrique* xlviii, Pardessus, *op. cit.*, vol. v, pp. 160-161.

diction, the Florentines were forbidden, under severe penalty, to trade with any foreigner who did not engage to submit to the consul's jurisdiction and to appear before him.[1]

IV. PERSONALITY OF LAWS AND DIPLOMATIC ASYLUM

That the principle of the personality of laws bears a causal relationship to the development of extraterritoriality is further manifested by a very interesting bit of evidence. In his study of diplomatic asylum, Professor John Bassett Moore has traced this extraordinary privilege of ambassadors to the time when territorial sovereignty was unknown to the intercourse of nations.[2] He shows further that the decline of diplomatic asylum has been a slow process and that in the history of modern Europe survivals of the decaying institution have not been uncommon, the practice being especially enduring in Spain, where, as late as 1873, a political refugee was sheltered by the British Minister at Madrid.[3] Practically the same thing may be said of extraterritoriality. Its origin is attributable to the absence of absolute territorial sovereignty and the accompanying tradition of the personality of laws, while its survivals in Europe, as will be shown later in this chapter, are equally reminiscent of the tardiness of its decline. But what is most interesting of all is the fact that just as diplomatic asylum lingered longest in Spain, so were extraterritorial rights maintained there at a very late date. By the Capitulations of 1782[4] and 1799,[5] Spain granted reciprocal extraterri-

[1] Miltitz, *op. cit.*, vol. ii, pt. i, p. 152. *Cf.* Bonfils, *Manuel de droit international* (7th ed., Paris, 1914), § 737n.

[2] Moore, *op. cit.*, vol. ii, p. 761.

[3] *Ibid.*, pp. 766 *et seq.*, esp. p. 770.

[4] Art. 5: "....it shall be the same with regard to the subjects and merchants of the Ottoman Empire in the dominions of Spain." Noradounghian, *Recueil d'actes internationaux de l'Empire Ottoman* (Paris, 1897-1903), vol. i, p. 346.

[5] Art. 6, Martens, *Recueil des principaux traités* (Gottingue, 1791-1801), vol. vi, p. 585. *Cf. infra*, p. 64, n. 2.

torial jurisdiction respectively to the Ottoman Empire and Morocco, both of which, be it remembered, were Mohammedan Powers. These Capitulations thus throw overboard the theory that extraterritoriality was in any way intended to derogate from the sovereignty of the State granting it, inasmuch as the notion of territorial sovereignty was as yet unknown when extraterritoriality took its root.

V. THE OFFICE OF THE JUDGE-CONSUL

The development of commerce made necessary special organs to take charge of foreign interests. Before the advent of the foreign consul, the various States created offices which exercised administrative and judicial supervision over foreign residents within their confines. The office of the *prætor peregrinus* in Rome has been mentioned above.[1] During the reigns of Theodosius the Great (379-395) and of Honorius (395-423), magistrates were created and invested with the right to decide cases of accidents of the sea and of salvage.[2] But the period during which the development of these judge-consuls, as they were sometimes called, assumed real importance was in the Middle Ages. Between the tenth and thirteenth centuries, the French, Italian, and Spanish cities set up courts with authority to decide commercial disputes and with jurisdiction over resident foreign merchants.[3] The members of these courts were given the generic name "consuls" and were variously designated as *consules mercatorum, consuls des marchands, consuls de commerce, juge-consuls,* and *juges-conservateurs.*[4] At about the same time, the Hanseatic cities, though they did not have consular courts like those in the French,

---

[1] *Supra*, p. 25.

[2] Miltitz, *op. cit.*, vol. i, p. 160.

[3] *Ibid.*, pp. 162-175.

[4] *Ibid.*, p. 6.

Italian and Spanish cities, conferred upon their deputies in the diet the authority to decide all commercial and maritime questions. In 1447, the Hanseatic cities instituted a tribunal of commerce sitting at Lübeck, of which the President was known as the Alderman, his functions being similar to those of the judge-consul in the other countries.[1] The fact to be noted is that, of the functions of these magistrates, judicial competence was invariably a part. It is more than probable that the extraterritorial jurisdiction granted to the European consuls in the Levant was but an extension of the functions assumed by the judge-consuls at home.[2]

VI. THE FOREIGN CONSULATE IN MEDIAEVAL EUROPE

The Crusades, it will be seen later, afforded an effective medium for the transplantation of the system of judge-consuls. But in Europe itself, during the same period, the office of the foreign consul was generally invested with judicial functions.

The merchants of the Italian cities who traded in France were subject to the jurisdiction of special judges of their own nationality, called *Captains of the University of Lombard and Tuscan Merchants,* who decided all cases between them.[3] In 1277, a treaty concluded with the French established the Genoese at Nimes and granted to them the right to be judged by their *recteur* according to their own laws.[4]

---

[1] *Ibid.*, pp. 175-176.

[2] *Cf.* Martens, *Das Consularwesen und die Consularjurisdiction im Orient* (Berlin, 1874), p. 100; also Depping, *Histoire du Commerce entre le Levant et l'Europe* (Paris, 1830), vol. ii, p. 52, where the author says: " It is from a remote antiquity that there were, in all the States on the shores of the Mediterranean, courts of commerce, where nearly the same rules were followed. The consulates were nothing but courts of this nature transported to foreign countries."

[3] Miltitz, *op. cit.*, vol. ii, pt. i, p. 77.

[4] Vincens, *Histoire de la République de Gênes* (Paris, 1842), vol. i, p. 389.

In the act of privilege which Ferdinand III of Castile accorded in 1251 to the Genoese at Seville, it is stipulated that the latter should have consuls of their own nationality, with the right to decide without appeal, disputes between themselves.[1] In the history of Pisa, the consulate is known to have been maintained from the twelfth century onward under the name *consules maris,* with jurisdictional rights.[2]

An interesting treaty between Frederick II, Emperor and King of Sicily and Abbuissac, Prince of the Saracens of Africa, dated 1230, provided that in the island of Corsica there should be a Mohammedan consul or prefect to administer justice to the Mohammedan merchants residing there, although the consul should be established by the Emperor and administer justice in his name.[3]

The French cities likewise enjoyed rights of jurisdiction in Italy and in Spain.[4] The Aragonians in Seville were granted by King Alfonso I in 1282 the same rights as had been accorded previously to the Genoese in the same city.[5]

As has been seen, the Hanseatic League was particularly jealous of the right of its own members to be exempt from any foreign jurisdiction.[6] In actual practice, many efforts were made to secure the safeguard of this right. In Scania, which now belongs to Sweden, privileges were granted to the Hanseatic merchants in 1361 and 1368, including the right to choose from among themselves judges to decide their disputes according to the law of Lübeck.[7] By the peace of 1285, it was stipulated that disputes between Ger-

---

[1] Depping, *op. cit.,* vol. ii, p. 47.

[2] Pardessus, *op. cit.,* vol. iv, p. 557.

[3] Dumont, *Corps universel diplomatique* (Amsterdam, 1726-31), vol. i, pt. i, p. 168.

[4] Miltitz, *op. cit.,* vol. ii, pt. i, p. 203.

[5] *Ibid.,* p. 294.

[6] *Supra,* p. 29.

[7] Miltitz, *op. cit.,* vol. ii, pt. i, pp. 343-344.

mans in Norway were to be decided by their own judges.[1]
Even in England, King Edward IV granted to the merchants of Hansa the right to be judged by their own magistrates according to their own laws. The treaty of 1474
permitted the Hanseatic merchants in London to hold in
perpetuity their special community known as the Steelyard.
Cases of contract in which Englishmen proceeded against
Germans were to be heard before two specially appointed
English judges, and the same practice was to be observed
in Germany. Within the Steelyard, the merchants were to
have exclusive administration, and, what is more important,
they were completely freed from any judicial process em-
anating from the local authorities (*"Dampnis, Injuris,
Spoliationibus, Rapinis, Incarcerationibus, Arrestationibus
Personarum, Bonorum, & Mercandisarum . . . per viam
Facti, per viam Judici & Sententiae, seu Executionis . . .
absolvunt firmitir per praesentes"*). The special nature of
the privileges granted is indicated by the promise of King
Edward IV not to concede them to other foreigners.[2]

In England, the office of the foreign consul did not make
its appearance until the beginning of the fifteenth century.
But long before England sent consuls abroad to protect the
interests of her nationals, she had made efforts to safeguard
the security of foreign life and property within her own
borders. Even before the Hanseatic treaty of 1474, King
Edward I had issued his great Charter, in 1303, commonly
known as the *Carta Mercatoria*, which contained a provision
that in all cases, except those entailing the death penalty,
in which a foreign merchant was implicated, the jury to be
charged with the trial of the cause should be composed of
an equal number of foreign merchants and natives.[3] Al-

---

[1] *Ibid.*, p. 344.

[2] Rymer, *Foedera* (2nd ed., London, 1726-35), vol. ix, pp. 795, 796, 797.

[3] "6. Item, that in all maner of pleas, sauing in case where punish-

though the nature of the grant differed considerably from a concession of consular jurisdiction, it nevertheless throws some light on the general privileges enjoyed by the foreigner in the Middle Ages. Indeed, the institution of the mixed jury is so important that some writers have regarded it as the origin of the modern mixed court.[1]

In 1404, King Henry IV accorded to the merchants of England in the Hanseatic towns the power to choose a certain number of individuals to be known as " *Gubernatores mercatorum* " and to exercise, in the name of the King, judicial authority over their compatriots. The same power was conferred on English merchants in the Netherlands in 1406, and in Norway, Sweden and Denmark in 1408. In 1485, King Richard III bestowed upon one Lorenzo Strozzi the office of the consul in Italy, with power to decide disputes between the Englishmen resident there.[2] In the letters-patent issued to the consul, it was stated that in creating the office, the King had consulted the experience of other nations,[3] thereby showing the trend of international practice at the time. There is little doubt, therefore, that one of the most important and common functions of the consul during this period was his judicial competence.

ment of death is to be inflicted, where a marchant is impleaded, or sueth another, of what condition soeuer hee bee which is sued, whether stranger or home borne, in fayres, cities, or boroughs, where sufficient numbers of marchants of the foresayd countreis are, and where the triall ought to bee made, let the one halfe of the Iurie be of the sayd marchants, and the other halfe of good and lawfull men of the place where the suite shall fall out to bee: and if sufficient number of marchants of the sayd countries cannot bee found, those which shall be found fit in that place shall be put vpon the iurie, and the rest shall be chosen of good and fit men of the places where such suit shall chance to be." Hakluyt, *The Principal Navigations, Voyages, Traffiques, and Discoveries of the English Nation* (ed. by E. Goldsmid, Edinburgh, 1885-90), vol. i, p. 121.

[1] Lippmann, *Die Konsularjurisdiktion im Orient* (Leipzig, 1898), p. 10.

[2] Miltitz, *op. cit.*, vol. ii, pt. i, pp. 385-386.

[3] *Ibid.*, p. 385.

VII. MODERN SURVIVALS

During the sixteenth and seventeenth centuries, an era of dynastic and colonial rivalry set in. The discovery of America initiated among the more powerful maritime Powers of Europe the struggle for colonial possessions. The ascendancy of these Powers aided their assertion of an exclusive territorial sovereignty, until in 1648 the treaties making up the Peace of Westphalia accepted the latter as a fundamental principle of international intercourse. This development of territorial sovereignty was distinctly fatal to the existence of the system of consular jurisdiction, and facilitated considerably its decadence in Europe, because it was founded on the opposite theory of the personality of laws.

But even from this period some documents have been handed down, which show the persistence of consular jurisdiction in Europe. In the *Principal Navigations of the English Nation*, Hakluyt gives the text of " a copie of the first priuileges graunted by the Emperour of Russia to the English Marchants in the yeere 1555." Among the provisions of this document is the following remarkable article:

4. Item, we giue and graunt vnto the saide Marchants and their successours, that such person as is, or shalbe commended vnto vs, our heires or successours by the Gouernour, Consuls and assistants of the said fellowship residant within the citie of London within the realme of England, to be their chiefe Factor within this our empire and dominions, may and shal haue ful power and authoritie to gouerne and rule all Englishmen that haue had, or shall haue accesse, or repaire in or to this said Empire and iurisdictions, or any part thereof, and shal and may minister vnto them, and euery of them good iustice in all their causes, plaints, quarrels, and disorders betweene them moued, and to be moued, and assemble, deliberate, consult, conclude, define, determine, and make such actes, and ordinances, as he so commended with his associates shall thinke good and meete for the good order, gouernment and rule of the said

Marchants, and all other Englishmen repairing to this our saide empire or dominions, or any part thereof, and to set and leuie vpon all, and euery Englishman, offender or offenders, of such their acts and ordinances made, and to be made, penalties and mulcts by fine and imprisonment.[1]

The letters-patent granted by Francis II, King of France, in 1559, to the Swedish subjects trading within his territory recognized the right of the latter to be judged by their own magistrates in all differences that might arise among them, although in mixed cases of any sort they were placed under the jurisdiction of the local authorities.[2]

By the treaty of February 24, 1606, between Henry IV of France and James I of England, it was arranged that all commercial disputes involving nationals of one party in certain portions of the other should be heard and decided by a mixed tribunal, composed of four merchants, two French and two English.   In case they could not agree, they should choose a French merchant if it was in France, or an English merchant if it was in England, " so that the Judgment pass'd by the Plurality of Voices shall be follow'd and put in execution."   These merchant judges were to be known as " Conservators of Commerce," and in each country the two foreign Conservators were to be appointed by their Ambassador.[3]   Later, the system was altered in such a way that no foreign merchants were to have jurisdictional rights in either country, the ambassador or his deputy only being permitted to " assist at any Judgment and Trials whatsoever which concern the Goods and Life of a Subject of his Prince, and especially when a Definitive Judgment is to be made or pass'd." [4]

[1] Hakluyt, *op. cit.*, vol. iii, p. 99.

[2] Dumont, *op. cit.*, vol. v, pt. i, p. 61.

[3] Arts. 7, 8, 9, *A General Collection of Treatys* (London, 1732), vol. ii, pp. 150-151.

[4] Art. 43, *ibid.*, p. 175.

What is most remarkable, perhaps, is the treaty of September 24, 1631, between Louis XIII, Emperor of France, and Molei Elqualid, Emperor of Morocco, which contains terms of absolute reciprocity, so far as extraterritorial jurisdiction was concerned.[1] The most interesting provision of this document is article 9, which stipulates that the ambassador of the Emperor of Morocco in France and the ambassador or consul of France in Morocco should determine all disputes respectively between Moroccans in France and Frenchmen in Morocco.[2] In cases between Frenchmen and Moors, the local authorities on either side were alone competent,[3] and to make mutual intervention in territorial jurisdiction impossible, article 12 contains the admonition that all judgments and sentences given by the local authorities should be " validly executed " without interference on the part of the other contracting party.[4] Here, then, is a treaty of perfect equality and reciprocity between a Christian and a Mohammedan Power, bearing a strikingly modern date, which assures to the parties thereto reciprocal extraterritorial jurisdiction of a limited sort. The arrangement is all the more significant when it is remembered that France, of all the continental European Powers, was the first in which national sovereignty was most completely established and a systematic jurisprudence most fully developed.[5] It

[1] Dumont, *op. cit.*, vol. vi, pt. i, p. 20.

[2] " That if any difference should arise between the Moorish merchants who are in France, the Ambassador of the Emperor of Morocco residing in France shall terminate them, and the same shall be done by the Ambassador or Consul of France in Africa."

[3] Art. 10.

[4] " That all the judgments and sentences given by the Judges and Officers of the Emperor of Morocco [in disputes] between the subjects of His Christian Majesty and the subjects of the said Emperor, shall be validly executed, without any complaint to the Kingdom of France, and the same shall be practised between the subjects of Morocco and the Frenchmen in France."

[5] Moore, *op. cit.*, vol. ii, p. 762.

ought to go far to prove that the institution of extraterritoriality was not contrived, at the beginning at any rate, and for a long time in the modern period, to meet the special situation of a defective legal system in non-Christian Powers. The explanation must be sought, if anywhere, in the tradition of the personality of laws long prevalent in Europe.[1]

As late as the eighteenth century, a number of interesting survivals of the decadent jurisdiction of the consul invite our attention. It is noteworthy that in the treaty of January 23, 1721, between Great Britain and Morocco, a measure of extraterritorial jurisdiction was granted to the Moors in England.[2] This privilege was repeatedly renewed and confirmed by later treaties.[3]

In the treaty of 1740 between the Ottoman Empire and the Kingdom of the Two Sicilies, there is a reciprocal provision regarding the adjudication of cases arising between Sicilians in Turkey and between Turks in Sicily. According to article 5, these cases should be disposed of by their respective consuls according to their own laws and customs.

---

[1] In some of the peace treaties of the seventeenth century, provision was made for the remission of prize cases to the home courts of the defendant's nationality. See art. 32, Anglo-French treaty of 1604, *A General Collection of Treatys*, vol. ii, p. 145; art. 30, Anglo-Spanish treaty of Nov. 15, 1630, *ibid.*, p. 289; art. 23, Peace of the Pyrenees, Nov. 7, 1659, *ibid.*, vol. i, p. 49. In later treaties any provision of such a nature was conspicuously absent. See art. 27, Treaty of Nymeguen, Aug. 10, 1678, Dumont, *op. cit.*, vol. vii, pt. i, p. 360; art. 32, Treaty of Ryswik, Sep. 20, 1697, ibid., pt. ii, p. 289.

[2] Art. IX. "... and if any quarrel or dispute shall happen between Musselmen in England, or in any of the English Dominions, by which hurt may ensue, the same to be heard before 1 Christian and 1 Musselman, and to be determined according to the Laws of Great Britain." *British and Foreign State Papers* (hereafter referred to as *State Papers*), vol. i, p. 430.

[3] Art. 4, treaty of May 10, 1729; art. 4, Feb. 1, 1751; art. 9, July 28, 1760; art. 8, April 8, 1791; and art. 8, June 14, 1801. *Ibid.*, pp. 431, 435, 439, 447, 457.

[4] Noradounghian, *Recueil d'actes internationaux de l'empire ottoman* (Paris, 1897-1903), vol. i, p. 272.

The treaty of 1787 between France and Russia stipulated
that the consul of one or the other party might decide disputes between his nationals when they submitted to his
jurisdiction by mutual consent.[1]

Still more interesting is the treaty of 1788 between France
and the United States, article 12 of which provides:

All differences and suits between the subjects of the Most
Christian King in the United States, or between the citizens of
the United States within the dominions of the Most Christian
King . . . shall be determined by the respective Consuls and
Vice-Consuls, either by a reference to arbitrators, or by a summary judgment, and without costs. No officer of the country,
civil or military, shall interfere therein, or take any part whatever in the matter; and the appeals from the said consular sentences shall be carried before the tribunals of France or of the
United States, to whom it may appertain to take cognizance
thereof.[2]

In 1825, Sardinia and Morocco mutually engaged to permit consular intervention in cases which involved the subjects of either country in the other. The pertinent provision
is quoted below:

XXII. If, in the States of Morocco, disturbances should
arise between our subjects and subjects of Morocco, the difficulties shall be settled in equity and justice, for which purposes
our subjects may present themselves before the Court, assisted
by our Consul or other Consular official, or may be represented

---

[1] Art. 7, Martens, *Recueil de traités* (2nd ed., Gottingen, 1817-35), vol.
iv, p. 199.

[2] U. S. *Treaties, Conventions,* etc. (hereafter referred to as Malloy),
Washington, 1910, vol. i, p. 495. In *Villeneuve v. Barron,* it was held
that the consular jurisdiction of France did "not extend generally to
all differences and suits between Frenchmen." Moore, *op. cit.,* vol. ii,
p. 84. The convention of 1788 was abrogated by Act of Congress, July
7, 1798, Malloy, vol. i, p. 490 n.

by an attorney. Appeal from the decision, whether favorable
or otherwise, may be made to the Emperor.

On the other hand, should a question arise in our States,
it shall be determined by the competent authority in the presence of the Consul of Morocco, or his agent or attorney, and if
justice is not accorded, appeal shall be made to a Supreme
Judge, to whom shall appertain the jurisdiction in such a case.[1]

The system of judges conservators enjoyed by the English
in Portugal is a close approximation to the present-day
régime of consular jurisdiction. According to Shillington
and Chapman, the system goes as far back as the fifteenth
century.[2] A specific provision for the office and functions
of the judges conservators is contained in the treaty of July
10, 1654, Article VII of which lays down:

Also, for judging all causes which shall relate to the people
of this Republic [England], a judge conservator shall be deputed, from whom no appeal shall be granted, unless to a committee of senators where the disputes shall be determined within
the space of four months, at most, after the appeals.[3]

By the treaty of February 19, 1810, it was arranged to give
the English merchants " the privilege of nominating and
having special magistrates to act for them as Judges Conservator," with jurisdiction over " all causes brought before
them by British subjects." It must be pointed out, however,
that the selection of these judges conservators, though they
were chosen by the British subjects in the locality, had to
be approved by the Prince Regent of Portugal.[4] The privi-

[1] *State Papers,* vol. xcviii, p. 979.

[2] Shillington and Chapman, *Commercial Relations of England and
Portugal* (New York, 1907), p. 182.

[3] Chalmers, *A Collection of Treaties between Great Britain and Other
Powers* (London, 1790), vol. ii, p. 271.

[4] Martens, *Nouveau supplémens au recueil de traités* (Gottingue, 1839-
42), vol. ii, p. 158.

lege of maintaining judges conservators was enjoyed by the English in Brazil until 1827, when a treaty between the Emperor of Brazil and the King of England abolished it.[1] In Portugal proper, it is interesting to note, the system of judge conservators was not formally abolished until 1842.[2]

That the system of judges conservators existed in the seventeenth and eighteenth centuries in Spanish America is evidenced by a number of " assiento " treaties or contracts. The Portuguese, French and English agreements, dated respectively July 12, 1696,[3] August 27, 1701,[4] and March 26, 1713,[5] all provide for these officers.[6] They were to be chosen by the merchants concerned, with the approval of the King of Spain, and were " to have cognizance, exclusive of all others, of all causes, affairs and suits, relating to the Assiento, with full authority and jurisdiction," but from their decisions an appeal lay to the supreme council of the Indies.[7] The author has attempted in vain to ascertain the actual operation of the system, to which all the available material gives no clue.

[1] Art. 6, *Annuaire historique universel*, 1827, p. 159.

[2] Art. 17, Martens, *Nouveau recueil général de traités* (Gottingue, 1843-75), vol. iii, p. 338.

[3] Art. 8, Castro, *Colleçcão de tradados* (Lisbon, 1856-58), vol. i, p. 53.

[4] Art. 13, Dumont, *op. cit.*, vol. viii, pt. i, p. 85.

[5] Art. 13, Jenkinson, *A Collection of All the Treaties* (London, 1785), vol. i, p. 382.

[6] The treaty of peace signed at Utrecht on June 26, 1714, between Spain and the United Provinces contained a similar provision (art. 29); Dumont, *op. cit.*, vol. viii, pt. i, p. 430.

[7] *Cf.* Ortega, *Questiones del derecho publico* (Madrid, 1747), pp. 314 *et seq.* In this connection, a nineteenth century survival of consular jurisdiction in Europe may be mentioned. The treaty of May 2, 1889, between Italy and Ethiopia, provided for the reciprocal exercise of consular jurisdiction in regard to criminal matters. After setting forth the rights of the Italians in Ethiopia, the agreement goes on to say: " Similarly, the Ethiopians accused of a crime committed in Italian territory shall be tried by the Ethiopian authorities." Art. 12, *State Papers*, vol. lxxxi, p. 735.

In the municipal legislation and orders of some European States, similar survivals were for a time equally evident. The Patent of John Chandler, as English consul to Spain, dated 1631, gave him the power " by way of interposition to compound . . . all contentions . . . that may arise amongst them [English merchants] and may be conveniently ordered without further proceeding to Lawe." [1]

The instructions of Peter the Great to one Jewreinoff, Russian consul at Cadiz, dated 1723, mentioned specifically among his functions the decision of differences between the subjects of the Czar in Spain.[2]   Likewise, the consular instructions issued by the King of Denmark and Norway, February 10, 1749, contained a provision ordering the consul to assume jurisdiction not only over the masters and crews of the Danish vessels, but also over the Danish merchants trading abroad.[3]   According to the French edict of June, 1778, regulating the judicial and police functions of French consuls abroad, the latter were empowered to take cognizance of all disputes between their compatriots, and all French merchants were prohibited from bringing their fellow-citizens before any other tribunal.[4]   In his History of Genoa, M. Vincens confirms the actual enforcement of this edict by relating that, in 1797, the French consul was the magistrate of first instance in Genoa for all civil disputes in which one of his nationals was defendant.[5]

These late survivals of extraterritoriality in Europe are to be explained partly by the as yet deficient judicial systems

[1] Shillington and Chapman, op. cit., app. ii, p. 327.

[2] Borel, De l'Origine et des fonctions des consuls (St. Petersburg, 1807), p. 90.

[3] Moser, Versuch des neuesten europäischen Völkerrechts (Frankfurt a. M., 1777-80), vol. vii, p. 833.

[4] Arts. 1, 2, Martens, Recueil de traités, vol. ii, pp. 632-633.

[5] Vincens, Hist. de la République de Gênes, vol. i, p. 86.

of some of the European Powers and partly by the abiding
influence of the theory of the personality of laws. An example of the former is the situation in Portugal. In this
country, according to Shillington and Chapman, " the general desire of the English, in fact, was to escape from the
ordinary Portuguese courts. The administration in Portugal seems to have been both corrupt and arbitrary, and
strangers, ill-acquainted with the customs and language of
the country, suffered considerably." [1] Consequently, the
system of judges conservators was maintained in Portugal
to protect the English against the injustices of the native
courts. That this statement is well-founded is shown by
the treaty which abolished the system in Portugal. This
instrument, dated 1842, gives as the reason for the abolition
" the state of progress in which the system of legislation and
administration of justice in Portugal was found." [2] This
is significant, because in the decline of extraterritoriality,
the improvement of the native judicial system has always
been an important factor. In the discussion to follow, we
shall have repeated occasion to take note of this fact.

In other instances, however, the persistence of extraterritoriality could not be ascribed to judicial deficiency. As we
have pointed out above,[3] to France belonged the honor of
being the continental European Power in which law and
sovereignty received their earliest development. Yet France
made a treaty with Morocco in 1631, in which reciprocal
extraterritorial privileges were provided for. This must
have been due, if anything, to the existence of deep-seated
custom having its basis in the time-honored theory of the
personality of laws.

[1] *Op. cit.*, p. 182.
[2] Art. 17, Martens, *N. R. G.*, vol. iii, p. 338.
[3] *Supra*, p. 39.

VIII. TESTIMONY OF PUBLICISTS

The works of the early writers on international law seem to betray the influence of the once prevalent practice. Wicquefort, whose treatise on *l'Embassadeur* was published in 1681, denied to the consul any public character, but made special mention of his judicial function.[1] Bynkershoek, in his *De Foro Legatorum*, 1721, speaks of the consuls as protectors and sometimes judges of the merchants of their nation.[2] Wolff, whose work was published in 1754, defines the consul as one who is sent abroad to safeguard the privileges and rights of his compatriots and to decide their disputes.[3] In his *Droit des Gens*, published in 1758, Vattel follows closely the definition of Wolff.[4] Of these early writers Moser was the latest to describe the judicial compe-

[1] "Consuls are only merchants, who notwithstanding their Office of *Judge in the Controversies* that may arise among those of their own Nation...are liable to the Justice of the Place where they reside...." *The Ambassador and His Functions*, trans. by Digby (London, 1716), p. 40.

[2] "Et à dire le vrai, ces Consuls ne sont autrechose que des Protecteurs, quelquefois Juges des Marchands de leur Nations:.. d'ordinaire même ce ne sont que des Marchands, que l'on envoie non pour représenter leur Prince auprès d'une autre Puissance Souveraine, mais pour protéger les Sujets de leur Prince, en ce qui regarde le Négoce, souvent aussi pour connoître & décider des differens qu'il pourra y avoir entr'eux au sujet de ces fortes d'affaires." Bynkershoek, *Traité du juge competent*, trans. by Barbeyrac (The Hague, 1723), ch. x, § vi, p. 112.

[3] "Consul sind solche Personen, welchen in den See-Handelsstäpten oder den Haafen aufgetragen ist, die Privilegien und Rechte der Nation, oder ihres Volkes zu bewahren, und die Streitigkeiten der Kaufleute zu scnlichten." Wolff, *Grundsätze des Natur- und Völkerrechts* (Halle, 1754), § 1118, p. 815.

[4] "L'une des institutions modernes les plus utiles au commerce est celle des consuls. Ce sont des gens qui dans les grandes places de commerce, & surtout dans les ports de mer, en pays étrangers, ont la commission de veiller à la conservation des droits et des privileges de leur nation, & de terminer les difficultés qui peuvent naître entre ses marchands." Vattel, *Le Droit des Gens*, (London, 1758), vol. i, bk. ii, ch. ii, § 34.

tence of the consul, and he was also the most specific of them all. He says that consuls are judges of first instance in cases involving their compatriots, but that in mixed cases in which natives of the country where the consuls reside or foreigners of a third country are concerned, the local authorities have jurisdiction.[1] It is not altogether easy to ascertain the exact limits of consular jurisdiction in mediaeval Europe.[2] But while Moser's conclusions might reasonably be established as a general proposition, instances are not lacking, as we have seen, in which it was arranged to settle even mixed cases according to the principle *actor sequitur forum rei*, one of the basic formulae of modern extraterritoriality.

That the judicial competence of the foreign consul was treated by these writers as of equal importance to his commercial powers is at once indicative of two things, which must have been responsible for their views on the subject as cited above. First, it is suggestive of the fact that the principle of territorial sovereignty is only a recent conception, reaching its full development after a painfully slow process of transformation. Secondly—and this is but a corollary of the first consideration—the widely prevalent theory of the personality of laws held its sway in Europe long after the inception of the countervailing principle of territorial sovereignty, and in its decadence left many survivals which have existed in Europe well into the end of the last century.

[1] " Seynd sie [consuln] die Richtere in erster Instanz, wann zwischen ihren Landesleuten in Handlungssachen in dem jedem Consul angewisenen Districkt Streitigkeiten entstehen. Wann aber die Streitigkeiten sich zwischen ihren Landesleuten einer-und denen Eingesessenen oder dritten Fremden, anderer Seits enthalten; so gehören sie für den Souverain des Orts, und dessen Gerichte." Moser, *Versuch des neuesten europäischen Völkerrechts,* 1777-80, vol. vii, pp. 840-841.

[2] Un Ancien Diplomate, *Le Régime des capitulations* (Paris, 1898), p. 27.

CHAPTER II

IN THE LEVANT PRIOR TO 1453

I. EARLY USAGE

IN the preceding chapter the judicial powers of the consul in Europe were briefly considered. The present chapter will deal with the rise of the consulate with its jurisdictional rights in the Levant and in the Mohammedan states prior to 1453.

In Sir Paul Rycaut's *The Present State of the Ottoman Empire* there was published for the first time a document known as the Testament of Mohammed, dated 625, which gave the Christians certain privileges and concessions, one of which was the protection accorded to Christian judges in the Mohammedan provinces.[1] The authenticity of the document is questioned by some writers,[2] but the fact that the Capitulation of Omar, which is referred to below, mentions an act of the Prophet giving security to Christians may be regarded as confirmation of its existence.[3]

---

[1] " By this Covenant... I promise to defend their judges in my Provinces, with my Horse and Foot, Auxiliaries, and other my faithful Followers..." Rycaut, *op. cit.*, p. 100; Van Dyck, " Report on the Capitulations of the Ottoman Empire," U. S. *Sen. Ex. Doc. 3, 46th Cong., Sp. Sess.*, (Appendix I).

[2] Ravndal, *The Origin of the Capitulations* (Washington, 1921), p. 12

[3] " Ils [the Christians] méritent tous les égards, parce qu'ils furent déjà autrefois honorés par le Prophète d'un Document muni de son Sceau, par lequel il nous exhorte à les ménager et à leur accorder la sureté." Text in Miltitz, *op. cit.*, vol. ii, pt. i, p. 500. *Cf.* Féraud-Giraud, *De la Juridiction française dans les Échelles du Levant* (Paris, 1866), vol. i, p. 36, n. 1.

The same apochryphal character is ascribed to the Capitulation granted by Caliph Omar Ibn-Khattâb to the Christians in Syria in 636.[1] But although the document may have been fictitious, it is of great historical importance, because in the later disputes between Christians and Turks it was constantly referred to, and it contained many of the stipulations of the later Turkish Capitulations.[2] The Capitulation of Omar granted equal security to the Christian churches, companies and places of pilgrimage. It ordained the Christians to be respected on account of the honor that had been bestowed upon them by the Prophet. Moreover, they were exempted from the capitation tax and all other tolls in the Moslem states, and on their entry into the Holy Sepulchre no one should receive anything from them. But the Christians who visited the Holy Sepulchre should deposit with the Patriarch one and a half drams (*drachme*) of white silver. Finally, it was ordered that the true followers of both sexes, whether rich or poor, should observe this law.

In the ninth century, Charlemagne is said to have obtained from Caliph Haroun-el-Raschid privileges for the Frankish merchants at Jerusalem, but unfortunately the text of the agreement is not in existence.[3]

That the Mohammedans stood for exemption from territorial jurisdiction was confirmed not only by their own concessions to the Christians, but also by their status in some of the foreign countries. An Arab merchant by the name of Soleyman relates that in the city of Canfu,[4] which is the

---

[1] See a French translation of the text in Miltitz, *op. cit.*, vol. ii, pt. i, p 500.

[2] Charrière, *Négociations de la France dans le Levant*, vol. i, pp. lxvi-lxix.

[3] Miltitz, *op. cit.*, vol. ii, pt. i, p. 7; Pardessus, *Collection de lois maritimes*, vol. i, p. lxv.

[4] Klaproth, "*Renseignemens sur les ports de Gampou et de Zaithoum,*

present Haiyen, Chekiang, a Mussulman was charged by
the Emperor of China with power to decide the disputes
which arose among the men of the Mohammedan religion
in the ninth century.[1]   This shows that the Mohammedans
of that age were just as jealous of their own rights abroad
as they were willing to let foreigners in their realm heed
their own affairs.   The reason for this state of affairs lies
in the fundamental religious beliefs which mark off the
Mohammedan from the " infidel " and which will be treated
of when we come to the later Christian consulates in the
Mohammedan Levant.[2]

In the tenth century, Capitulations were entered into between the Byzantine Emperor and the Varangians or Russians.   The agreement of 912 provided, *inter alia,* that " He
who strikes any one with a sword or any other instrument
shall pay for the act a fine of five pounds of silver according
to Russian law." [3]   In the treaty of 945, we find the following significant provision :

déscrits par Marco Polo," Journal Asiatique, vol. v, pp. 35 *et seq.*
Many writers have erroneously taken Canfu for Canton.   Even such a
learned scholar as Sir Travers Twiss has fallen into this mistake.   Twiss,
Law of Nations, vol. i, p. 447.

[1] Reinaud, *Relation des voyages* (Paris,, 1845), vol. i, p. 13.   *Cf.* Pardessus, *op. cit.,* vol. ii, p. xxviij.   Of the authority for the existence of a
Mohammedan judge in China in the ninth century, Sir Travers Twiss
says : " This interesting fact was first made generally known by a nar-
rative purporting to be the work of two ancient Arab travelers which was
translated into French by Eusebius Renaudot in 1718, and subsequently
translated into English in 1733.   The MS., however, of which there is
preserved in the Bibliothèque Nationale in Paris a perfect example, has
been subsequently ascertained to be an extract from a larger work by
a most famous Arab historian, Ali Abou'l Hassan Mas'oudy, who
died in Egypt A. D. 956, and who was a contemporary of the Arab
travelers, whose voyage he has handed down to us." *On Consular
Jurisdiction in the Levant* (London, 1880), p. 6.

[2] *Infra,* p. 55.

[3] *La Chronique de Nestor,* trans. by L. Paris (Paris, 1834-35), vol. i,
p. 40.

If a Russian should attempt to steal from any one in our Empire, he shall be severely punished for that act; and if he shall have accomplished the theft, he shall pay double the value of the object stolen.   It shall be the same for the Greek in respect of the Russians; the guilty person, moreover, shall be punished according to the laws of his country.[1]

The reciprocal nature of this treaty inevitably points to the degree of tolerance with which the exemption was regarded on both sides and shows that there was a time when even in the relations of one Christian Power with another the practice of extraterritoriality was by no means such an anomaly as it is now.

II. THE CRUSADES AND THE RISE OF EXTRATERRITORIALITY

The influence of the Crusades upon the development of international commerce is well-known.   While the transcendent motive of this great armed movement, which pervaded all classes of men who participated in it, was religious, there were also other considerations which lured them on to their final goal.   These latter differed according as the social status of the participants differed: with the princes, it was the love of conquest and adventure; with the lower classes, it was the desire to elevate their social status; and with the bourgeois, it was the thirst for gain.[2]   As a result of the notable rôle played by the bourgeois, a great increase in the volume and scope of overseas trade was brought about.

The reasons for this unusual development of international commerce are not far to seek.   In a large part the progress is to be ascribed to the favorable situation of Constantinople and of its environs.   For a long time, due to their advantageous position, the Byzantines had held in the Mediterranean

[1] *Ibid.,* p. 61.

[2] Heyd, *Histoire de commerce du Levant* (Leipzig, 1885-86), vol. i, p. 131.

a supremacy undisputed by the Occidentals. In the south, there was Egypt, where the Red Sea commanded the merchandise of the Levant; in Asia Minor, Syria, where caravan parties from the Arabian Sea, the Persian Gulf or the center of Asia came to discharge their burdens; and on the Black Sea, there were many places of commercial interest.[1]

Brought into contact by the Crusades with this land of opportunity, the Italian and other maritime peoples of the West sought to fortify themselves still further by obtaining numerous privileges and concessions from the Christian princes who planted themselves in the Levant during this period. To the ambitions of the merchants the circumstances of the time were peculiarly favorable, for in the conquests made by the crusading princes, the Italian fleets were constantly called upon to render invaluable services, without which all the bravery and military tactics of the knights would have been in vain. Moreover, even after the taking of the well fortified ports of Syria, the assistance of the Italian fleets was needed for their retention. Evidently, the possession of these ports was a matter of life and death to the Crusaders, as through them unobstructed communication was maintained with the Occident, whence only resources of man power and money could come. The sovereigns of the conquered States could, therefore, hardly be oblivious of the assistance rendered by the Italians, and it was in recognition of this that many concessions were granted to them in their respective establishments. On their side, it was also not uncommon, nor was it unnatural, that the Italians felt at times conscious of the importance of their aid, and in many an instance, made their help conditional on promises of extravagant remuneration. Thus, a large number of *colonies* were founded, which, in the course of time, became commercial centers of greater or less impor-

[1] Heyd, *op. cit.*, p. 24; Nys, *Les Origines du droit international* (Brussels, 1894), p. 281.

tance in the Levant.[1]   In the grants made by the Prince of
Tyre to the Pisans in 1188[2] and 1189,[3] for instance, it was
expressly stated that the privileges were conceded on account
of military services rendered by the Pisans.

In the States of the Levant under Christian sovereignty
during the Crusades, special privileges of consular jurisdiction existed in the Byzantine Empire,[4] Syria,[5] and
Cyprus.[6]   As it is to be expected, the provisions of the early

---

[1] Heyd, *op. cit.*, vol. i, pp. 131-132, 135-136. *Cf.* Martens, *Das Consularwesen* (Berlin, 1874), p. 61; Nys. *Les Origines*, p. 283.

[2] Lünig, *Codex Ital. Dip.* (Francfort, 1725-34), vol. i, c. 1060.

[3] Muratori, *Antiq. Ital.* (Avetti, 1773-80), vol. vi, c. 279.

[4] Venice, Nov., 1199, Tafel und Thomas, *Urkunden zur älteren Han-
dels- und Staatsgeschichte der Republik Venedig* (Vienna, 1856-57),
vol. i, pp. 273-276; Genoa, Venice and Pisa, 1265, Pachymeres, *Michael
Palaologus* (Rome, 1666), p. 105; Turkey, 1391, Ducas, *Historia Byzan-
tina* (Paris, 1649), p. 30. According to the last-mentioned grant, the
Turks were to have a *cadi* in Constantinople to decide their own cases.
This is important, as it constitutes a significant basis for the later Turkish
Capitulations, especially as it was granted by a Christian to a Moham-
medan Power. *Cf. infra*, p. 64.

[5] Venice: Jerusalem, 1123, Tafel und Thomas, *op. cit.*, vol. i, p. 87;
May, 1125, *ibid.*, p. 92; 1130, Muratori, *op. cit.*, vol. vi, c. 288; Beirut,
Dec., 1221, Tafel und Thomas, *op. cit.*, vol. ii, p. 231; Tyre, 1275,
Muratori, *Rerum italicarum scriptores* (Mediolani, 1723-51), vol. xii,
c. 382-383.

Pisa: Antioch, 1154, Lünig, *op. cit.*, vol. i, c. 1046; Jerusalem, 1157,
ibid., c. 1047; Antioch, 1170, Muratori, *Antiquitates Italicae*, vol. vi, c.
268; Tripoli, 1187, *ibid.*, c. 271; Tyre, Oct. 6, 1187, Ughelli, *Italia Sacra*
(Venice, 1717-22), vol. iii, c. 415-416; 1188, Lünig, *op. cit.*, vol. i, 1060;
1189, Muratori, *op. cit.*, vol. vi, c. 278; 1191, *ibid.*, c. 281; Antioch, 1216,
ibid., c. 284.

Genoa: Antioch, Sep. 1, 1190, Dumont, *Corps universel diplomatique*,
vol. i, pt. i, p. 115.

Marseilles: Syria, Nov. 8, 1226, *ibid.*, p. 164.

[6] Genoa: July 12, 1218, Mas-Latrie, *Histoire de l'île de Chypre* (Paris,
1852-61), vol. ii, Doc., p. 39; June 10, 1232, *ibid.*, pp. 51-52; Dec. 25,
1233, *ibid.*, p. 58; Feb. 16, 1329 (art. 2), *ibid.*, p. 153; April 18, 1365,
(art. 3), *ibid.*, pp. 258-9.

Venice: June 3, 1306 (art. 7), *ibid.*, pp. 105-6; Sep. 4, 1328, *ibid.*, pp.
142-3; Aug. 16, 1360, *ibid.*, p. 232.

grants were not always specific or comprehensive, but in a general way the rights conceded were in strict accord with the principle *actor sequitur forum rei.* With few exceptions,[1] the Italians in the Levant, who were commonly allowed to dwell in special quarters provided for them, were placed under the exclusive jurisdiction of their own consular courts in cases affecting themselves alone.[2] Mixed cases were assigned by some of the earlier grants to the competence of the local courts,[3] but later practice differed in no wise from the modern rule that the plaintiff should follow the defendant into his court. Cases of natives against Christians were under the jurisdiction of the consular court concerned, and cases of Christians against natives, under that of the local courts.[4]

It should be pointed out in passing that independently of these acts of privilege, there existed in Jerusalem a régime in the nature of a mixed court system. When the Christians of the First Crusade conquered Palestine and formed the kingdom of Jerusalem in 1099, they established the military and feudal constitution known as the "*Assises de Jérusalem.*" The "*Assises*" set up a Commercial Court and a *Cour des Bourgeois.* The Commercial Court was composed of a bailiff and six jurors, two of whom were Christians and four Syrians. All civil and commercial disputes were brought before this court; but criminal matters were within

[1] The excepted cases were those of murder, rape, assault, treason and robbery. See Venice-Beirut, 1221; Pisa-Tripoli, 1187; Genoa-Cyprus, 1218, 1365 (art. 3); Venice-Cyprus, 1306 (art. 7).

[2] See all the acts listed in notes 1-3 on the preceding page.

[3] Pisa-Antioch, 1154, 1170. The Byzantine grant of 1199 to Venice stated that only the more important cases between Venetians and Greeks were to be tried by the local court.

[4] Venice-Byzantium, 1199; Venice-Jerusalem, 1123, 1125, 1130; Venice-Tyre, 1275; Pisa, 1187, 1189; Genoa-Cyprus, 1365 (art. 3); Venice-Cyprus, 1306 (art. 7).

the sole competence of the *Cour des Bourgeois*, which was composed of the Viscount and jurors.[1]

III. EXTRATERRITORIALITY IN THE MOHAMMEDAN STATES PRIOR TO 1453

The Testament of Mohammed and the Capitulation of Omar furnish the customary basis of Mussulman practice with regard to jurisdiction over foreigners. The explanation for the position held by the Mussulman on this subject, as has been intimated above, has to be sought in his religious beliefs. According to the *Koran*, which is at once a gospel, a code and a constitution, all those who were not followers of the Mohammedan religion were to be treated as enemies and to be slaughtered without mercy.[2] But the exigencies of commerce demanded and effected a mitigation of this rule. " The innate and invincible aversion of the Mohammedans," says Pradier-Fodéré,[3] " to do business outside their country; their inexperience in navigation, which forced them to recruit their crews only from among foreign seamen; the need, which the political chiefs of Islamism felt, of utilizing their extended coast, their fine harbors, the rich products of their fertile soil, and of reaping the numerous advantages of maritime commerce, were early destined to inspire the Sultans with a favorable disposition towards the

---

[1] Miltitz, *Manuel des consuls*, vol. i, pp. 42-48, 168, n. 6; vol. ii, pt. i, p. 16; Ancien Diplomate, *Le Régime des Capitulations*, pp. 38-39; Depping, *Histoire du commerce* (Paris, 1830), vol. ii, p. 210. *Cf.* Foucher, *Assises de Royaume de Jérusalem*, 1 vol. in 2 (Rennes, 1839-41); Beugnot, *Assises de Jérusalem*, 2 vols. (Paris, 1841-43).

[2] *Koran*, sura xlvii, verse 4, " When ye encounter the infidels, strike off their heads till ye have made a great slaughter among them, and of the rest make fast and fetters."

[3] " *La Question des Capitulations*," *Révue de droit international et de législation comparée* (hereafter referred to as *R. D. I.*), vol. i, p. 119. *Cf.* Féraud-Giraud, *De la Jurisdiction française dans les Echelles du Levant*, vol. i, pp. 33-35.

foreigners.   It was necessary to invite the Christians to the
exploitation of so many resources and, in the interest of the
State, to encourage them to make settlements in the Levant."
The writer is here discussing the origin of the Turkish Capitulations, but what he says is, in a general way, applicable
to all the Mohammedan States prior to the conquest of
Constantinople.   The Mussulman's desire to develop commerce and navigation, therefore, saved the unbeliever from
the Damoclean sword of Islam.

Indeed, the commercial motive, before which even religious bigotry gave way, was so overwhelming that it has left
its imprint in the very Capitulations granted by the Mussulman rulers.   It is a remarkable fact that all these Capitulations are unilateral or one-sided, dispensing favors without
exacting any consideration.   The explanation is again to be
sought in the exuberant zeal for commercial development or
nowhere.   The object of the Capitulations was to regulate
the conditions under which Europeans were to do business
in the Levant; the interests of the Mussulman, whether at
sea or abroad in a Christian country, were ignored in the
scramble for the benefit of European commerce at home.[1]
Thus, the element of reciprocity was conspicuously absent,
but its absence, though conspicuous, ought not to betray any
derogation from sovereignty on the part of the proud Saracens.   The fact is that during the period under examination,

[1] Mas-Latrie, *Traités de paix et de commerce* (Paris, 1865), Introduction Historique, pp. 114, 115. According to M. Mas-Latrie, who has
made an exhaustive study of the documents bearing on the commercial
relations between the Christian States of Europe and the Mohammedans
of North Africa, a condition of reciprocity in all but one respect, could
have come about. " Save this case [of religion] and this case alone,
perhaps, the Mussulmans would probably have obtained in Europe
complete equality of treatment, if the Arab plenipotentiaries, nearly
always charged with the first draft of the treaties, of which the Latin
text was only an interpretative version, had felt it opportune to stipu-
late for it." *Ibid.*, p. 115.

the notion of exclusive sovereignty was still unborn, and it is highly improbable that much attention could have been paid to it by the negotiators on either side. Be this as it may, the consul, who was usually invested with the judicial authority, occupied a not at all exalted position in the Levant at the time.[1]

Saved as the foreigner was from the fate of the infidel, by the Mohammedan quest after the boon of European commerce, he was nevertheless outside the pale of the Mohammedan religion. In the *Koran,* we find a passage to the following effect:

> Say: O ye Unbelievers!
> I worship not what ye worship,
> And ye are not worshippers of what I worship;
> And I am not a worshipper of what ye have worshipped,
> And ye are not worshippers of what I worship.
> To you your religion; and to me my religion.[2]

Inasmuch as the *Koran* was a judicial as well as a moral or religious code, one who was not a follower of the religion was naturally not amenable to the law. Hence, it was necessary to submit the foreigner to a special jurisdiction, the most reasonable being that of his own country.[3]

---

[1] In the writings of Khalil ben-Schahin Dhahéri occurs a passage, which is translated by M. Silvestre de Sacy into French as follows: "Dans cette ville [Alexandria] sont otages des consuls, c'est-à-dire, de grands seigneurs d'entre les Francs des diverses nations: toutes les fois que la nation de l'un d'eux fait quelque chose de nuisible a l'islamisme, on en demande compte à son consul, qu'on en rend responsable." Silvestre de Sacy, *Christomathie arabe* (Paris, 1806), vol. ii, p. 318.

[2] Sura cix.

[3] *Cf.* Pelissié du Rausas, *Le Régime des Capitulations dans l'Empire Ottoman* (2nd ed., Paris, 1910-11), vol. i, p. 21, where it is said: "The Mussulman law was not made for the foreigner, since he is a non-Mussulman; it is necessary that he remain subject to his own law. The Mussulman law can neither protect him nor judge him nor punish him, since it protects, judges and punishes only Mussulmans; it is necessary

Amalfi is said to have been the first Christian Power to enter into commercial relations with Egypt. According to Sir Travers Twiss, the merchants of that city obtained from the Caliphs of Egypt towards the end of the ninth century the privilege of trading at Alexandria under a consul of their own nationality, though the text of such a grant does not exist.[1]

The earliest grant made by Egypt to a Christian Power, which has been preserved is a letter of 1154 addressed by an Egyptian official to Pisa, which guaranteed to the Pisans their own jurisdiction.[2]   In this letter, allusion was made to the maintenance of old rights,[3] which indicates the existence of consular jurisdiction in Egypt prior to 1154. Other Italian republics which enjoyed extraterritorial privileges in Egypt at this time were Venice,[4] Genoa [5] and Florence.[6]

Outside of Egypt, rights of consular jurisdiction existed also in the Barbary States in favor of the Italian and Spanish States.[7]

that he be protected, judged and punished by his own law. The Mussulman law is the *Jus Quiritium;* it is the exclusive right, the privilege of the Mussulmans; and it it is the *Jus Gentium* that rules the foreigner."

[1] Twiss, *Law of Nations* (2nd ed., Oxford, 1884), vol. i, p. 446.

[2] Amari, *I Diplomi Arabi* (Firenze, 1863), p. 247. This letter was confirmed by another letter from Saladin dated Sep. 25, 1173, *ibid.*, p. 257, and a treaty of 1215-16 (art. 33), *ibid.*, p. 287.

[3] *Ibid.*, p. 248.

[4] Nov. 14, 1238, Tafel und Thomas, *op. cit.*, vol. ii, p. 338.

[5] 1290, *Notices et extraits des manuscrits de la Bibliothèque Nationale et autres bibliothèques,* vol. xi, p. 35.

[6] June 14, 1422, Amari, *op. cit.*, p. 333; 1488 (arts. 11, 12, 14), *ibid.*, p. 384; 1496, *ibid.*, p. 212; 1509, *ibid.*, p. 223.

[7] Tunis: Venice, 1251 (arts. 4, 23), Mas-Latrie, *Traités de paix et de commerce,* Doc., pp. 200, 202; 1271 (art. 3), *ibid.*, p. 204; 1305 (art. 3), *ibid.*, p. 212; 1317 (art. 3), *ibid.*, p. 217; 1392 (art. 3), *ibid.*, p. 233; 1438 (art. 3), *ibid.*, p. 251; 1456, *ibid.*, p. 255; Genoa, June 10, 1236 (art. 15), *ibid.*, p. 117; Oct. 18, 1250 (art. 15), *ibid.*, p. 120; Oct. 17, 1391, *ibid.*, p. 132; Oct. 19, 1433 (arts. 3, 15), *ibid.*, p. 135; 1445, *ibid.*,

According to these Capitulations, the Christians were
allowed to dwell in specially provided quarters under their
own administration. Cases, whether civil or criminal, involving Christians of the same nationality were within the
exclusive competence of their consul administering their own
laws.[1] In mixed cases, the principle *actor sequitur forum
rei* was generally adopted, but not without vagueness and
confusion at times. Thus, while the Pisans were completely
exempted from local interference in any cases involving
them[2] and were required to proceed against criminals in
the court of the admiral of Alexandria,[3] and while the
Venetian consul was to take cognizance of cases between
Venetians and other Christians in Egypt,[4] the Florentines,
when they succeeded to the rights of the Pisans, were subjected to the jurisdiction of the sultan in their litigations
with other Christians in Egypt.[5] This deviation from the
general principle was removed by the treaty of 1496, which
granted to the Pisans the same rights as had been enjoyed
by the Venetians.[6] In general, cases involving foreigners
of different nationalities were to be disposed of by their
consuls, and cases between natives and Christians were likewise placed under the jurisdiction of the defendant's court.[7]

p. 142; Pisa, May 16, 1353 (arts. 9, 35), *ibid.*, pp. 58, 62; Dec. 14, 1397
(art. 5), *ibid.*, p. 74; Florence, 1421 (arts. 2, 3, 5), *ibid.*, p. 347; Aragon,
1271 (arts. 9, 28), *ibid.*, p. 283; 1285 (art. 28), *ibid.*, p. 289; 1314 (art.
15), *ibid.*, p. 309; 1323 (arts. 16, 17, 18), *ibid.*, p. 322.
Morocco: Pisa, 1358 (art. 11), *ibid.*, p. 68.

[1] See all the Captulations listed in notes 4-7 on the preceding page.

[2] Letter of Saladin, Sep. 25, 1173.

[3] 1215-16, art. 33.

[4] 1238.

[5] 1488, art. 24.

[6] Amari, *op. cit.*, p. 212.

[7] Venice-Egypt, 1238; Genoa-Egypt, 1290; Venice-Tunis, 1251, art. 23;
1305, art. 3; 1317, art. 3; 1392, art. 3; 1438, art. 3; Genoa-Tunis and

In some of the treaties, a right of appeal was allowed to the local courts in cases where natives proceeded against Christians in their consular courts.[1]

Tripoli, 1236, art. 15; Genoa-Tunis, 1250, art. 15; 1433, art. 3; Pisa-Tunis, 1353, art. 9; 1397, art. 5; Florence-Tunis, 1421, arts. 2, 3, 5; Aragon-Tunis, 1271, art. 9; 1323, art. 16; Pisa-Morocco, 1358, art. 11. The treaty of 1356 between Venice and Tripoli contained the peculiar provision that cases between Saracens and Christians should be tried by special local judges, according to the laws of each party (art. 4).

[1] Venice-Tunis, 1305, art. 3; 1317, art. 3; 1392, art. 3; 1438, art. 3; Pisa-Tunis, 1397, art. 5; Florence-Tunis, 1421, art. 5; Aragon-Tunis, 1323, art. 16.

CHAPTER III

In the Levant and Africa After 1453

I. ORIGIN OF EXTRATERRITORIALITY IN THE OTTOMAN EMPIRE AND THE LEVANT

IN explaining the development of consular jurisdiction in the Ottoman Empire and the Levant, writers have attached an almost undue amount of importance to the differences between the Christian and Mohamemdan religions. They have sought to ascribe the special status of the foreigner in Turkey principally, if not wholly, to the fundamental discrepancies between the two faiths. A typical pronouncement to this effect is that made by M. Féraud-Giraud:

When there exists between two peoples a very great difference in respect of religion, manners, laws, and customs, lasting and proper [*suivis*] relations are possible only when one of these peoples, drawn to the territory of the other by their activity, finds there exceptional guarantees, without which security of person and property cannot exist.[1]

In the footsteps of this eminent jurist has followed many a subsequent writer.[2]

It is true that the Mohammedan religion makes certain discriminations against the infidel, but to say that this was the principal ground on which the right of extraterritoriality

[1] *De la Juridiction française dans les Échelles du Levant et de Barbarie*, vol. i., p. 29.

[2] See, e. g., Pradier-Fodéré, *Traité de droit international* (Paris, 1885-1906), vol. iv, p. 713; Bonfils, *Manuel de droit international public* (Paris, 1914), p. 514.

was imposed upon or wrested from the sultans would be inconsistent with the facts of the case. The first Capitulations granted to France, on which all later claims of Europe to extraterritorial jurisdiction in the Ottoman Empire are chiefly based, bear the date of 1535. In the instructions which Francis I issued to his envoy in Constantinople, M. Jean de la Forêt,[1] one would look in vain for the slightest intimation of a demand for special judicial status. As a matter of fact, had any demand of the sort been made, it would have been categorically rejected, for it must be remembered that when it granted the Capitulations of 1535, Turkey was at the zenith of its power. True, the idea of exclusive sovereignty had not yet emerged, but had it been suggested that the rights accorded were to be a derogation from Ottoman sovereignty, they could scarcely have been acceded to. No such suggestion was ventured, however, no exorbitant demand was made upon the Porte, which gratuitously conferred upon the Christians their judicial rights. And it is of great interest to note in this connection that seven years before France obtained her first Capitulations in the Ottoman Empire, Sultan Suleyman II confirmed the treaty between the Mameluke Sultans and the French and Catalonian consuls,[2] at a time when Francis I was in captivity at Madrid and was in no position to ride roughshod over the Turks.

That the Capitulations were not imposed upon the sultans at the beginning and were but gratuitous concessions on their part may further be corroborated by the exemption of the sultan's non-Moslem subjects from Ottoman justice. Immediately after the conquest of Constantinople, Sultan Mohammed II granted to the Armenians, Greeks and Jews

---

[1] Charrière, *Négociations de la France dans le Levant,* vol. i, pp. 255 *et seq.*

[2] *Cf. infra*, p. 66.

their special rights of jurisdiction. At Constantinople, a
Greek patriarch was chosen as chief of the nation, president
of the synod, and supreme judge of all the civil and religious
affairs of the Greeks. The Armenians had at Constantinople, Caesarea, and Jerusalem three patriarchs invested with
the right of deciding civil disputes. The Jews likewise had
their courts, and a triumvirate composed of three rabbis
served as their supreme court at Constantinople.[1] This was
in accord with the Mohammedan theory that those who were
outside the pale of religion were also outside the pale of
law.[2]

The influence of religious differences on the development
of extraterritoriality in the Ottoman Empire can, of course,
hardly be denied. But what these differences did was not
to furnish the Franks with a ground for demanding special
concessions, but rather to give the sultans an additional impetus to make these concessions.[3]

The aversion of the Mohammedans to overseas commerce
has been referred to above.[4] Its effect on the attitude of
the Sultans towards foreigners was, to say the least, considerable, but its importance as a factor in bringing about
their special status is assuredly second to yet other considerations.

Of all the explanations which have been given for the
existence of the capitulatory régime in the Ottoman Empire, none is as near an approximation to the truth as the
one based on the force of custom. Whatever may have
been the intention of the Sultans in doling out privileges to
their foreign residents without exacting any consideration,
the motivating force of long-established custom must have

---

[1] Féraud-Giraud, *op. cit.*, vol. i, pp. 31-32.

[2] *Supra*, p. 57.

[3] *Cf.* Twiss, *On Consular Jurisdiction in the Levant*, p. 4.

[4] *Supra*, p. 55.

been the strongest and the most persuasive. Here was an institution of several centuries of standing. It had been in vogue in Christian as well as in non-Christian countries and prominent in the relations between non-Christians and Christians and even between Christians and Christians. Furthermore, it was a system in perfect accord with Mohammedan theories of law and religion. Was the Ottoman Empire to throw overboard this long prevalent usage? The answer to this question was self-evident, and the sultans chose the line of least resistance.

In discussing the same question, M. Renault makes the following observation:

Suleyman the Magnificent, with whom Francis I sought an alliance in 1535, did not make a concession which could have been regarded as humiliating. It must be considered that in the early days, territorial sovereignty had a less exclusive character than it does to-day and was not repugnant to the exercise of jurisdiction by foreign authorities. Thus, the curious fact has been noted that sixty years before Constantinople passed under the domination of the Turks, a Mussulman community had resided there under the administration of the *Cadi* who rendered justice according to Mohammedan laws.[1] It is then not surprising that Mohammed II, after the conquest, accorded to the merchants of Genoa and of Venice the continuation of the privileges which they had enjoyed under the Christian emperors.[2]

Another writer goes even farther than M. Renault and dismisses all the other explanations, expressing himself in favor of the customary origin of the Capitulations in the Levant. He says:

I repeat that there has existed no period in the history of

[1] *Supra*, p. 53, n. 4.

[2] L. Renault, Article on "Capitulations," *Grand Encyclopédie*, vol. ix, p. 213.

Constantinople in which foreigners have not enjoyed the advantages, and been subject to the disabilities, of exterritoriality. The
existing system of Capitulations is a survival rather than, as it
is generally represented, a new invention specially adapted to
Turkey. Still less is it a system, as it is often said to be, of
magnanimous concessions made by far-sighted sultans of Turkey
in order to encourage foreigners to trade with and reside in the
empire. The Capitulations were neither badges of inferiority
imposed on foreigners, as they have been described, nor proofs
of exceptional wisdom peculiar to the sultans. As a fact, foreigners have never held so important a position in the capital
under Ottoman rule as under that of the Christian emperors,
and especially at the close of the twelfth century.[1]

II. CAPITULATIONS AND TREATIES WITH THE LEVANT AND AFRICA

Having dealt with the circumstances which have con-
duced to the maintenance of the capitulatory régime in the
Ottoman Empire, we may now proceed to examine the in-
dividual acts which have established the rights of the various
European Powers in Turkey and in the Levant and Africa.

The first document which conferred extraterritorial rights
on Christians in the Ottoman Empire was the firman of
1453 respecting the Genoese in Galata. On May 29, a few
days after the conquest of Constantinople, the firman was
issued, which granted to the Genoese the right of retaining
their own laws and customs and of choosing from among
themselves an *ancien* to decide their own disputes.[2] This
act was renewed in 1612.[3]

In 1454, a treaty was concluded with Venice, giving the
latter the right to send to Constantinople a consul or *bailo*,
with his customary suite, who should exercise civil jurisdic-

[1] Pears, *Fall of Constantinople* (New York, 1886), p. 152.
[2] The text, with a French translation, is given in Hammer, *Histoire de l'Empire Ottoman* (Paris, 1835-43), vol. ii, pp. 523 *et seq.*
[3] Noradhounghian, *Recueil*, vol. i, p. 111.

tion over Venetians of every description, the *Grand Seigneur* engaging to accord to him protection and assistance whenever necessary.[1] The privileges were renewed in 1479, 1482, 1502, 1517, 1539, 1575, and 1595.[2]

On September 20, 1528, Sultan Suleyman II entered into a treaty with France, which confirmed the jurisdictional rights of the French and Catalonian consuls in Egypt granted to them by the Mameluke Sultans.[3]

So far as the Ottoman Empire as a whole was concerned, however, the first instrument which established the French régime in Turkey was the Capitulations of February, 1535.[4] It was the earliest treaty defining in detail the rights to which the foreigners were entitled in Turkey.

As it was the Turkish theory that treaties should not last longer than the lifetime of a single sultan, this document was renewed by each sultan in succession,[5] with occasional modifications, until, in 1740,[6] the treaties were given their final form, to constitute the principal basis of the European claim to extraterritorial privileges in Turkey.

The Capitulations of 1740 were also renewed repeatedly in 1802, 1838, and 1861.[7] The document of 1802 was the first engagement between France and Turkey in modern treaty form. Article 2 provided that " The treaties or capitulations which, before the War, determined respectively

[1] Daru, *Histoire de Venise* (2nd ed., Paris, 1821), vol. ii, p. 514; Miltitz, *op. cit.*, vol. ii, pt. i, pp. 217-218.

[2] *Ibid.*, pp. 76-77.

[3] Testa, *Recueil des traités de la Porte Ottomane* (Paris, 1864-1901), vol. i, p. 24; Charrière, *op. cit.*, vol. i, p. 116.

[4] Noradounghian, *Recueil*, vol. i, p. 83.

[5] Prior to 1740, renewals were made in 1569, 1581, 1597, 1604, 1607, 1609, 1618, 1624, 1640, 1673, and 1684. See Noradounghian, *Recueil*, vol. i, pp. 88, 35, 37, 93, 108, 40, 43, 45, 47, 49, 136, 54.

[6] Arts. 15, 26, 52, 65, *ibid.*, pp. 282, 285, 290, 294.

[7] *Ibid.*, vol. ii, pp. 52, 257, vol. iii, p. 131.

relations of every kind existing between the two Powers, are hereby renewed in their entirety."

For a long time after France obtained her first Capitulations, she was the protector of European merchants, who were required to trade under her flag.[1]   In the sixteenth and seventeenth centuries, the English sought to dispute the right of the French to protect non-treaty interests and to arrogate to themselves the same authority.[2]   But these attempts were for a time fruitless, and as late as the Capitulations of 1740, France was allowed to retain the right.[3]   It was only in 1607 that England herself was exempted from the obligation of trading under the French flag.[4]   In 1675, however, Great Britain was given the authority to exercise protection over the merchants of Spain, Portugal, Ancona, Sicily, Florence, Catalonia and the Netherlands.[5]

Following the example of France, other Powers obtained capitulatory rights from the Ottoman Empire in rapid succession.   These included Great Britain,[6] the Netherlands,[7]

---

[1] See article 1 of the Capitulations of 1581: " That henceforth Venetian, Genoese, English, Portuguese, Catalonian, Sicilian, Anconian, Ragusian merchants, and all those who have traded [*cheminé*] under the name and flag of France, from antiquity to to-day, shall trade in the same manner." Hauterive et Cussy, *Recueil des traités de commerce et de navigation* (Paris, 1834-44), vol. ii, pt. i, p. 446.

[2] On the controversy between France and England regarding the privilege of protection, see *Mémoires de St. Priest* (Paris, 1877), p. 287; *Ambassade en Turquie de Jean de Contaut Biron, Baron de Salignac, 1605 à 1610* (Paris, 1888-89), pp. 136, 143, 146, 155, 156, 160, 184, 415, 419, 422; Additional Act of 1607, Noradounghian, *op. cit.*, vol. i, p. 108.

[3] Arts. 32, 38, *ibid.*, pp. 286, 288.

[4] *Ibid.*, p. 110.

[5] Art. 33, *ibid.*, p. 154.

[6] Treaty of June, 1580, Hakluyt, *op. cit.*, vol. v, p. 264; Oct. 28, 1641, Noradounghian, *op. cit.*, vol. i, p. 48; Sep., 1675 (arts. 15, 16, 24, 42), *ibid.*, pp. 149, 151, 156. The last was renewed in 1838 and 1861, *ibid.*, vol. ii, p. 249; vol. iii, p. 136.

[7] 1612 (arts. 3, 11, 38), Dumont, *Corps univ. dip.*, vol. v, pt. ii, pp. 207, 208, 211; renewals in 1680, 1840, and 1862, Noradounghian, *op. cit.*, vol. i, p. 169; vol. ii, p. 298; vol. iii, p. 180.

Austria-Hungary,[1] Sweden,[2] Italy,[3] Denmark,[4] Prussia and
later Germany,[5] Russia,[6] Spain,[7] Persia,[8] Belgium,[9] Portugal,[10] Greece,[11] the United States,[12] Brazil,[13] and Mexico.[14]

[1] July 27, 1718 (art. 5), *ibid.,* vol. i, p. 224; renewals in 1784, 1862,
ibid., p. 379; vol. iii, p. 194.

[2] Jan. 10, 1737 (arts. 6, 8), *ibid.,* vol. i, p. 240; renewals in 1840 and
1862, *ibid.,* vol. ii, p. 298; vol. iii, p. 182.

[3] Treaty with the Two Sicilies, April 7, 1740 (art. 5), *ibid.,* vol. i, p
272, which was renewed in 1851, *ibid.,* vol. ii, p. 395; treaty with
Tuscany, May 25, 1747 (art. 4), Martens, *Supplément au Recueil,* vol.
i, p. 293, which was renewed in 1833 and 1841, Noradounghian, *op. cit.,*
vol. ii, pp. 219, 338; treaty with Sardinia, Oct. 25, 1823 (art. 8), *ibid.,*
p. 101, which was renewed in 1839 and 1854, *ibid.,* pp. 283, 425.
The Kingdom of Italy succeeded to all these treaties by virtue of
article 1 of the treaty of July 10, 1861, *ibid.,* vol. iii, p. 152.

[4] Oct. 14, 1746 (art. 10), *ibid.,* vol. i, p. 311; renewals in 1841 and 1862,
ibid., vol. ii, p. 330; vol. iii, p. 183.

[5] Treaty with Prussia, Mar. 23, 1761 (art. 5), *ibid.,* vol. i, p. 317, which
was renewed in 1840 and 1862, *ibid.,* vol. ii, p. 314; vol. iii, p. 185; treaty
with the Hanseatic League, 1839 (art. 8), *State Papers,* vol. xxviii, p.
450, which was renewed in 1841 and 1862, Noradounghian, *op. cit.,* vol.
ii, p. 345; vol. iii, p. 206. The German Empire succeeded to these
treaties by virtue of article 24 of the treaty of Aug. 26, 1890, *ibid.,*
vol. iv, p. 493.

[6] July 10/21, 1774 (art. 11), *ibid.,* vol. i, p. 325; June 10/21, 1783 (art.
63), p. 369; renewals in 1792, 1812, 1829, 1846, and 1862, *ibid.,* vol. ii,
pp. 16, 86, 166, 371; vol. iii, p. 171.

[7] Sept. 14, 1782 (art. 5), *ibid.,* vol. i, p. 345, which was renewed in
1840 and 1862, *ibid.,* vol. ii, p. 298; vol. iii, p. 184.

[8] July 28, 1823 (art. 2), *State Papers,* vol. xi, p. 838; May 20, 1847
(art. 7), Noradounghian, *op. cit.,* vol. ii, p. 384; Dec. 20, 1875 (arts. 1,
7, 10), *ibid.,* vol. iii, pp. 391, 393, 394.

[9] Aug. 3, 1838 (art. 8), *ibid.,* vol. ii, p. 245; renewals 1839, 1840, 1861,
ibid., pp. 276, 302; vol. iii, p. 160.

[10] March 20, 1843 (art. 8), *ibid.,* vol. ii, p, 356; renewal in 1868, *ibid.,*
vol. iii, p. 263.

[11] May 23, 1855 (arts. 24, 25), *ibid.,* vol. ii, p. 443.

[12] May 7, 1830 (art. 4), Malloy, vol. ii, p. 1319; renewal in 1862, *ibid.,*
p. 1321.

[13] Feb. 5, 1858 (art. 7), Noradounghian, *op. cit.,* vol. iii, p. 107.

[14] May 6, 1866 (arts. 10, 13), *ibid.,* p. 249.

The extraterritorial rights conferred by these treaties were formally abolished in 1923.[1]

Outside of the Ottoman Empire, extraterritoriality has also existed in the following States of the Levant and Africa: Algiers,[2] Morocco,[3] Tripoli,[4] Tunis,[5] Persia,[6] Mus-

[1] *Cf. infra*, pp. 185 *et seq.*

[2] Great Britain, April 10, 1682 (arts. 15, 16), *State Papers*, vol. i, p. 358; April 5, 1686 (arts. 15, 16), *ibid.*, p. 364; France, May 17, 1666 (art. 11), Rouard de Card, *Les Traités de la France avec les pays d'Afrique du Nord* (Paris, 1906), p. 36; April 25, 1684 (arts. 17, 19, 22), *ibid.*, p. 49; Sep. 24, 1689 (arts. 18, 21, 24), *ibid.*, p. 58; Dec. 28, 1801 (arts. 2, 12), *ibid.*, pp. 83, 84; U. S., Sep. 5, 1795 (arts. 15, 16), Malloy, vol. i, p. 4; June 30/July 6, 1815 (arts. 19, 20), *ibid.*, p. 10; Portugal, June 14, 1813 (art. 10), *State Papers*, vol. i, p. 187; Sicily, April 3, 1816 (art. 9), *ibid.*, vol. iii, p. 525. When France occupied Algiers in 1830, these treaties came to an end. *Cf. infra*, p. 104.

[3] France, Sep. 17, 1631 (art. 9), Dumont, *op. cit.*, vol. vi, pt. i, p. 20; Sep. 24, 1631 (arts. 9, 10, 12), *ibid.;* Jan. 29, 1682 (arts. 12, 13, 16), Rouard de Card, *op. cit.*, p. 318; May 28, 1767 (arts. 12, 13), *ibid.*, p. 324; Great Britain, Jan. 23, 1721 (art. 9), *State Papers*, vol. i, p. 430; Add. Articles, July 10, 1729 (art. 3), *ibid.*, p. 431; Jan. 15, 1750 (art. 3), *ibid.*, p. 433; Feb. 1, 1751 (art. 3), *ibid.*, p. 435; July 28, 1760 (art. 9), *ibid.*, p. 439; April 8, 1791 (arts. 7, 8), *ibid.*, pp. 447, 448; June 14, 1801 (arts. 7, 8), *ibid.*, pp. 456, 457; Jan. 19, 1824, *ibid.* vol. xiv, p. 641; Dec. 9, 1856 (arts. 8, 9, 14), *ibid.*, vol. xlvi, pp. 179-181; U. S., Jan., 1787 (arts. 20, 21), Malloy, vol. i, p. 1210; Sep. 16, 1836 (arts. 20, 21), *ibid.*, p. 1215; The Netherlands, May 26, 1683 (arts. 15, 16), Dumont, *op. cit.*, vol. vii, pt. ii, p. 68; Denmark, July 25, 1767 (art. 14), *State Papers*, vol. ci, p. 285; Spain, March 1, 1799 (art. 6), Martens, *Recueil des principaux traités*, vol. vi, p. 585; Nov. 20, 1861 (arts. 9, 10, 11), *State Papers*, vol. liii, p. 1093; Sardinia, June 30, 1825 (art. 22), *ibid.*, vol. xcviii, p. 979. The majority of these States, except Great Britain and the United States, have suspended their extraterritorial rights in Morocco. *Cf. infra*, pp. 161 *et seq.*

[4] Great Britain, Oct. 18, 1662 (arts, 8, 10), *State Papers*, vol. i, p. 712; March 5, 1675 (arts. 14, 15), *ibid.*, p. 716; July 19, 1716 (arts. 11, 12), *ibid.*, p. 722; Sep. 19, 1751 (arts. 11, 12), *ibid.*, p. 727; France, Jan. 29, 1685 (arts. 18, 20, 23), Rouard de Card, *op. cit.*, pp. 249, 250; July 4, 1720 (arts. 15, 17, 20), *ibid.*, pp. 259, 260; June 9, 1729 (arts. 23, 25, 29), *ibid.*, pp. 268, 269; June 18, 1801 (arts. 18, 19, 23), *ibid.*, pp. 281, 282, 283; Aug. 11, 1830 (art. 8), *ibid.*, p. 292; Spain, Sep. 10, 1784 (arts. 31, 32, 34), Martens, *Recueil de traités*, vol. iii, pp. 773, 775; U. S., Nov.

cat,[7] Zanzibar,[8] Senna (in Arabia),[9] Egypt,[10] Congo,[11] Ethiopia,[12] and Madagascar.[13]

4, 1796 (art. 9), Malloy, vol. ii, p. 1786; June 4, 1805 (arts. 18, 19), *ibid.,* p. 1792. When Tripoli was annexed by Italy in 1912, the extraterritorial régime in that country came to an end. *Cf. infra,* p. 113.

[5] France, Nov. 25, 1665 (arts. 21, 22, 23), Rouard de Card, *op. cit.,* pp. 121, 122; June 28, 1672 (arts. 21, 22, 23), *ibid.,* p. 135; Aug. 30, 1685 (arts. 18, 21, 24), *ibid.,* pp. 146, 147; Dec. 16, 1710 (arts. 13, 16, 19), *ibid.,* p. 159; Feb. 20, 1720 (arts. 14, 16, 19), *ibid.,* pp. 166, 167; Nov. 9, 1742 (arts. 13, 16, 19), *ibid.,* pp. 177, 178; renewals in 1743 (art. 1), 1802 (art. 2), 1824 (art. 2), and 1830 (art. 7), *ibid.,* pp. 182, 204, 208, 215; Great Britain, Oct. 5, 1662 (art. 8), *State Papers,* vol. i, p. 734; Aug. 30, 1716 (art. 8), *ibid.,* p. 736; Oct. 19, 1751 (art. 8), *ibid.,* p. 740; July 19, 1875 (arts. 24-26), *ibid.,* vol. lxvi, p. 101; U. S., Aug., 1797 (arts. 20, 21, 22), Malloy, vol. ii, p. 1799. The texts or extracts of all the principal treaties between Tunis and the European Powers prior to the year 1881 are given in *Documents diplomatiques, revision des traités tunisiens, 1881-1897,* pp. 7-41. Since that date, the majority of the Powers have suspended their rights of jurisdiction in Tunis. Great Britain claims, however, that these rights are subject to resumption. *Cf. infra,* pp. 142 *et seq.*

[6] France, Sep., 1708 (arts. 16, 18, 24), Hauterive et Cussy, *Recueil des traités* (Paris, 1834-44), pt. i, vol. ii, pp. 385, 386, 388, confirmed in 1715 and 1808, *ibid.,* pp. 402, 410; July 12, 1855 (art. 5), Martens et Cussy, *Recueil manuel et pratique,* (Leipzig, 1885-88), vol. vii, p. 578; Russia, Feb. 10/22, 1828 (arts. 7, 8), *State Papers,* vol. xlv, pp. 867, 868; Great Britain, July 2, 1763 (art. 4), Martens, *N. R. G.,* vol. xvi, pt. ii, p. 94; Spain, March 4, 1842 (art. 5), *State Papers,* vol. lviii, p. 594; U. S., Dec. 13, 1856 (art. 5), Malloy, vol. ii, p. 1372; Sardinia, April 26, 1857 (art. 5), *State Papers,* vol. xlix, p. 1343; Austria, May 17, 1857 (art. 9), *ibid.,* vol. xlvii, p. 1162; Prussia, June 25, 1857 (art. 5), *ibid.,* vol. lix, p. 910; Belgium, July 31, 1857 (art. 5), *ibid.,* vol. xlvii, p. 624; Greece, Oct. 16/28, 1861 (art. 9), *ibid.,* vol. li, p. 537; Italy, Sept. 24/29, 1862 (art. 5), *ibid.,* vol. lvii, p. 319; Germany, June 11, 1873 (art. 13), *ibid.,* vol. lxiii, p. 49; Switzerland, July 23, 1873 (art. 5), *ibid.,* p. 626; Turkey, Dec. 16, 1873 (arts. 7, 10), *Archives diplomatiques,* 1875, vol. iv, p. 142. The extraterritorial privileges of the following States in Persia rest on most-favored-nation clauses: Great Britain, March 4, 1857 (art. 9), *State Papers,* vol. xlvii, p. 44; Sweden & Norway, Nov. 17, 1857 (art. 3), *ibid.,* vol. lxxv, p. 907; Denmark, Nov. 30, 1857 (art. 3), *ibid.,* vol. xlvii, p. 1157; Argentina, July 27, 1902 (art. 3), *ibid.,* vol. xcvi, p. 1240; Mexico, May 14, 1902 (art. 3), *ibid.,* p. 174; Chile, Mar. 30, 1903 (art. 3), *ibid.,* vol. c, p. 827.

[7] U. S., Sep. 21, 1833 (art. 9), Malloy, vol. i, p. 1230; Great Britain,

The rights of jurisdiction granted by the above Capitula-

May 31, 1839 (art. 5), *State Papers*, vol. xxviii, p. 1082; March 19, 1891 (arts. 13, 14), *ibid.*, vol. lxxxiii, pp. 15-16; France, Nov. 17, 1844 (art. 6), *ibid.*, vol. xxxv, p. 1012.

[8] Hanseatic Republics, June 13, 1859 (art. 12), *ibid.*, vol. l, p. 1121; Portugal, Oct. 25, 1879 (art. 12), *ibid.*, vol. lxx, p. 1249; Italy, May 28, 1885 (art. 5), *ibid.*, vol. lxxvi, p. 270; Belgium, May 30, 1885 (art. 1), *ibid.*, p. 291; Germany, Dec. 20, 1885 (art. 16), *ibid.*, p. 253; Great Britain, April 30, 1886 (arts. 16, 17), *ibid.*, vol. lxxvii, p. 60; U. S., July 3, 1886, (art. 2), Malloy, vol. ii, p. 1900; Austria-Hungary, Aug. 11, 1887 (art. 1), *State Papers*, vol. lxxviii, p. 943. Extraterritoriality ended in Zanzibar soon after the British protectorate over that country took effect in 1890. *Cf. infra*, pp. 140 *et seq.*

[9] Great Britain, Jan. 15, 1821 (art. 6), *State Papers*, vol. xii, p. 503; France, Firman of the Iman, Dec. 26, 1824, Martens et Cussy, *Recueil manuel et pratique*, vol. iii, p. 616.

[10] Sec. 5 of the Separate Act annexed to the Convention of London, 1840, stipulated for the application of all the treaties and laws of the Ottoman Empire in Egypt. *State Papers*, vol. xxviii, p. 346. Since Egypt was placed under British protection in 1914, some of the Powers have abandoned their capitulatory rights in Egypt. *Cf. infra*, pp. 173-174.

[11] Great Britain, Dec. 16, 1884 (arts. 5-8), *State Papers*, vol. lxxv, p. 32; Sweden & Norway, Feb. 10, 1885 (arts. 7-9), *ibid.*, vol. lxxvi, p. 581; Turkey, June 25, 1885 (art. 6), *ibid.*, vol. ci, p. 632. Most-favored-nation treatment was extended to Germany, Nov. 8, 1884 (art. 2); Italy, Dec. 19, 1884 (art. 2); the Netherlands, Dec. 27, 1884 (art. 2); Austria-Hungary, Dec. 24, 1884 (art. 2); Spain, Jan. 7, 1885 (art. 2); Russia, Feb. 5, 1885 (art. 2); France, Feb. 5, 1885 (art. 1); Portugal, Feb. 14, 1885 (art. 1); Denmark, Feb. 23, 1885 (art. 3); and the United States, Jan. 24, 1891 (art. 1). For these treaties see *State Papers*, vol. lxxv, pp. 355, 634, 323, 991; vol. lxxvi, pp. 576, 1010, 578, 583, 587; Malloy, vol. i, p. 329. The régime of extraterritoriality in Congo came to an end when the country was placed under the sovereignty of Belgium in 1908. *Cf. infra*, p. 111.

[12] Great Britain, Nov. 2, 1849 (art. 17), *State Papers*, vol. xxxvii, p. 6; Italy, May 2, 1889 (arts. 10, 12), *ibid.*, vol. lxxxi, pp. 734, 735; U. S., Dec. 27, 1903 (art. 3), Malloy, vol. i, p. 466; June 27, 1914 (art. 3), *ibid.*, vol. iii (Washington, 1923), p. 2578. The American treaties contain most-favored-nation clauses "in respect to customs duties, imposts and jurisdiction."

[13] France, Sep. 12, 1862 (art. 9), *State Papers*, vol. liii, p. 155; Aug. 8,

tions and treaties may be summarized in three categories:
(1) in cases between foreigners of the same nationality;
(2) in cases between natives and foreigners; and (3) in
cases between foreigners of different nationalities. In none
of these agreements was there any provision made for the
jurisdiction over cases between natives exclusively, the implication being, however, that it was reserved to the local
authorities.

(1) In cases between foreigners of the same nationality,
all the treaties conferred the jurisdiction upon the diplomatic or consular representative of their own country, to
be exercised according to its laws, all interference and moles-
tation on the part of the local magistrates being disallowed.[1]

1868 (arts. 6, 7), *ibid.*, vol. lviii, p. 192; Great Britain, June 27, 1865
(art. 11), *ibid.*, vol. lv, p. 23; U. S., Feb. 14, 1867 (art. 5), Malloy, vol.
i, p. 1060; May 13, 1881 (art. 6), *ibid.*, p. 1067. The following treaties
contained most-favored-nation clauses: Germany, May 15, 1883 (art. 2),
State Papers, vol. lxxiv, p. 717; Italy, July 6, 1883 (art. 2), *ibid.* vol.
lxxvi, p. 301. The system of consular jurisdiction ceased to operate in
Madagascar soon after the island was occupied by France in 1896. *Cf.
infra*, pp. 105 *et seq.*

[1] Turkey: France, 1535; 1604 (arts. 24, 43); 1673 (arts. 16, 37); 1740
(art. 15); Great Britain, 1675 (art. 16); the Netherlands, 1612 (art. 11),
1680 (art. 5); Austria, 1718 (art. 5); Sweden, 1737 (art. 6); Sicily,
1740 (art. 5); Sardinia, 1823 (art. 8); Tuscany, 1833 (art. 6); Denmark, 1746 (art. 10). Prussia, 1761 (art. 5); Hanseatic League, 1839
(art. 8); Russia, 1783 (art. 63); Persia, 1823 (art. 2); 1875 (art. 7);
Greece, 1855 (art. 24); Mexico, 1866 (art. 10).

Algiers: Great Britain, 1682 (art. 15); 1686 (art. 15); France, 1684
art. 17); 1689 (art. 18); U. S., 1795 (art. 15); 1815 (art 19); Portugal,
1813 (art. 10); Sicily, 1816 (art. 9).

Morocco: France, Sep. 17, 1631 (art. 9); Sep. 24, 1631 (art. 9);
1682 (art. 12); Great Britain, 1721 (art. 9); 1760 (art. 9); 1791 (art.
7); 1856 (art. 8), U. S., 1787 (art. 20); 1836 (art. 20); the Netherlands, 1683 (art. 15); Spain, 1861 (art. 10).

Tripoli: Great Britain, 1662 (art. 8); 1675 (art. 14); 1716 (art. 11);
1751 (art. 11); France, 1685 (art. 18); 1720 (art. 15); 1729 (art. 23);
1801 (art. 18); Spain, 1784 (art. 34); U. S., 1805 (art. 18).

Tunis: France, 1665 (art. 23); 1672 (art. 23); 1685 (art. 18); 1710

(2) Mixed cases between natives and foreigners were assigned by the earlier treaties, as by the Turkish, to the competence of the local authorities, who should, however, try them in the presence of the foreign diplomatic or consular officer concerned; but it was expressly provided that the pretext of the absence of the foreign representative should not be abused.[1] In general, the principle *actor sequi-*

(art. 13); 1720 (art. 14); 1742 (art. 13); Great Britain, 1716 (art. 8); 1751 (art. 8); 1875 (art. 24); U. S., 1797 (art. 20).

Persia: France, 1708 (art. 16); 1855 (art. 5); Russia, 1828 (arts. 7, 8); U. S., 1856 (art. 5); Sardinia, 1857 (art. 5); Austria, 1857 (art. 9); Prussia, 1857 (art. 5); Belgium, 1857 (art. 5); Italy, 1862 (art. 5); Germany, 1873 (art. 13); Switzerland, 1873 (art. 5); Turkey, 1873 (art. 7).

Muscat: U. S., 1833 (art. 9); Great Britain, 1839 (art. 5); 1891 (art. 13); France, 1844 (art. 6).

Zanzibar: Hanseatic Republics, 1859 (art. 12); Portugal, 1879 (art. 12); Italy, 1885 (art. 5); Germany, 1885 (art. 16); Great Britain, 1886 (art. 16).

Congo: Great Britain, 1884 (art. 5); Sweden and Norway, 1885 (art. 6); Turkey, 1885 (art. 6).

Ethiopia: Great Britain, 1849 (art. 17); Italy, 1889 (art. 10).

Madagascar: France, 1862 (art. 9); 1868 (art. 6); Great Britain, 1865 (art. 11); U. S., 1867 (art. 5); 1881 (art. 6, §2).

[1] Turkey: France, 1535; 1604 (art. 42); 1673 (art. 36); 1740 (arts. 26, 65); Great Britain, 1675 (arts. 24, 42); the Netherlands, 1612 (art. 38); 1680 (art. 36); Sweden, 1737 (art. 8); Sicily, 1740 (art. 5); Sardinia, 1823 (art. 8); Denmark, 1746 (art. 10); Prussia, 1761 (art. 5); the Hanseatic League, 1839 (art. 8); Russia, 1783 (art. 63); Spain, 1782 (art. 5); Belgium, 1838 (art. 8); Portugal, 1843 (art. 8); U. S., 1830 (art. 4); Mexico, 1866 (arts. 10, 13).

Algiers: France, 1666 (art. 11); 1684 (art. 22); 1689 (art. 24); 1801 (art. 12); U. S., 1815 (art. 20); Portugal, 1813 (art. 10); Sicily, 1816 (art. 9).

Morocco: France, 1682 (art. 16); 1767 (art. 13); Great Britain, 1750 (art. 3); 1791 (art. 7); 1801 (art. 7); 1824 (art. 7). U. S., 1787 (art. 21); 1836 (art. 21); Denmark, 1767 (art. 14); Sardinia, 1825 (art. 22).

Tripoli: France, 1685 (arts. 20, 23): 1720 (arts. 18, 20); 1729 (arts. 25, 29); 1801 (arts. 19, 23); Spain, 1784 (arts. 31, 32); U. S., 1805 (art. 19).

Tunis: France, 1685 (arts. 21, 24); 1710 (arts. 16, 19); 1720 (art. 19);

tur forum rei was adhered to, and in a number of the treaties mentioned, it was laid down that in all mixed cases, civil or criminal, the plaintiff should be brought under the jurisdiction and laws of the defendant's courts, an officer of the plaintiff's nationality being deputed to attend the proceedings in the interests of justice.[1]

(3) Finally, mixed cases involving foreigners of different nationalities were left to be disposed of by their respective diplomatic or consular officers, all local interference being disallowed.[2]

1742 (arts. 16, 19); Great Britain, 1875 (arts. 25, 26); U. S., 1797 (arts. 21, 22).

Persia: France, 1708 (art. 18); 1855 (art. 5); Russia, 1828 (arts. 7, 8); Spain, 1842 (art. 5); U. S., 1856 (art. 5); Sardinia, 1857 (art. 5); Belgium, 1857 (art. 5); Greece, 1861 (art. 9); Italy, 1862 (art. 5); Germany, 1873 (art. 13); Switzerland, 1873 (art. 5).

Ethiopia: Italy, 1889 (art. 11).

Madagascar: France, 1862 (art. 9); 1868 (art. 6); Great Britain, 1865 (art. 11); U. S., 1867 (art. 5).

In many cases, it was specified that only the higher authorities of the native administration could have cognizance of mixed cases between foreigners and natives. See the following treaties:

Algiers: Great Britain, 1682 (arts. 15, 16); 1686 (art. 11); France, 1666 (art. 11); 1684 (art. 19); 1689 (arts. 21, 24); 1801 (art. 12); U. S., 1795 (arts. 15, 16).

Morocco: France, 1682 (art. 13); 1767 (art. 12); Great Britain, 1721 (art. 9); 1760 (art. 9); 1791 (art. 8); 1801 (art. 8); 1824 (art. 8).

Tripoli: Great Britain, 1675 (art. 14); 1716 (art. 11); 1751 (art. 11).

Tunis: France, 1665 (art. 22); 1672 (art. 22); 1685 (art. 21); 1710 (art. 16); 1720 (art. 16).

[1] Morocco: Great Britain, 1856 (art. 9); Spain, 1861 (art. 11).

Muscat: Great Britain, 1839 (art. 5); 1891 (art. 13); France, 1844 (art. 6).

Zanzibar: Hanseatic League, 1859 (art. 12); Portugal, 1879 (art. 12); Italy, 1885 (art. 5); Germany, 1885 (art. 16); Great Britain, 1886 (art. 16).

Madagascar: U. S., 1881 (art. 6, §§ 7-14).

[2] Turkey: France, 1740 (art. 52).

Algiers: U. S., 1815 (art. 19).

Morocco: Great Britain, 1856 (art. 14).

Tunis: France, 1665 (art. 23); 1672 (art. 23); Great Britain, 1875 (art. 24).

Persia: France, 1855 (art. 5); Sardinia, 1857 (art. 5); Austria, 1857 (art. 9). Prussia, 1857 (art. 5); Belgium, 1857 (art. 5); Italy, 1862 (art. 5); Germany, 1873 (art. 13); Switzerland, 1873 (art. 5).

Muscat: Great Britain, 1839 (art. 5); 1891 (art. 13); France, 1844 (art. 6).

Zanzibar: Hanseatic League, 1859 (art. 12); Portugal, 1879 (art. 12); Italy, 1885 (art. 5); Germany, 1885 (art. 16); Great Britain, 1886 (art. 16).

Ethiopia: Great Britain, 1849 (art. 17).

Madagascar: France, 1862 (art. 9); 1868 (art. 6); Great Britain, 1865 (art. 11); U. S., 1881 (art. 6, § 3).

CHAPTER IV

In the Far East

I. ORIGIN OF EXTRATERRITORIALITY IN THE FAR EAST

In Turkey and the Levant, as has been seen above, the concession of capitulatory rights to foreigners may be ascribed to various factors. The union of Mohammedan law and religion, the desire of Islam to invite foreign commerce, and, above all, the existence of long-established custom and usage have all contributed to perpetuate the system of consular jurisdiction in the Mohammedan world.

A different story, however, must be told of the establishment of extraterritoriality in the Far East. There, religious differences did not necessitate a special jurisdiction, the motive of foreign intercourse was by no means persistent, and the force of custom was distinctly averse to the assertion of judicial competence by foreign magistrates.

As is well known, Confucianism and Buddhism, the dominant systems of philosophy and religion in the Far East, make no discriminating distinctions between the native and the alien. They teach tolerance and indulgence to all alike. For this reason, the peculiar situation to which the Mohammedan religion gave rise in regard to the unbeliever did not exist in Eastern Asia.

In the matter of world intercourse, the Far East is noted for its excessive indifference. Vast empires lived in a state of splendid isolation for countless ages, and had it not been for the insistence of the foreign merchant—an insistence often amounting to open violence—it is difficult to speculate how soon the East would have waked up to the need of contact with the Occident. Thus, it is not within the realm of possibility that the countries of the East could have been disposed to induce Western nations to trade with them by extending such special privileges as those of consular jurisdiction.

When we come to the consideration of custom as a motivating force in bringing about the establishment of extraterritoriality in the Far East, a preponderance of the evidence leads us to a conclusion different from that reached in connection with the Capitulations of the Ottoman Empire and the Levant. With the possible exception of Japan,[1] the assertion of territorial jurisdiction was quite general in the more important countries of Asia prior to the introduction of extraterritoriality in the nineteenth century. Let us examine the prevailing practice of the pre-conventional period in Siam and in China.

Siam had exercised complete jurisdiction over foreigners prior to the year 1664, when a treaty with the Dutch United East India Company, dated August 22, provided that cases of grave crime committed by Dutch merchants were to be disposed of by the Company's chief according to Dutch law.[2]

---

[1] "The Shogun's government, in the beginning of the seventeenth century, left the Portuguese, Spanish, English, and Dutch traders to their own law. This privilege, which was granted to them by letters-patent, was held at the pleasure of the Shogun, and was liable to be annulled. The Japanese, however, were more familiar with the idea of personal than of territorial law; and when, in a later age, they formed treaty relations with the West, they seem not to have insisted upon the principle of territoriality. Harris states that, when he proposed that Americans should be subject to the jurisdiction of their consuls, 'to my great and agreeable surprise this was agreed to without demur.'" Hishida, *The International Position of Japan as a Great Power* (New York, 1905), p. 133. The entry from Harris's diary is quoted from Griffis, *Townsend Harris* (Boston and New York, 1895), p. 124.

[2] *Records of the Relations between Siam and Foreign Countries in the 17th Century*, vol. ii, p. 66.

In 1685, M. de Chaumont, heading an embassy from France, negotiated two treaties with Siam, one on religious and the other on commercial matters. The first, dated December 10, granted the French request for a special " mandarin " empowered to hear and judge all cases involving Christian converts, with the proviso that the mandarin must refer such matters to one of the judges of the king of Siam before passing sentence.[1] The second treaty, dated December 11, 1685, is as yet unpublished, but is referred to by a writer on foreign jurisdiction in Siam, according to whom "the second treaty of M. de Chaumont provided for the adjudication by the captain of the *Compagnie des Indes Orientales* of cases between French alone and of cases of theft or any other offense committed by them, and for the joint competence of the captain and the Siamese judges in cases, civil or criminal, between the merchants and others not French."[2] Mr. James also mentions another treaty between France and Siam, dated December 11, 1687, which contained stipulations on extraterritorial jurisdiction. The principal officer of the company was to have complete civil and criminal jurisdiction over those in the employ of the company, regardless of their nationality. If one of the parties was not in the service of the company, the case was within the competence of the king of Siam, but the principal officer of the company was to sit in the court and to have a definite voice in the determination of the case, after taking an oath to judge according to right and justice.[3]

Later practice, however, was directly contrary to the spirit of these treaties. In the treaty of June 20, 1826, be-

---

[1] Art. 5, Dumont, *op. cit.,* vol. vii, pt. ii, p. 120.

[2] James, "Jurisdiction over Foreigners in Siam," *American Journal of International Law* (hereafter referred to as *A. J. I. L.*), vol. xvi, p. 588.

[3] Art. 5, *Journal of the Siam Society*, vol. xiv, pt. ii, p. 32.

tween England and Siam, it was expressly provided that
" Should a Siamese or English merchant have any complaint or suit, he must complain to the Officers and Gov-
ernors, on either side; and they will examine and settle the
same according to the established Laws of the place or
Country, on either side." [1] In the first American treaty
with Siam, dated March 20, 1833, it was likewise provided
that " Merchants of the United States trading in the Kingdom of Siam shall respect and follow the laws and customs
of the country in all respects." [2]

Prior to the definitive establishment of the extraterritorial system in Siam in the middle of the nineteenth century, therefore, the most recent practice was on the side of
subjecting the foreigner to the local laws and jurisdiction.
Thus, after a careful study of the early period, a competent
writer comes to this conclusion: " While the treaties of the
seventeenth century undoubtedly contained the germs of an
exterritorial system, they had long since become obsolete
and inoperative, and it is not, therefore, too much to say
that in 1855 exterritoriality was unknown in Siam." [3]

Before China entered into formal treaty relations with
the European nations, it had been customary for her to
assume over all foreigners resident within her territory a
measure of protection and control commensurate with her
own sovereignty and independence. The idea of personal
law was never conceded by the Chinese Government, until
it was forced upon it by treaty. " The Chinese notion of
territorial sovereignty and jurisdiction," observed Dr. Wel-
lington Koo, " as entertained, though at times vaguely, by
the officials of the Empire in the early days, was not essentially different from that which is maintained by modern

[1] Art. 6, *State Papers,* vol. xxiii, p. 1156.

[2] Art. 9, Malloy, vol. ii, p. 1628

[3] James, *A. J. I. L., loc. cit.,* p. 589.

international jurists." [1]   Up to the middle of the nineteenth century, this principle was tenaciously adhered to, so that even on the eve of the Opium War, when Captain Elliott, British Superintendent of Trade at Canton, questioned the subjection of opium smugglers to penalties laid down by Chinese law, Commissioner Lin asked him this pertinent question: " How can you bring the laws of your nation with you to the Celestial Empire? " [2]

To be sure, there were exceptions to the claim on China's part to territorial jurisdiction over the foreign residents. Mention has already been made of the grant of an exemption from the local laws to the Arabians at Canfu in the ninth century.[3]   But from all later evidence, this tradition seems to have been forgotten and fallen into disuse long before the formal introduction of extraterritoriality into China.   It could not have constituted an authoritative precedent, inasmuch as it was a mere unilateral grant, and could have been revoked at the pleasure of the grantor.   As a matter of fact, no claim to special jurisdiction appears to have ever been entertained by any Power on the basis of this early grant.

Another important exception to the Chinese rule of territorial jurisdiction was the series of treaties entered into with Russia.   Article 4 of the Treaty of Nipchu or Nerchinsk, 1689, provides: " If hereafter any of the subjects of either nation pass the frontier and commit crimes of violence against property or life, they are at once to be arrested and sent to the frontier of their country and handed over to the chief local authority for punishment." [4]

[1] *The Status of Aliens in China* (New York, 1912), p. 47.

[2] Sargent, *Anglo-Chinese Commerce and Diplomacy* (Oxford, 1907), pp. 75-76.

[3] *Supra*, p. 49.

[4] China.   The Maritime Customs.   *Treaties, Conventions, etc., between China and Foreign States* (hereafter referred to as China, *Maritime Treaties*) 2nd ed., Shanghai, 1917, vol. i, p. 6.

The " Treaty of the Frontier," signed at Kiakhta in 1727,[1] and the Supplementary Treaty of Kiakhta, signed in 1768,[2] contained similar provisions relative to the suppression of brigandage and other disturbances along the coterminous frontiers. These treaties are regarded by some writers as constituting a recognition of the principle of extraterritoriality in China.[3] As a matter of fact, however, nothing of the kind was intended. Being reciprocal in nature, the whole arrangement was merely a temporary expedient to facilitate the administration of the frontiers on the part of the two Governments, which, as Dr. Koo points out, " far from establishing the principle of extraterritoriality, seems to have involved nothing more than an application, in exceptional circumstances, of the principle of personal law, which is found in the criminal jurisprudence of substantially all civilized nations to a greater or less extent." [4]

Quite in keeping with her territorial sovereignty, China had always asserted a complete control over the foreign residents. This is illustrated unequivocally by the insistence on the exercise of criminal jurisdiction.[5] Section 34 of the Penal Code, in force before the introduction of extraterritoriality, provided: " In general, all foreigners who come to submit themselves to the government of the Empire, shall,

---

[1] Art. 10, *ibid.*, p. 36.

[2] Art. 10, *ibid.*, p. 62.

[3] See, e. g., Morse, *International Relations of the Chinese Empire* (London, New York, etc., 1910-18), vol. i, p. 60; *Trade and Administration of the Chinese Empire* (London, New York & Calcutta, 1908), p. 181. In the latter place, the author declares, " Here, then, for one to two centuries before the first of the treaties with any of the maritime powers, we have the principle of extraterritoriality accepted. . ."

[4] Koo, *op. cit.*, p. 53.

[5] In civil matters, the Chinese courts had little occasion to exercise jurisdiction over disputes between Chinese and foreigners, these being usually settled by direct negotiations between the parties concerned and by arbitration. *Cf.* Morse, *International Relations*, vol. i, p. 96.

when guilty of offences, be tried and sentenced according to the established laws." [1]   Instances abound in which the rule was applied with an uncompromising uniformity and strictness.   Space does not allow a detailed examination of them all, and for this the reader is referred to other authoritative accounts.[2]

One interesting fact, however, must be pointed out at this juncture.   In the assertion of territorial jurisdiction, the Chinese Government received the unconditional submission of some Powers, such as the United States.   When the well-known case of Terranova was being tried in 1821, the American merchants made this remark to the Chinese authorities: "We are bound to submit to your laws while we are in your waters, be they ever so unjust.   We will not resist them." [3]

In another instance, not only was open confession made of the customary American obedience to Chinese law and jurisdiction, but the responsibility was laid on the Chinese Government for prosecuting violations of her territorial sovereignty.   During the first quarter of the nineteenth century, British naval authorities were in the habit of searching American vessels for deserters.   After a fruitless demand for the surrender of certain seamen taken on one of these occasions, a meeting was held by the Americans in 1805, as a result of which a formal representation was drawn up and signed by the consul and twenty-seven other Americans and addressed to the governor of Canton.   After reciting the facts of the controversy, the letter continued:

The undersigned further respectfully represent to Your Excellency that the citizens of the United States have for many

[1] Geo. Staunton, *Penal Code of China* (London, 1810), p. 36.

[2] Morse, *op. cit.,* vol. i, pp. 100-107; Koo, *op. cit.,* pp. 50-55.

[3] *North American Review,* vol. xl, p. 66.

years visited the city of Canton in the pursuit of honest commerce, that their conduct during the whole period of intercourse
has been regulated by a strict regard and respect for the laws
and usages of this Empire, as well as the general law of nations.
and that by their fidelity in trade, and their peaceable demeanor,
the most perfect harmony, confidence, and good understanding
has ever been maintained between the subjects of this country
and the citizens of the United States, from which has flowed a
very extensive and rapidly increasing commerce, mutually advantageous and honorable to both parties.

That by the ancient and well-established laws and usages of
all civilized nations, the persons and property of friendly foreigners within the territory and jurisdiction of a sovereign and
independent Empire, are under the special protection of the
Government thereof, and any violence or indignity offered to
such persons or to the flag of the nation to which they belong,
is justly considered as done to the government within whose
territory the outrage is committed.

That by the same law of nations, the civil and military agents
of the government are strictly prohibited from assuming any
authority whatever within the territory of the other, nor can
they seize the person of the highest state criminal, who may
have eluded the justice of their own.[1]

Nothing can be more explicit than these voluntary admis-
sions, and as one reads them to-day, one is struck by the
radical departure from them when, a generation later, far-
reaching limitations were imposed on the operation of territorial jurisdiction in China. The reason for the change will
be dealt with shortly; for the present, it is sufficient to note
that it is not to be sought in the force of custom. With
the exception of Japan, the Powers of Eastern Asia, prior
to the middle of the nineteenth century, assumed their territorial jurisdiction and were not in the habit of granting to
foreigners extraterritorial privileges.

[1] Dennett, *Americans in Eastern Asia* (New York, 1922), pp. 81-84.
Passage quoted is on p. 84.

Just as the above considerations cannot explain the rise of extraterritoriality in the Far East, so the differences of civilization between the Orient and the Occident give no clue to the explanation. It is recognized by all that the countries of the Far East had attained a high degree of civilization long before the system of extraterritoriality was established there. Claims to special treatment could hardly have been advanced by the Westerners on this ground, and they were not advanced. Even Caleb Cushing, who regarded the extension of extraterritoriality to non-Christian peoples as a rule of international law, refuted the argument of civilization. " Europeans and Americans," he said, " had a vague idea that they ought not to be subject to the local jurisdiction of barbarian Governments, and that the question of jurisdiction depended on the question, whether the country was a civilized one or not; and this erroneous idea confused all their reasonings in opposition to the claims of the Chinese; for it is impossible to deny to China a high degree of civilization, though the civilization is, in many respects, different from ours." [1]

Failing to find the original justification of the extraterritorial régime in the Far East in any of the circumstances enumerated above, we have but one alternative left, i. e., to seek an explanation in the alleged deficiency of the Oriental legal systems. Rightly or wrongly, there lurked in the hidden nooks of every Western mind a vague notion that Oriental jurisprudence could not possibly be in keeping with Western ideas of justice, and that an Occidental would certainly do violence to his dignity and pride by rendering obeisance to a deficient judicial régime. That this was the dominant state of mind, of which the Europeans in the Far East were possessed, is evidenced by a number of facts.

[1] Mr. Cushing to Mr. Calhoun, Sep. 29, 1844, U. S. *Sen. Doc. no. 58, 28th Cong., 2d Sess.*

In spite of the vigorous attempts made by the Chinese
Government to assert its territorial sovereignty, there was
an equally strong tendency on the part of the nationals of
some foreign Powers, especially of Great Britain, to set
Chinese law and jurisdiction at defiance.[1] The reasons
given for their resistance center around the imperfections
of the Chinese legal system.[2] The justice or injustice of
these contentions is of no concern to our present study;[3]
what we aim to ascertain is whether the foreign governments were conscious of the same reluctance to enjoin compliance with the laws of China.

Writing in 1836, Sir George Staunton, although he depre-
cated the proposals then made for aggressive hostilities with
China in order to force on her certain concessions,[4] and
although he advocated the treatment of China on a footing
of equality with the other Powers,[5] admitting the defective-
ness of her judicial system. " The Chinese laws," he declared, " as specially applied, and endeavored to be enforced,
in cases of homicide, committed by foreigners, are not only
unjust, but absolutely *intolerable.* The demand of blood
for blood, in all cases, without reference to circumstances,
whether palliative or even justifying, is undoubtedly an intolerable grievance." [6]

The remarks of Sir George are of greater interest and
importance when we recall that it was he who was instru-
mental in framing and introducing to the House of Com-

[1] For specific cases see Koo, *op. cit.,* pp. 68-79.

[2] *Ibid.,* pp. 79-95; Morse, *op. cit.,* vol. i, pp. 109 *et seq.*

[3] Dr. Koo gives an excellent critical account of these reasons in the
section of his work just referred to.

[4] *Remarks on the British Relations with China and the Proposed Plans
for Improving Them* (2nd ed., London, 1836).

[5] *Ibid.,* p. 20.

[6] *Ibid.,* p. 18. It must be pointed out that the last assertion is grossly
inaccurate. See Koo, *op. cit.,* pp. 80-84.

mons, in 1833, a set of resolutions, looking, *inter alia,* to the glaringly illegal measure of establishing a British court of justice on Chinese soil without the consent of the territorial sovereign. In the body of the resolutions, complaint was again made against the unsatisfactory state of Chinese laws. The pertinent section reads:

That, lastly, the state of the trade under the operation of the Chinese laws in respect to homicides committed by foreigners in that country, calls for the early interposition of the Legislature, those laws being practically so unjust and intolerable that they have in no instance for the last forty-nine years been submitted to by British subjects; great loss and injury to their commercial interests accruing from the suspension of trade in consequence of such resistance, and the guilty as well as the innocent escape with impunity; and that, it is, therefore, expedient to put an end to this anomalous state of law by the creation of a British naval tribunal upon the spot, with competent authority for the trial and punishment of such offences.[1]

The resolutions failed of adoption, but in their stead a bill was introduced on July 1, 1833, under the title of " an act to regulate the trade to China and India," which was adopted by both Houses and became an act of Parliament on August 28, 1833. Article 6 authorized the creation of a British court of justice with criminal and admiralty jurisdiction for the trial of offenses committed by British subjects in China.[2] In pursuance of this act, a number of Orders in Council were issued on December 9, 1833, bringing the legislation into effect.[3] But although the machinery was thus set up for the administration of justice by Great

[1] Hansard, *Parliamentary Debates,* 3rd ser., vol. xviii, p. 700.

[2] 3 & 4 Will. IV, c. 93. The act does not state where the court was to sit, but from the context the general intention was to set it up on Chinese soil.

[3] *State Papers,* vol. xx, pp. 260, 262.

Britain in China—a machinery that had no legal sanction at
all, inasmuch as it was not consented to by China—yet as a
matter of fact, the powers assumed were never actually
exercised, due partly to the vigorous resistance of the Chinese and partly to the hesitancy on the part of the British
authorities themselves.[1]

. In 1838, a new bill was introduced by Lord Palmerston,
suggesting the establishment of a court in China, with even
larger powers than those authorized by the act of 1833, for
the new bill contemplated a court with civil as well as criminal and admiralty jurisdiction.[2] On this bill a long debate
ensued in the House of Commons, with Lord Palmerston
defending it and Sir James Graham taking the opposite
side. The arguments advanced by the former were again
in accord with the indictments made by the British merchants against the legal system of China.[3] Due to the lack
of support and the general opposition to the bill, Lord Palmerston stated that he had "no objection to postponing it
until the next session," whereupon the bill was withdrawn.[4]

The record of the British attempts to introduce extraterritorial jurisdiction into China by means of legislative
enactment prior to the Opium War was, therefore, one of
failure and disappointment to their sponsors. In the midst
of an obstinate resistance to the assertion and exercise, on
China's part, of her rightful territorial sovereignty, there
was not lacking an enlightened public opinion, which, while
crying against certain imperfections in the operation of Chinese laws, insisted upon a strict regard for the rules of international law.[5] It was only after the termination of the

---

[1] See Koo, *op. cit.*, p. 109.

[2] *Journal of the House of Commons,* vol. xciii, p. 476.

[3] Dr. Koo gives a critical review of the arguments on both sides,
op. cit., pp. 114-30.

[4] Hansard, *op. cit.*, 3rd ser., vol. xliv, p. 751.

[5] In the debate of the House of Commons on July 28, 1838, on the

Opium War in 1842 that extraterritoriality was formally
introduced into China by a treaty premised upon her independence and sovereignty. For this treaty the bitter controversy of the previous decade between the Chinese and
British authorities on the question of jurisdiction undoubtedly prepared the ground, and it is only in this light that we
have dealt briefly with the events of this period. No matter
what is to be said of the accusations of the foreign merchants and governments against Chinese jurisprudence, the
important fact for us to note in this connection is that such
accusations were made and were influential in contributing
to the establishment of extraterritoriality in China.[1]

Later developments in the history of extraterritoriality in
China throw still more light on the relation between a defective judicial system and the establishment of foreign
jurisdiction in the Orient. Ever since the opening of the
present century, treaties have been concluded by China with

bill looking toward the establishment of a British court in China, Mr.
Hawes said that " he had carefully looked over the papers, the noble
Lord [Palmerston] had laid before the House, and he could not dis-
cover in them the smallest trace of the smallest consent on the part of
the authorities of China to the jurisdiction proposed to be given by
the noble Lord. He wished to ask the noble Lord, whether the
authorities of China recognized this interference with their laws?"
Ibid., p. 744. Another speaker, Sir James Graham, while approving a
part of the bill felt that consistently with the whole course of British
policy, with international law and past experience, it would be unad-
visable to pass the remainder of the bill, including the part on the
creation of a British court in China. *Ibid.*, p. 751. When the House
went into committee on the bill, Mr. Hawes again rose to move its
omission, saying that there could be no objection to the establishment
of a court for the trial of offenses committed by British subjects, but
protesting against the court's interfering with an independent power like
China. *Ibid.*, p. 752. On account of this opposition, the bill was withdrawn on Lord Palmerston's own motion. *Cf. supra*, p. 87.

[1] It is to be admitted that there were some irregularities in the administration of justice in China at the time; but, to say the least, they
were unduly exaggerated. *Cf.* Koo, *op. cit.*, pp. 79-95.

foreign Powers, which, while granting them extraterritorial
rights, embody at the same time promises for their abandonment on condition that certain reforms were carried out.[1]
From these stipulations one can hardly resist the logical in-
ference that judicial deficiency has been at the very foundation of the installation of the extraterritorial system in the
Far East.

In Siam, as in China, the principal ground on which the
European claim to extraterritorial jurisdiction was originally
based seems to have been the discrepancy between European
and Siamese laws. This statement finds its corroboration in
official pronouncements as well as in treaty provisions. In
the Memorandum prepared by the British Minister in Siam,
in 1909, explanatory of the origin and modification of
British jurisdiction in Siam, it is said:

By the Anglo-Siamese Treaty of 1855 full extra-territorial
privileges were guaranteed to British subjects in Siam. Comparatively little being then known concerning Siamese laws and
customs, it was considered necessary by the British negotiators
that British subjects for their security should be placed under
the sole jurisdiction and control of their consular authorities.[2]

Again, when Japan first obtained her extraterritorial
rights in Siam, by virtue of the treaty of February 25, 1898,
the protocol granting the said rights provides:

1. The Siamese Government consent that Japanese officers
shall exercise jurisdiction over Japanese subjects in Siam, until
the judicial reforms of Siam shall have been completed, that is,
until a Criminal Code, a Code of Criminal Procedure, a Civil

---

[1] Treaty with Sweden, July 2, 1908, art. 10, MacMurray, *Treaties and
Agreements with and concerning China, 1894-1919* (New York, 1921), vol.
i, 1908/11, p. 745; treaty with Switzerland, July 13, 1918, Declaration,
ibid., vol. ii, 1918/8, p. 1430.

[2] *Parliamentary Papers*, 1909 [cd. 4646], Siam, no. 1 (1909), p. 7.

Code, . . . a Code of Civil Procedure, and a Law of Constitution of the Courts of Justice will come into force.[1]

The necessary implication of this provision is, of course, that at the time of the conclusion of the treaty, Siamese laws were imperfect, because of which extraterritorial jurisdiction was conferred on Japan over her own nationals.

The treaties which Corea [2] had with the Western Powers granting extraterritoriality to them all embodied provisions for its abandonment upon the completion of Corea's legal reform. A representative provision to this effect is that contained in the protocol attached to the British treaty of November 26, 1883:

1. With reference to Article III of this Treaty, it is hereby declared that the right of extraterritorial jurisdiction over British subjects in Corea granted by this Treaty shall be relinquished when, in the judgment of the British Government, the laws and legal procedure of Corea shall have been so far modified and reformed as to remove the objections which exist to British subjects being placed under Corean jurisdiction, and Corean Judges shall have attained similar legal qualifications and a similar independent position to those of British Judges.[3]

[1] *State Papers,* vol. xc, p. 70.

[2] Although Corea was at first a vassal state to China, she was fully independent in her relations with the foreign Powers, and the latter were regulated by Corea's own treaties. In 1870, the American Minister at Peking wrote to his government: "Corea is substantially an independent nation. To be sure, it sends tribute to China annually, but from the information I am able to obtain, the tribute is sent rather as a *quid pro quo* for the privilege of trading with the Chinese than as a governmental tribute." Mr. F. F. Low to Mr. Fish, July 16, 1870, U. S. *For. Rel.,* 1870, p. 362. This opinion was later confirmed by a statement of the Chinese Foreign Office, dated March 28, 1871, to the effect " that although Corea is regarded as a country subordinate to China, yet she is wholly independent in everything that relates to her government, her religion, her prohibitions, and her laws; in none of these things has China hitherto interfered." *Ibid.,* 1871, p. 112.

[3] *State Papers,* vol. lxxiv, p. 105. *Cf.* U. S., May 22, 1882, art. 4.

II. Rights of Extraterritoriality Conferred by the Treaties with the Far Eastern Countries

In the Far East, extraterritorial rights have been enjoyed by foreign Powers in China, Japan, Corea, Siam, Borneo, Tonga and Samoa. The earliest grant of such rights made by China to Great Britain was contained in the supplemental treaty of July, 1843.[1] The first treaty entered into by Japan

Malloy, vol. i, p. 336; Germany, Nov. 22, 1883, Protocol, *State Papers*, vol. lxxiv, p. 649; Russia, June 25/July 5, 1884, Protocol, *ibid.*, vol. lxxv, p. 527; China, Sep. 11, 1899, art. 5, *ibid.*, vol. xcii, p. 1049; Belgium, March 23, 1901, art. 3, § 11, *ibid.*, vol. xciv, p. 541; and Denmark, July 15, 1902, art. 3, § 11, *ibid.*, vol. xcv, p. 172.

[1] Art. 13 of General Regulations, China, *Maritime Treaties*, vol. i, p. 388. Other Powers which had extraterritorial treaties with China are the United States (July 3, 1844, arts. 21, 25, Malloy, vol. i, pp. 202, 203; June 8, 1858, arts. 11, 27, *ibid.*, pp. 215, 220; Nov. 17, 1880, art. 4, *ibid.*, p. 240), France (Oct. 24, 1844, arts. 25, 27, 28, China, *Maritime Treaties*, vol. i, pp. 785, 786; June 28, 1858, arts. 35, 38, 39, *ibid.*, pp. 831, 833), Norway and Sweden (March 20, 1847, arts. 21, 25, *ibid.* pp. 56, 58), Russia (June 1/13, 1858, art. 7, *ibid.*, p. 88), Germany (Sep. 2, 1861, arts. 35, 38, 39, *ibid.*, vol. ii, pp. 132, 133, 134), Denmark (July 13, 1863, arts. 15, 16, 17, *ibid.*, pp. 318-319), the Netherlands (Oct. 6, 1863, art. 6, *ibid.*, p. 343), Spain (Oct. 10, 1864, arts. 12-13, *ibid.*, p. 364), Belgium (Nov. 2, 1865, arts. 16, 19, *ibid.*, pp. 11, 12), Italy (Oct. 26, 1866, arts. 15-17, *ibid.*, pp. 408-9), Austria-Hungary (Sep. 2, 1869, arts. 38-40, *ibid.*, p. 473), Peru (June 26, 1874, arts. 12-14, *ibid.*, 804-5), Brazil (Oct. 3, 1881, arts. 9-11, *ibid.*, pp. 818-9), Portugal (Dec. 1, 1887, arts. 47, 48, 51, *ibid.*, pp. 291, 292), Japan (July 21, 1896, arts. 20-22, *ibid.*, pp. 611-2), Mexico (Dec. 14, 1899, arts. 13-15, *ibid.*, pp. 840-1), Sweden (May 24, 1908, art. 10, MacMurray, *Treaties*, vol. i, 1908/11, p. 744), and Switzerland (July 13, 1918, Declaration annexed, *ibid.*, vol. ii, 1918/8, p. 1430). The provisions of these treaties will be summarized presently. The German treaty was abolished by a Presidential Proclamation of Aug. 14, 1917, making a declaration of war against Germany and Austria-Hungary, *ibid.*, 1917/7, p. 1363, and by the treaty of May 20, 1921, art. 3. *China Year Book*, 1921-22, p. 739. The same Presidential Proclamation also abrogated China's treaty with Austria-Hungary. The Treaty of St. Germain, Sep. 10, 1919, which concluded peace between China and Austria, does not mention extraterritorial rights. The Mexican treaty was denounced by the Mexican Government on Nov. 11, 1920, *State Papers*, vol. cxiv, p. 878.

In this connection, the doubtful case of Chile may be mentioned.

was that of March 31, 1854, with the United States,[1] but it included no provision regarding extraterritorial jurisdiction. Of all the European treaties the Russian, dated Jan-

According to article 2 of the treaty of Feb. 18, 1915, the Diplomatic and Consular Agents of Chile and China "shall enjoy the same rights, privileges, favors, immunities, and exemptions as are or may be conceded to the Diplomatic and Consular Agents of the most favored Powers." MacMurray, *op. cit.,* vol. ii, p. 1190. No specific mention is made of the grant of extraterritorial rights. Whether this is implied in article 2 or not is not certain. But inasmuch as the same article appears in the British treaty of 1858 (art. 7), which makes express provision for extraterritorial jurisdiction in other parts of the same agreement, it is reasonable to infer that the article comprehends only the ordinary privileges and immunities of diplomatic and consular agents which are sanctioned by international law, and does not *ipso facto* carry with it an exceptional right such as that of extraterritoriality. In order to lay claim to the latter in China, it is, in the author's opinion, essential that the claimant should be able to invoke an express treaty provision to that effect, the omission of which in the agreement of 1915 would seem to imply the denial of the right to Chile. "Even if there were commercial treaties with other countries," says Hinckley, "containing most-favored-nation clauses, such clauses would probably not extend the extraterritorial exemption... The substantial fact is that China has continuously maintained her jurisdiction sovereignty, excepting as specifically abrogated by treaty." Hinckley, "Extraterritoriality in China," *American Academy of Political and Social Science, Annals,* vol. xxxix, p. 97. Recently, an attempt was made by the Chilean consul at Shanghai to exercise jurisdiction over a Chinese claiming Chilean nationality. The claim was made on the basis of the most-favored-nation clause referred to. The Chinese Government having refused to entertain the Chilean point of view, the Chilean consul appealed to the Diplomatic Corps at Peking, which seems to have espoused the cause of Chile. The Chinese Government, however, still regards it as an open question. The diplomatic correspondence on this subject has not yet been made available, but whatever may have been the facts involved, the assertion by Chile of extraterritoriality in China on the basis of a most-favored-nation clause would be contrary to established usage in that country. That this is so is further shown by the notes exchanged between China and Bolivia, also a South American Republic, in 1919, to the effect that the most-favored-nation clause embodied in the new treaty between the two countries should not affect the question of extraterritoriality. *Cf. infra,* p. 221.

[1] Malloy, vol. i, p. 996.

uary 26/February 7, 1855, appears to have contained the earliest germs of extraterritorial jurisdiction in Japan.[1] In Corea, Japan was the first foreign Power to secure extraterritorial rights.[2] The formal establishment of extraterritoriality in Siam dates from the treaty of April 18, 1855, with Great Britain.[3] The United States and Great Britain

[1] Art. 8 of this treaty provides that criminals should be judged according to the laws of their own country. *State Papers*, vol. lvii, p. 1055. Other Powers which had extraterritoriality treaties with Japan were the United States (June 17, 1857, art. 4, Malloy, vol. i, p. 999; July 29, 1858, art. 6, *ibid.*, p. 1033), Great Britain (Aug. 26, 1858, arts. 4-6, *State Papers*, vol. xlviii, p. 30), France (Oct. 9, 1858, arts. 5-7, *ibid.*, vol. l, p. 402), Portugal (Aug. 3, 1860, arts. 4-6, *ibid.*, vol. lix, p. 510), Prussia (Jan. 24, 1861, arts. 5-6, *ibid.*, pp. 520-1), the Netherlands (Nov. 9, 1855, arts. 2-3, *ibid.*, vol. xlvii, p. 1087), Switzerland (Feb. 6, 1864, arts. 5-6, *ibid.*, vol. liv, pp. 513-4), Belgium (Aug. 1, 1866, arts. 5-6, *ibid.*, vol. lix, p. 557), Italy (Aug. 25, 1866, arts. 5-6, *ibid.*, p. 866), Denmark (Jan. 12, 1867, arts. 5-6, *ibid.*, vol. lxii, p. 292), Sweden and Norway (Nov. 11, 1868, arts. 5-6, *ibid.*, vol. lxi, p. 561), Spain (Nov. 12, 1868, arts. 5-7, *ibid.*, vol. lviii, p. 197), Austria-Hungary (Oct. 18, 1869, arts. 5-6, *ibid.*, vol. lix, p. 531), Hawaii (Aug. 19, 1871, art. 4, *ibid.*, vol. lxii, p. 1013), China (Sep. 13, 1871, arts. 8-9, China, *Maritime Treaties*, vol. ii, p. 510), and Peru (Aug. 21, 1873, art. 6, *State Papers*, vol. lxiii, p. 54). These treaties were superseded by the treaties concluded by Japan with the various Powers between 1894 and 1899. *Cf. infra,* pp. 208 *et seq.*

[2] Treaty of Feb. 26, 1876, art. 10, *State Papers*, vol. lxvii, p. 533. Other Powers which enjoyed extraterritorial rights in Corea prior to 1910 were China (Sep. 11, 1899, art. 5, China, *Maritime Treaties*, vol. ii, p. 867), the United States (May 22, 1882, art. 4, Malloy, vol. i, p. 336), Great Britain (Nov. 26, 1883, art. 3, *State Papers*, vol. lxxiv, p. 87), Germany (Nov. 26, 1886, art. 3, *ibid.*, p. 634), Russia (June 25/July 7, 1884, art. 3, *ibid.*, vol. lxxv, p. 511), Italy (June 26, 1884, art. 3, *ibid.*, p. 310), Austria-Hungary (June 23, 1892, art. 3, *ibid.*, vol. lxxxiv, p. 121), Belgium (March 23, 1901, art. 3, *ibid.*, vol. xciv, p. 540), and Denmark (July 15, 1902, art. 3, *ibid.*, vol. xcv, p. 171). These treaties came to an end when Corea was annexed by Japan in 1910. *Cf. infra,* pp. 112-113.

[3] Art. 2, *State Papers*, vol. xlvi, p. 139. Other Powers which had similar treaties with Siam were the United States (May 29, 1856, art. 2, Malloy, vol. ii, p. 1630), France (Aug. 15, 1856, arts. 8-9, *State Papers*, vol. xlvii, p. 997), Denmark (May 21, 1858, arts. 9-10, *ibid.*,

have enjoyed extraterritorial rights in Borneo since the middle of the last century.[1] Before the Tongo Islands fell under the protection of Great Britain, various Powers obtained title to rights of jurisdiction in that country. The first treaty containing a specific grant of this nature was that with Great Britain, dated November 29, 1879.[2] Finally, in Samoa, the United States, Germany and Great Britain enjoyed extraterritorial rights [3] before the islands were divided up between Germany and the United States in 1899.[4]

The provisions of the above-mentioned treaties respecting extraterritorial jurisdiction may be divided into four categories: (1) jurisdiction in cases between natives exclusively; (2) jurisdiction in cases between foreigners of the same

vol. i, p. 1077), Portugal (Feb. 10, 1859, art. 6, *ibid.* vol. lxxii, p. 111), the Netherlands (Dec. 17, 1860, art. 9, *ibid.*, vol. lviii, p. 266), Prussia, etc. (Feb. 7, 1862, arts. 9-10, *ibid.*, vol liii, p. 745), Sweden and Norway (May 18, 1868, arts. 9-10, *ibid.*, vol. lxix, p. 1139), Belgium (Aug. 29, 1868, arts. 9-10, *ibid.*, vol. lix, p. 409), Italy (Oct. 3, 1868, art. 9, *ibid.*, vol. lx, p. 775), Austria-Hungary (May 17, 1869, arts 9-10, *ibid.*, vol. lxi, p. 1312), Spain (Feb. 23, 1870, arts. 6-7, *ibid.*, p. 484), and Japan (Feb. 25, 1898, Protocol, art. 1, *ibid.*, vol. xc, p. 70). The United States abolished her extraterritoriality in Siam conditionally by the treaty of Dec. 16, 1920, while Great Britain, France, and Denmark subsequently agreed to a substantial curtailment of their judicial rights in Siam. *Cf. infra*, pp. 213 *et seq.*

[1] U. S., June 23, 1850, art. 9, Malloy, vol. i, p. 132; Great Britain, Nov. 26, 1856, *State Papers*, vol. lxv, p. 1170.

[2] Art. 3, *ibid.*, vol. lxx, p. 10. Other Powers which enjoyed extraterritorial rights in Tonga were the United States (Oct. 2, 1886, art. 12, Malloy, vol. ii, p. 1784) and Germany (Nov. 1, 1876, art. 9, *Reichsgesetzblatt*, 1877, p. 521). After Tonga became a protectorate of Great Britain, the German and American Governments were deprived of their extraterritorial privileges there. *Cf. infra*, p. 142.

[3] U. S., Jan. 17, 1878, art. 4, Malloy, vol. ii, p. 1575; Germany, Jan. 24, 1879, art. 7, *State Papers*, vol. lxx, p. 244; Great Britain, Aug. 28, 1879, arts. 4, 5, *ibid.*, p. 134.

[4] *Infra*, p. 111.

nationality; (3) jurisdiction in cases between natives and foreigners; and (4) jurisdiction in cases between foreigners of different nationalities.

(1) In civil and criminal cases between natives exclusively, it is generally implied and, in some instances expressly provided, that the native authorities should administer justice according to their own laws and usages without interference on the part of the foreign representatives.[1]

(2) Cases, civil or criminal, between foreigners of the same nationality were placed under the exclusive jurisdiction of their own officials, to be decided according to their laws and usages, without interference on the part of the native authorities.[2] In Borneo, the procedure laid down by the British treaty of November 26, 1856, differs somewhat from the general practice observed in the countries of the Far East. According to this treaty, crimes committed by

---

[1] Siam: Great Britain, 1855, art. 2; U. S., 1856, art. 2; France, 1856, art. 8; Portugal, 1859, art, 6; the Netherlands, 1860, art. 9; Italy, 1868, art. 9.

[2] China: U. S., 1844, art. 25; 1858, art. 27; Great Britain, 1858, art. 15; France, 1844, art. 27; 1858, art. 39; Sweden and Norway, 1847, art. 25; Germany, 1861, art. 39; Denmark, 1863, art. 15; the Netherlands, 1863, art. 6; Spain, 1864, art. 12; Italy, 1866, art. 15; Austria-Hungary, 1869, art. 40; Peru, 1874, art. 14; Brazil, 1881, art. 11; Portugal, 1887, art. 47; Japan, 1896, art. 20; Mexico, 1899, art. 15; Sweden, 1908, art. 10.

Japan: Great Britain, 1858, art. 4; France, 1858, art. 5; Portugal, 1860, art. 4; Prussia, 1861, art. 5; Switzerland, 1864, art. 5; Belgium, 1866, art. 5; Italy, 1866, art. 5; Denmark, 1867, art. 5; Spain, 1868, art. 5; Germany, 1869, art. 5; Austria-Hungary, 1869, art. 5; China, 1871, art. 8.

Corea: Great Britain, 1883, art. 3; Germany, 1883, art. 3; Russia, 1884, art. 3; Italy, 1884, art. 3; Austria-Hungary, 1892, art. 3; Belgium, 1901, art. 3; Denmark, 1902, art. 3.

Siam: Great Britain, 1855, art. 2; U. S., 1856, art. 2; France, 1856, art. 8; Portugal, 1859, art. 6; the Netherlands, 1860, art. 9; Italy, 1868, art. 9.

Borneo: U. S., 1850, art. 9.

Tonga: U. S., 1886, art. 17.

Samoa: U. S., 1878, art. 4; Great Britain, 1879, art. 4.

British subjects—the treaty does not specify the nationality of the victims, nor does it state whether this makes any difference—should be tried and adjudicated jointly by the British consular representative and " an officer chosen by His Highness." In civil disputes between British subjects, the same authorities should have jurisdiction, but " according to the customs of Borneo." [1]

(3) In mixed cases, the principle *actor sequitur forum rei* was generally adopted,[2] that is to say, that the plaintiff should follow the defendant into his court. Crimes committed by the natives against the nationals of a Treaty Power should be tried and punished by the native authorities according to their own laws, and crimes committed by the nationals of a Treaty Power against the natives, by the consular representatives of the defendant's nationality according to the latter's laws and customs.[3] In civil matters

[1] *State Papers,* vol. lxv, p. 1170.

[2] See, e. g., China-Mexico, 1899, art. 14, which provides: "As a general rule, every civil or criminal suit instituted in China between the subjects or citizens of the two Contracting Parties shall be tried according to the laws and by the authorities of the country to which the defendant or accused belongs."

[3] China: Great Britain, 1843, Gen. Reg., art. 13; 1858, art. 16; U. S., 1844, art. 21; 1858, art. 11; France, 1844, art. 27; 1858; art. 38; Sweden and Norway, 1847, art. 21; Germany, 1861, art. 38; Denmark, 1863. art. 16; the Netherlands, 1863, art. 6; Spain, 1864, art. 13; Belgium, 1865, art. 19; Italy, 1866, art. 16; Austria-Hungary, 1869, art. 39; Peru, 1874, art. 13; Brazil, 1881, art. 10; Portugal, 1887, art. 48; Japan, 1896, art. 22; Mexico, 1899, art. 14; Sweden, 1908, art. 10.

Japan: the Netherlands, 1858, art. 5; U. S., 1857, art. 4; 1858, art. 6; Russia, 1858, art. 14; Great Britain, 1858, art. 5; France, 1858, art. 6; Portugal, 1860, art. 6; Prussia, 1861, art. 6; Switzerland, 1864, art. 6; Belgium, 1866, art. 6; Italy, 1866, art. 6; Denmark, 1867, art. 6; Sweden and Norway, 1868, art. 6; Spain, 1868, art. 7; Germany, 1869, art. 6; Austria-Hungary, 1869, art. 6.

Corea: U. S., 1882, art. 4; Germany, 1883, art. 3; Russia, 1884, art. 3; Italy, 1884, art. 3; Austria-Hungary, 1892, art. 3; Belgium, 1901, art. 3; Denmark, 1902, art. 3.

Siam: Great Britain, 1855, art. 2; U. S., 1856, art. 2; France, 1856,

of this nature, the self-same rule was applied.[1]   The procedure laid down by the treaties was briefly as follows: In
all civil cases between natives and foreigners, the consul was
charged with the duty of hearing the complaint on either
side and of settling it amicably without causing litigation.
In case of failure to placate the parties, the consul should
have recourse to the assistance of the local authorities, that
they might together examine into the merits of the case and
decide it equitably.[2]   Subsequently, the joint competence of

art. 9; Denmark, 1858, art. 10; Portugal, 1859, art. 6; the Netherlands,
1860, art. 9; Prussia, 1862, art. 10; Sweden and Norway, 1868, art. 10;
Belgium, 1868, art. 6; Italy, 1868, art. 9; Austria-Hungary, 1869, art.
10; Spain, 1870, art. 7.

Borneo: Great Britain, 1856.

Tonga: Great Britain, 1879, art. 3; U. S., 1866, art. 12.

Samoa: U. S., 1878, art. 4; Great Britain, 1879, art. 4. In Samoa,
the Germans had a special system, whereby the German authorities in
Samoa and the Samoan judges exercised a joint jurisdiction over penal
matters. See the German treaty, 1884, art. 4, *State Papers,* vol. lxxv,
p. 508.

[1] China: Japan, 1896, art. 21; Sweden, 1908, art. 10.

Japan: Austria-Hungary, 1869, art. 5.

Corea: All the treaties referred to in the preceding note.

Siam: Portugal, 1859, art. 6; the Netherlands, 1860, art. 9.

Borneo: U. S., 1850, art. 9.

Tonga: Great Britain, 1879, art. 3 (d); U. S., 1886, art. 12.

Samoa: Great Britain, 1879, art. 5.

[2]   China: Great Britain, 1843, Gen. Reg., art. 13; 1858, art. 17;
France, 1844, art. 25; 1858, art. 35; Russia, 1858, art. 7; Germany, 1861,
art. 35; Denmark, 1863, art. 17; Spain, 1864, art. 14; Belgium, 1865,
art. 16; Italy, 1866, art. 17; Austria-Hungary, 1869, art. 38; Peru, 1874,
art. 12; Brazil, 1881, art. 9; Portugal, 1887, art. 51; Mexico, 1899,
art. 13.

Japan: Great Britain, 1858, art. 6; France, 1858, art. 7; Portugal,
1860, art. 5; Belgium, 1866, art. 5; Italy, 1866, art. 5; Denmark, 1867,
art. 5; Sweden and Norway, 1868, art. 5.

Siam: Great Britain, 1855, art. 2; U. S., 1856, art. 2; France, 1856,
art. 8; Denmark, 1858, art. 9; Prussia, 1862, art. 9; Sweden and Norway,
1868, art. 9; Belgium, 1868, art. 9; Italy, 1868, art. 9; Austria-Hungary,
1869, art. 9; Spain, 1870, art. 6.

the consul and the local authorities was brought into accord with the rule embodied in the principle *actor sequitur forum rei* by an interpretative provision to the effect that " the case is tried by the official of the defendant's nationality, the official of the plaintiff's nationality merely attending to watch the proceedings in the interest of justice," and that " the law administered will be the law of the nationality of the officer trying the case." [1]   The privileges of the " assessor ", i. e., the officer of the plaintiff's nationality watching the proceedings of a mixed civil case, were described in the Sino-American treaty of November 17, 1880, as follows :

The properly authorized official of the plaintiff's nationality shall be freely permitted to attend the trial, and shall be treated with the courtesy due to his position.   He shall be granted all proper facilities for watching the proceedings in the interests of justice.   If he so desires, he shall have the right to present, to examine, and to cross-examine witnesses.   If he is dissatisfied with the proceedings, he shall be permitted to protest against them in detail.[2]

It is a lamentable fact that in the case of some countries, as in that of China, the foreign assessor, instead of stopping with the treaty right of attending to watch the proceedings

---

Samoa : U. S., 1878, art. 4.

Art. 8 of the Sino-Japanese treaty, Sep. 13, 1871, provided that in questions where subjects of both parties were concerned, the complainant should address a petition to the consul of the accused, who should acquaint the local authorities, the latter being charged with the duty of investigating the case, arresting offenders, and recovering debts. *State Papers,* vol. lxii, p. 322.

[1] China : Great Britain, 1876, sec. ii (3).

Corea : U. S., 1882, art. 4; Great Britain, 1883, art. 3; Germany, 1883, art. 3; Russia, 1884, art. 3; Italy, 1884, art. 3; Austria-Hungary, 1892, art. 3; Belgium, 1901, art. 3; Denmark, 1902, art. 3.

Siam : Portugal, 1859, art. 6.

[2] Art. 4, Malloy, vol. i, p. 240.   *Cf.* China-Britain, 1876, sec. ii (3) and all the Corean treaties referred to in the preceding note.

IN THE FAR EAST

in the interests of justice, has gradually arrogated to himself the rôle of the principal magistrate.[1]   What is equally an unjustifiable violation of treaty is the usurpation by the foreign Powers in 1911 of the Shanghai International Mixed Court, which will be treated of later.[2]

(4) In civil and criminal cases between foreigners of different nationalities, the jurisdiction is said to be regulated by the treaties between the foreign Powers concerned, and no interference on the part of the territorial sovereign is allowed.[3]   In actual practice, no such treaties have ever been entered into, but the settled rule is again that embodied in the principle *actor sequitur forum rei.*

[1] Hinckley, "Extraterritoriality in China," *Am. Acad. of Poli. and Soc. Science, Annals,* vol. xxxix, p. 97.

[2] *Infra,* pp. 225 *et seq.*

[3] China: U. S., 1844, art. 25; 1858, art. 27; France, 1844, art. 28; 1858, art. 39; Sweden and Norway, 1847, art. 25; Germany, 1861, art. 39; Denmark, 1863, art. 15; Spain, 1864, art. 12; Italy, 1866, art. 15; Austria-Hungary, 1869, art. 40; Peru, 1874, art. 14; Brazil, 1881, art. 11; Japan, 1896, art. 20; Mexico, 1899, art. 15; Sweden, 1908, art. 10.

PART II
THE DECLINE OF EXTRATERRITORIALITY

CHAPTER V

Annexation

With the growth of the territorial theory of law, States fettered with the anomaly of extraterritoriality have labored again and again to throw it off. Little by little, the statesmen of these countries have awakened to the fact that what had once been a normal practice had become a distinct limitation and derogation of their sovereignty. They have come to realize that the system is regarded as a humiliating sign of backwardness, which the Christian States had seen fit to put an end to, and which the non-Christian States should also claim a right to depart from. But the attempts of the latter have not been greeted with uniform success, and it is only by fulfilling many conditions that some States have been able to rid themselves of the increasingly distasteful anomaly.

The methods by means of which the abolition of extraterritoriality has been accomplished or attempted are varied. Broadly speaking, they may be classified under the following six categories:—(1) by passing under the sovereignty of States which do not recognize or grant the right of exemption from local jurisdiction; (2) by passing under the temporary jurisdiction of such a State; (3) by breaking off from a State in which the extraterritorial system exists; (4) by becoming a protectorate of a State which does not concede rights of extraterritoriality; (5) by unilateral cancellation; and (6) by diplomatic negotiation leading to a mutual agreement on the abolition or the preliminaries to it.

Extraterritoriality ceases when part or all of a country with such a system passes under the permanent sovereignty of a country without it.

I. ALGIERS

In 1830, Algiers was captured by France, and consular jurisdiction forthwith came to an end. The Algerians were clothed with French citizenship and came under French jurisdiction in the Ottoman Empire. On August 10, 1834, an ordinance was issued, concerning the organization of the judicial system in the French possessions of North Africa. Article 4 of this ordinance sets forth that "the jurisdiction of the tribunals of Algiers, Bone, and Oran extends over all the territory occupied by each of these Provinces up to the limits which shall be determined by a special order of the Governor." [1]

II. MADAGASCAR

On December 17, 1885, the island of Madagascar was by treaty placed under the protection of France.[2] It was understood, however, that this treaty "changes nothing in the Treaties already existing between the Hova Government and other States." [3]

Shortly after the establishment of the French protectorate over Madagascar, the French Government contemplated the inauguration of a French tribunal in the island and was desirous of receiving an assurance from the British Government that the latter would be prepared to accept for British subjects the jurisdiction of such a tribunal and to forego in its favor the extraterritorial privileges which they enjoyed

---

[1] *State Papers*, vol. xxii, p. 351.

[2] *Parliamentary Papers*, 1886 [C. 4652], Africa, no. 2 (1886), p. 4; *State Papers*, vol. lxxvi, p. 477.

[3] M. de Freycinet to the French Ambassadors abroad, Dec. 27, 1885, *ibid.*, p. 7.

under existing treaties with Madagascar.[1]   To this proposition, the Marquess of Salisbury showed himself to be favorably inclined.   He stated that his government was willing to give the assurance and to consent to the establishment in Madagascar of a jurisdiction similar to that which was introduced in Tunis in 1883,[2] and that the procedure adopted in that year regarding the waiver of British jurisdiction in Tunis would be followed closely.[3]

On February 11, 1896, the British Government was informed of a military occupation of Madagascar by France.[4] In taking cognizance of this information, the British Government reserved all its rights in the island pending the communication of the terms of the treaty understood to have been concluded between France and Madagascar.[5]   It was later brought to the knowledge of the British Government that no treaty had been concluded between France and the Malagasy Government, but that " in consequence of the military operations rendered necessary by the resistance of the Malagasy authorities to the exercise of the French Protectorate, the French Government have simply taken possession of the island.   The Queen of Madagascar," it was added, " to whom the annexation was notified, has submitted to this decision, and accepted conditions which it was thought needful to impose in order to secure the proper administration of the country." [6]   Under these circumstances, the French Government proposed to exercise jurisdiction over foreigners in Madagascar, and to that end had organized

[1] The following summary is made from *Parliamentary Papers*, 1898 [C. 8700], Africa, no. 8 (1897).

[2] *Infra*, p. 145.

[3] The Marquess of Salisbury to M. Waddington, May 6, 1892.

[4] Baron de Courcel to the Marquess of Salisbury, Feb. 11, 1896.

[5] The Marquess of Salisbury to Baron de Courcel, Feb. 20, 1896.

[6] See the Declaration of the Queen, Jan. 18, 1896, *ibid.*, p. 14.

French courts in that country, by a decree of December 28, 1895.[1] Consequently, the British consent to surrender consular jurisdiction was requested.[2]

In his instructions to the British Ambassador at Paris relative to the above French note, Lord Salisbury alluded to the treaty of 1865 between Great Britain and Madagascar giving the British subjects their extraterritorial rights in the island; to the assurance made by the French Government in 1885 that the protectorate did not affect the treaty rights of foreign Powers; to the declaration exchanged between the British and French Governments on August 5, 1890, in which the former agreed to recognize the protectorate of France over Madagascar " with its consequences," and the latter engaged that the establishment of the protectorate should not " affect any rights or immunities enjoyed by British subjects in that island; "[3] and to later declarations to the same effect. It was contended by Great Britain that the Act signed by the Queen of Madagascar on January 18, 1896, did not confer sovereignty on France, and that " the position of the Queen remains in every respect the same as it was under the October treaty, in which it was expressly recorded that the status of her kingdom was that of a protectorate."[4] To the argument that there was a similarity between the status of Madagascar and that of the protected States of India, the British note replied:

The States of India are not annexed to, nor incorporated in, the possessions of the Crown. The rulers have the right of internal administration subject to the control of the Protecting Power for the maintenance of peace and order and the suppression of abuses. The latter conducts all external relations. The

[1] *Parliamentary Papers*, 1898 [C. 8700], Africa, no. 8 (1897), p. 17.

[2] M. Geoffray to the Marquess of Salisbury, Apr. 10, 1896.

[3] See *Parliamentary Papers*, 1890 [C. 6130], Africa, no. 9 (1890).

[4] Art. 1, *State Papers*, vol. lxxxviii, p. 447.

position has been defined as that of subordinate alliance. It has, however, never been contended that if those States had had pre-existing treaties with foreign Powers the assumption of Protectorate by Great Britain would have abrogated these treaties.

In conclusion, it was reiterated that " the treaty between Great Britain and Madagascar is still in full and undiminished force," but France was given to understand that the British Government would give its consent to the cessation of British extraterritoriality in Madagascar, on condition that a similar cessation of French extraterritoriality in Zanzibar, over which Great Britain exercised a protectorate, should take place.[1]

On August 18, 1896, the British Government was apprised of the final organization of the French courts in Madagascar by the Decree of June 9, 1896. " The French courts constituted by this Decree," it was pointed out by the note transmitting it, " take cognizance of all civil and criminal suits between Europeans or those in a similar position [*assimilés*], and between Europeans or those in a similar position [*assimilés*] and natives; likewise of all crimes, misdemeanors, and offences committed within the area of jurisdiction, whatever the nationality of the persons accused or inculpated." These courts were formally established, and necessary instructions had been sent for them to exercise their jurisdiction over all the inhabitants of the island of Madagascar. The British Government was, therefore, requested to notify the British Consul in Madagascar to that effect.[2]

In reply, the British Government stated that it would comply with the request on learning from the French Gov-

[1] The Marquess of Salisbury to the Marquess of Dufferin, Apr. 25, 1896.
[2] Baron de Courcel to the Marquess of Salisbury, Aug. 18, 1896.

ernment that instructions would also be given to the French consular officers in Zanzibar to terminate their exercise of extraterritorial jurisdiction in that country.[1] In the later negotiations between the British and French Governments, the former took the position that it would renounce the British rights in Madagascar on " receiving from the French Government a note undertaking to renounce their exterritorial rights in Zanzibar, as soon as they should be satisfied that adequate provision had been made for the administration of justice by the Tribunals, in cases where French subjects were concerned." The French Government contended that there was no analogy in this matter between Madagascar and Zanzibar, since Great Britain had not as yet established courts in the latter, and that when she had done so, France would make no difficulty about admitting their jurisdiction over French citizens. She would not, however, give an assurance as to a future contingency, of which there was then no prospect.[2]

Contrary to the apparent firmness of the above statement, the French Government shortly afterwards gave the assurance desired by the British Government, that " the Government of the Republic are prepared to abandon the exercise of their rights of jurisdiction over their nationals at Zanzibar, as soon as the administration of justice there, by regularly constituted British tribunals, shall be assured."[3] Consequently, the British Government gave instructions to the British consular officers in Madagascar to recognize the jurisdiction of the French courts over the British subjects in that island.[4] Thus, the British rights of extraterritoriality in Madagascar were formally renounced.

[1] The Marquess of Salisbury to Baron de Courcel, Aug. 24, 1896.
[2] The Marquess of Salisbury to the Marquess of Dufferin, Sept. 14, 1896.
[3] M. Hanotaux to Mr. Gosselin, Apr. 5, 1897.
[4] Sir E. Monson to M. Hanotaux, Apr. 12, 1897.

On February 12, 1896, the United States Government was informed of the French occupation of Madagascar.[1]   In his reply, Secretary Olney observed that "the Department has noted the contents of your note with due reserve as to the effect of the action of the Government of France upon the treaty rights of the United States."[2]   The American Ambassador at Paris was instructed to obtain from the French Government an "explicit statement" on the effect of the occupation upon American treaty rights.[3]

In the meantime, the French Resident at Tamatave had informed the United States Consul there of the raising of the siege of Madagascar and of the fact that "Madagascar having become a French possession, justice will be henceforth rendered to your nationality and those under its jurisdiction, by the French tribunals."[4]   In reply, Mr. Wetter, United States Consul at Tamatave, stated that as Consul of the United States he had received no formal notification of Madagascar having become a French possession, and that pending instructions from his government he could not "accept or acquiesce in any abridgment or change of American interests and of the powers of this consulate under the treaty of 1881-1883."[5]

In the subsequent negotiations, the French Government indicated "that in the opinion of the Government of the Republic, the maintenance of the treaty of May 13, 1881, is inconsistent with the new order of things created by the taking possession of Madagascar," and "that, on the other

[1] M. Patenôtre to Mr. Olney, Feb. 12, 1896, U. S. *Foreign Relations*, 1896, p. 118.

[2] Mr. Olney to M. Patenôtre, Feb. 26, 1896, *ibid.*, p. 119.

[3] Mr. Olney to Mr. Eustis, Mar. 30, 1896, *ibid.*

[4] M. Ferraud to Mr. Wetter, Feb. 18, 1896, *ibid.*, p. 120.

[5] Mr. Wetter to M. Ferraud, Feb. 18, 1896, *ibid.*, p. 120; *cf.* Same to Same, Feb. 20, 1896, *ibid.*, p. 121.

hand, the Government of the Republic is disposed to extend
to the great African island the whole (*ensemble*) of the conventions applicable to the Government or citizens of the
United States in France and in French possessions, and
which have enabled them to entertain their relations of all
kinds so profitable to both countries." [1] But the Government
of the United States desired a " categorical statement " that
the American treaty with Madagascar had been superseded
by those with France " in virtue of complete absorption of
Madagascar and the substitution of a wholly French government for that of the Hovas," with which the United
States had theretofore maintained relations. [2] Pending the
receipt of such a " categorical statement," Secretary Olney
instructed the American Consul at Tamatave by telegraph
to suspend, until further instruction, the exercise of his
judicial functions in all cases where the operation of an established French court was ascertained to be available for
the disposition of judicial cases affecting American citizens
or interests. [3]

On July 22, 1896, M. Patenôtre, French Ambassador at
Washington, informed the American Government of the
passing by the Chamber of Deputies and the ratification by
the Senate of a bill to the effect that " the island of Madagascar, with its dependent islands, is declared a French
colony."   The bill was promulgated by the President as
law on August 6. [5]   Thereupon, the French Ambassador inquired at the State Department whether further instructions

---

[1] M. Bourgeois to Mr. Eustis, Apr. 16, 1896, U. S. *Foreign Relations,*
1896, p. 123; *cf.* M. Patenôtre to Mr. Olney, Apr. 18, 1896, *ibid.*, p. 124.

[2] Mr. Olney to Mr. Eustis, Apr. 27, 1896, *ibid.*, p. 125; *cf.* Mr. Olney
to M. Patenôtre, May 2, 1896, *ibid.*, p. 126.

[3] Mr. Olney to M. Patenôtre, May 2, 1896, *ibid.*, p. 127.

[4] M. Patenôtre to Mr. Olney, July 22, 1896, *ibid.*, p. 133.

[5] *Ibid.*, p. 135.

were necessary to insure the transfer of the jurisdiction
exercised by the American Consul at Tamatave to the French
tribunals.[1] In reply, Mr. Rockhill, Acting Secretary of
State, stated that the instructions already given to the United
States consulate at Tamatave on the subject in question
were deemed sufficient by the Department.[2]

III. SAMOA

By the General Act of Berlin, June 14, 1889, Samoa was
recognized by Great Britain, Germany, and the United
States as an independent power, and a supreme court was
established, the chief justice of which was to be nominated
by the three governments in common accord and appointed
by the Samoan Government. With a few exceptions, the
court had jurisdiction over all the residents of Samoa.[3]

The régime established by the Berlin Act lasted only ten
years. In 1899, the Samoan Islands were divided between
Germany and the United States, and each renounced its extraterritorial rights in the part falling under the sovereignty
of the other.[4]

IV. CONGO

On April 28-30, 1885, resolutions were passed by the
Belgian Chamber of Representatives and Senate, authorizing
King Leopold II to be the Chief of the Congo Free State,
and declaring the union between Belgium and the Congo
Free State to be exclusively personal.[5] In 1908, the per-

---

[1] M. Patenôtre to Mr. Olney, Aug. 8, 1896, *ibid.*, p. 134.

[2] Mr. Rockhill to M. Patenôtre, Aug. 12, 1896, *ibid.*, p. 135.

[3] Malloy, vol. ii, pp. 1577-1579.

[4] Treaty of Dec. 2, 1899, between Great Britain, Germany and the United
States, art. 2, *State Papers,* vol. xci, p. 77; *cf.* arts. 1 and 3 of the treaty
between Great Britain and Germany, Nov. 14, 1899, *ibid.*, p. 71.

[5] *Ibid.*, vol. lxxvi, p. 327.

sonal union was dissolved, and the Congo Free State was placed under the sovereignty of Belgium as one of her colonies.[1] This put an end to the system of extraterritoriality in that country.

V. COREA

In 1910, Corea was annexed by Japan. Article 1 of the treaty of annexation, dated August 22, 1910, provided that the annexation covered " all rights of sovereignty over the whole of Corea." [2] On August 29, 1910, a Declaration was published by the Japanese Government, announcing that " The Imperial Government of Japan undertake the entire government and administration of Corea." A number of rules were drawn up relating to the status of foreigners in Corea, one of which abolished all the treaties of Corea with foreign Powers.[3] On the same day a statement was issued by the Japanese Foreign Office to the following effect:

At the same time, the right of extraterritoriality which foreigners have hitherto enjoyed in Corea comes definitely to an end from today. The Japanese Government believe that they are entirely justified in regarding such right of extraterritoriality as ended upon the termination of Corea's treaties in consequence of the annexation, considering that the continuance of that system would inevitably prove a serious obstacle and interfere with the unification of the administration of Corea. Moreover, it seems only natural that foreigners, being allowed to enjoy in Corea the same rights and privileges as in Japan proper, should be called upon to surrender the right of extraterritoriality which is not granted to them in Japan proper.[4]

All the Powers but the United States acquiesced in the

---

[1] Decree of Mar. 5, 1908, *State Papers,* vol. ci, p. 731.
[2] *Ibid.,* vol. ciii, p. 993.
[3] *Ibid.,* vol. cv, p. 687.
[4] *Ibid.,* p. 691.

Japanese announcement. The United States maintained that consular jurisdiction should be continued until the old Corean system was completely replaced, under Japanese supervision, by actually operating laws and courts, in substantial conformity to those of Japan itself; or that the trial of American citizens under Japanese laws should be limited to such courts in Corea as were maintained at a high standard of efficiency.[1] The Japanese reply was that the judicial system in Corea was substantially the same as in Japan, and that the system of consular jurisdiction being wholly unsuited to the new condition of things, its revival would be " both unnecessary and inadvisable." [2] The United States persisted for a while in its original attitude,[3] but although no agreement has been reached on the subject between the American and Japanese Governments, the former appears no longer to enjoy extraterritorial rights in Corea.[4]

VI. TRIPOLI

After the Turco-Italian War of 1911-1912, the Italian Government took possession of Tripoli. By a Decree of October 17, 1912, it was declared that in accordance with a Law of February 25, 1912, " Tripoli and Cyrenaica were

[1] The Acting Secretary of State to the American Ambassador, Sep. 18, 1910, U. S. *Foreign Relations*, 1911, p. 321.

[2] The Minister for Foreign Affairs to the American Ambassador, Oct. 6, 1910, *ibid.*, p. 324.

[3] " In all my conversations with Mr. Ishii [acting Japanese Minister for Foreign Affairs] and others since the Treaty of annexation was published, I have consistently made the point that American consular jurisdiction was not abolished and could not be so until some definite action to that end had been taken by the Government of the United States." The American Chargé d'Affaires to the Secretary of State, Nov. 29, 1910, *ibid.*, p. 327.

[4] In reply to an inquiry addressed by the author, the United States Department of State " regrets that it has no information on this subject available for dissemination."

placed under the full and entire sovereignty of the Kingdom of Italy." [1]   A year later, on February 28, 1913, the American Secretary of State informed the Italian Chargé d'Affaires that instructions had been issued to the diplomatic and consular representatives of the United States to conform to the judicial régime established by Italy in Libya and to discontinue their extraterritorial jurisdiction. [2]

[1] *State Papers*, vol. cvi, p. 1079.
[2] U. S. *Foreign Relations*, 1913, p. 609.

CHAPTER VI

Transfer of Jurisdiction

THE second method by means of which the abolition of extraterritoriality has been brought about consists in the subjection of portions of the territory of a country in which the system exists to the temporary occupation, administration or jurisdiction of a country in which it does not. In some cases, the temporary transfer of jurisdiction has ended in outright annexation, while in others, as in those of the leaseholds in China, the legal ownership of the territory has been retained to this day by the lessor sovereign. But in either case, the rights of jurisdiction have been exercised by the temporary occupant or usufructuary of the territory concerned, and the extraterritorial system has been suspended during the term of the temporary occupation, administration, or leasing.

I. PROVISIONAL OCCUPATION AND ADMINISTRATION

In 1878, the island of Cyprus was assigned by Turkey " to be occupied and administered by England." [1] Shortly afterwards, an additional article was agreed upon, declaring that for the term of the occupation, the Queen of England should have " full powers for making Laws and Conventions for the government of the Island in Her Majesty's name, and for the regulation of its commercial and consular relations and affairs free from the Porte's control." [2]

[1] Art. 1, Treaty of Constantinople, June 4, 1878, *State Papers*, vol. lxix, p. 745.

[2] Agreement of Aug. 14, 1878, *ibid.*, p. 769.

In accordance with these agreements, a British Order in Council, dated September 14, 1878, made provision for a High Commissioner for the administration of the island. Article 21 of the Order gave the High Commissioner power "to constitute and appoint" judges and other officials in the island.[1] Subsequently, the High Commissioner issued an Ordinance, establishing a High Court of Justice with "all jurisdiction, criminal and civil, over all persons and in all cases other than such as would have been under the sole jurisdiction and authority of the Ottoman Courts if the said Convention of June 4, 1878, had not been made."[2]

The British régime in Cyprus was recognized by Austria-Hungary by a declaration of the latter, dated September 14, 1880.[3] The other Powers have taken no action on this matter, but have apparently tacitly acquiesced in it as a *fait accompli.*[4]

In the same year that Cyprus was transferred to British occupation and administration, the provinces of Bosnia and Herzegovina were subjected to Austrian occupation and administration.[5] By an Ordinance of March 5, 1880, Austria-

---

[1] *State Papers*, vol. lxix, p. 724.

Ibid., vol. lxx, p. 661.

[3] *Ibid.*, vol. xciv, p. 838.

[4] The measure taken by the British Government to assume jurisdiction over all foreigners in Cyprus was adversely criticized by some writers at the time. An article in *The Law Magazine and Review*, 4th ser., vol. iv, declared that "wheresoever throughout the Ottoman Empire the Capitulations have not been 'totidem verbis,' suspended or abrogated, there they are still in force. And for Great Britain to assume the opposite would be, apart from the grave questions of Law and Fact, a very ungracious return towards at least one of her nearest neighbors on the Continent" (p. 139). M. Esperson, in an article in the *Révue de droit international*, vol. x, pp. 587-593, also maintained that the island of Cyprus was still an integral part of the Ottoman Empire even after the British occupation and that as such the Capitulations continued to be in force there.

[5] Art. 25, Treaty of Berlin, July 13, 1878, *State Papers*, vol. lxix, p. 758.

Hungary put an end to her consulates in both provinces and
to the extraterritorial régime there.[1] England acquiesced
in the Austro-Hungarian action on October 15, 1880, when
she made a declaration to the following effect:

Whereas Her Majesty's Government recognize that the
powers of the Government of His Imperial, Royal and Apostolic
Majesty with regard to the administration of Bosnia and of the
Herzegovina should not be restricted in matters of jurisdiction
by the anterior engagements of the Sublime Porte known as the
" Capitulations "; and whereas a judicial administration founded
on the principles of European law has been introduced by the
said Imperial and Royal Government in Bosnia and in the
Herzegovina, it is hereby declared that from the 1st November
next Her Majesty's Consuls in Bosnia and in the Herzegovina
shall be bound to respect in its full extent, and without regard
to the " Capitulations," the jurisdiction of the Tribunals established in Bosnia and in the Herzegovina by His Imperial and
Royal Majesty's Government, and that they shall not exercise
any rights and functions, nor claim any privileges, other than
those which appertain to other Consuls of Her Britannic Majesty residing in the Austro-Hungarian Monarchy.[2]

Russia, France, and Italy followed the example of England
in 1881,[3]

II. LEASEHOLDS IN CHINA

The leaseholds possessed by the various Powers in China
illustrate further the effect of the temporary transfer of
jurisdiction on the existence of extraterritoriality. With
the leasing of Kiaochow to Germany, of Port Arthur to

---

[1] J. Trigant-Geneste, " *Le Droit international privé en Bosnie et
Herzégovine*," *Journal du droit international privé* (hereafter referred
to as *J. D. I. P.*), vol. xviii, p. 783.

[2] *State Papers*, vol. xciv, p. 838.

[3] *Ibid.*, vol. lxxiii, pp. 643, 644.

Russia, and of Weihaiwei to Great Britain in 1898, a question was raised as to the status of consular jurisdiction in these territories. With the exception of Japan, all the Powers recognized that the transfer of jurisdiction over them by China to the respective Powers, though coupled with the retention of sovereignty, meant the abolition of the extraterritorial rights formerly enjoyed by foreigners therein.[1]

The question having been referred by the United States Secretary of State to the Solicitor of the Department of State, the latter rendered his opinion as follows:

As it is expressly stipulated in the leases that China retains sovereignty over the territory leased, it could doubtless be asserted that such territory is still *Chinese territory* and that the provisions of our treaties with China granting consular jurisdiction are still applicable. But in view of the express relinquishment of jurisdiction by China, I infer that the reservation of sovereignty is merely intended to cut off possible future claims of the lessees that the sovereignty of the territory is *permanently* vested in them. The intention and effect of these leases appear to me to have been the relinquishment by China, *during the term of the leases*, and the conferring upon the foreign power in each case of *all jurisdiction over the territory*. Such relinquishment would seem, also, to involve the loss by the United States of its right to exercise consular jurisdiction in the territories leased.[2]

In a recent case, decided by United States Commissioner Lurton, it was held that the United States Court for China had jurisdiction over Americans in the leasehold of Port Arthur and Dairen. The facts of this case were briefly as follows: When the S. S. *Patrick Henry*, an American vessel, was docked at Dairen, two of the crew were assaulted by

---

[1] See United States *Foreign Relations*, 1900, pp. 382, 390.

[2] *Ibid.*, p. 389.

the captain of the ship in a Japanese saloon on shore. Upon complaint to the American Consul at Dairen, the plaintiffs were advised to take the matter up in the United States Court for China when their steamer reached Shanghai. This was done, and at the preliminary hearing the question of jurisdiction was raised by defendant's counsel.[1]

The opinion of the Commissioner was based on the theory that sovereign rights were expressly retained by China in the territory leased to Japan, and that as long as China exercised such rights in Port Arthur and Dairen, her treaties with the United States, including those granting extraterritorial jurisdiction, should have force there until the rights conferred were waived by the United States. At first sight, the premises of the Commissioner's reasoning seem scarcely to differ from those of the Solicitor of the State Department, and one is at a loss to see why a difference of opinion should have existed with regard to the exercise of jurisdiction in the leased territories. Upon closer examination, however, one discovers that whereas what the Solicitor calls sovereignty *excludes* the right of jurisdiction (which is held to have been ceded, for the term of the lease, to the lessee), what the Commissioner calls sovereignty *includes* the right of jurisdiction (which is held not to have ceded to the lessee, in this case, Japan). An analysis of the arguments of the Commissioner will clarify the whole situation.

The opinion of Commissioner Lurton begins with an examination of the provisions of treaties between China and the United States bearing on the exercise of extraterritorial jurisdiction in the former. Then it proceeds to describe and explain the origin of the Japanese leasehold in Port Arthur and Dairen. A provision of the treaty of May 25, 1915, which extended the term of the lease, and constructions placed on the same are cited to show the retention of

---

[1] *China Weekly Review*, vol. xxvii, p. 384.

sovereign rights by China in the territory leased. The
American note of May 13, 1915, making reservations regarding American treaty rights, etc., in China, is produced
to prove that "the United States has not been a party to
or has in any way waived her extraterritorial rights given
to her by the various treaties with China, and took occasion
to so notify both China and Japan before this treaty [of
May 25, 1915] was actually signed." Moreover, at the
Washington Conference of 1921-22, it was argued, Japan
expressly announced her intention to respect China's sovereign rights and the principle of equal opportunity in South
Manchuria, and the United States reasserted its right to
most-favored-nation treatment, "showing conclusively that
it never has relinquished its extraterritorial rights in this
particular territory in question." The precedent of 1900
embodied in the instructions of Mr. John Hay and in the
Memorandum of the Solicitor of the State Department is
alluded to, and the position held that "before the United
States relinquished extraterritoriality in any portion of
China as existed in 1844, there must be definite action taken
by it." After citing the principles of international law
bearing on the validity of treaties, the Commissioner comes
to the following conclusion:

Having taken into consideration the various phases of this
novel case, I fail to find that the United States Court for China
has lost its jurisdiction over this defendant who is charged with
committing a crime within the Leased Territory of China, and
more particularly described as being in the City of Dairen. The
defendant's demurrer is accordingly overruled, and as there
appears to be sufficient evidence adduced to make out a *prima
facie* case of assault against him, he is required to answer the
information filed herein.[1]

The theory that sovereignty is expressly retained by

[1] *China Weekly Review*, vol. xxvii, pp. 384-385.

China in the leaseholds is indisputable, and it was so recognized by the Solicitor of the State Department in his opinion of 1900. So long as China retains her sovereign rights in the territory leased, the treaties between her and foreign States are in force there as they are everywhere else in China, and the rights conferred by these treaties can be waived only by the government to which they are granted. Such is the law, and the Commissioner adds nothing to it when he propounds the self-same principle. But the crucial point of the Commissioner's decision, as the author has suggested, seems to be in the inclusion of the right of jurisdiction in what he terms sovereignty. After dealing with the transfer of the Russian leasehold to Japan in 1905 and the extension of its term in 1915, Commissioner Lurton quotes the language of article 5 of the treaty of May 25, 1915, as follows:

Civil and criminal cases in which the defendants are Japanese shall be tried and adjudicated by the Japanese Consul; those in which the defendants are Chinese shall be tried and adjudicated by Chinese authorities. In either case, an officer may be deputed to the Court to attend the proceedings; but amongst [mixed] civil cause [cases] between Chinese and Japanese relating to land shall be tried and adjudicated by delegates of both nations conjointly in accordance with Chinese laws [law] and local usage.[1]

Commenting on this provision, the Commissioner says:

In construing this part of the treaty, it shows conclusively that Japan recognized the Sovereignty of China, and reiterated in specific terms her extraterritorial rights for her subjects and does not claim supreme powers to herself to the exclusion of Chinese Sovereignty in this particular territory.[2]

[1] The words in brackets are from the correct version of the provision cited. *Cf.* MacMurray, *Treaties*, vol. ii, 1915/8, p. 1220; also China, *Maritime Treaties*, vol. ii, p. 791.

[2] *China Weekly Review, loc cit.*, p. 384.

Here is in fact the crux of Commissioner Lurton's argument and here it is that he differs from the Solicitor of the State Department. What he is trying to drive home is not that China retained her sovereignty in the leasehold of Port Arthur and Dairen, stripped of her right of jurisdiction, as she did in the treaties with Great Britain, Germany, France,[1] and, in a qualified sense, also Russia,[2] in

---

[1] The case of France was not treated of by the Solicitor's Memorandum. It may be pointed out that in the treaty of 1898, leasing Kwanchow Wan to France, it was likewise provided: " The territory shall be governed and administered during the 99 years of the lease by France alone." Art. 3, MacMurray, *op. cit.*, vol. i, 1898/10, p. 129.

[2] The treaty of March 27, 1898, leasing Port Arthur and Dairen to Russia provided: " In the event of a Chinese subject committing any crime within the limits of the leased territory, the offender will be handed over to the nearest Chinese authorities for trial and punishment in accordance with Chinese laws, as laid down in Article VIII of the Treaty of Peking of 1860." Art. 4, MacMurray, *op. cit.*, vol. i, p. 120 (1898/5). In his despatch to Mr. Hay, dated Dec. 11, 1898, Mr. Conger, American Minister at Peking, reported: " The Russian legation informs me that that provision [cited above] is not correctly translated, and that construing it in connection with Article VIII of the treaty of 1860 they have the right and do try Chinese for crimes against Russians." U. S. *Foreign Relations*, 1900, p. 385. Reference to the Chinese version fails to reveal where the inaccuracy of translation occurs. See China, *Maritime Treaties*, vol. i, p. 220. The Russian claim to try crimes committed by Chinese against Russians, if it was made, rested on a questionable ground, since it is expressly provided by the article cited that Chinese criminals should be sent to the nearest Chinese authorities for trial and punishment. Even construing it with article 8 of the treaty of 1860, one can hardly reconcile the Russian claim to the actual grant. The reference to article 8 of the treaty of 1860 was directed apparently to that particular portion of the article which stipulated for the rendition of Russians guilty of grave crimes in China to Russia for trial and punishment. What was meant was that the procedure to be followed in the sending of Chinese criminals from the Russian leasehold to the nearest Chinese authorities should be the same as in the sending of Russian criminals to Russia, hence the phrase " as laid down in Article VIII of the Treaty of Peking of 1860." See China, *Maritime Treaties*, vol. i, p. 106. Leaving aside this point, we find further that this article 8 of the Treaty of Peking made express provision against the trial, punishment and imprisonment by either party

1898; but that she retained this sovereignty, together with the right of jurisdiction, as modified, of course, by her treaties of extraterritoriality. In 1898, China allowed the lessee Powers to exercise complete jurisdiction in the territories leased to them; in 1915, she failed to make the same concession to Japan in the case of Port Arthur and Dairen. The provision quoted by Commissioner Lurton from the treaty in question shows this; and that it admits of no question is further attested by what follows in the same article, a portion which the Commissioner omits to cite but which is of great importance in the present connection:

When, in future, the judicial system in the said region is completely reformed, all civil and criminal cases concerning Japanese subjects shall be tried and adjudicated entirely by Chinese law courts.[1]

of persons not its subjects in any criminal case whatever. "*En cas de crime, quelle qu'en soit la gravité, le Consul et le chef local ne peuvent prendre les mesures nécessaires que relativement au coupable appartenant à leur pays, et ni l'un ni l'autre n'a le droit d'incarcérer ni de juger séparément, et encore moins de châtier un individu non-sujet de son Gouvernement.*" *Ibid.* It appears, therefore, to be difficult, if not impossible, to justify the assumption by Russia of jurisdiction over Chinese criminals in Port Arthur and Dairen on any legal ground. Outside of such jurisdiction over Chinese criminals, however, the Russian Government was given complete administrative authority in the leased territory. To quote from another part of the same article of the treaty of May 27, 1898, cited above, "During the above-specified period, on the territory leased by the Russian Government and its adjacent water area, the entire military command of the land and naval forces and equally the supreme civil administration will be entirely given over to the Russian authorities." MacMurray, vol. i, p. 120. From this, it is clear that complete jurisdiction was ceded to Russia in the leased territory, except over Chinese criminals. Even in their case, as the treaty provided, they should simply be withdrawn from the Russian jurisdiction there, and sent to the nearest Chinese authorities for trial and punishment, the Chinese Government asserting no jurisdiction in Port Arthur and Dairen.

[1] MacMurray, *op. cit.*, vol. ii, 1915/8, p. 1220.

This is, of course, unequivocal language, and it is conclusive evidence that the leasing of the territory to Japan did not carry with it the transfer of jurisdiction, except in so far as it was conceded to her under the régime of extraterritoriality, applicable alike to this and to other portions of Chinese territory. As the cessation of extraterritoriality in a leasehold, according to the Memorandum of the Solicitor of the State Department, was ascribed to the transfer of jurisdiction from China to the lessee Powers, it could not take place unless such a transfer was made. Therefore, while the Solicitor decided in favor of the termination of American extraterritorial jurisdiction in the British, German and Russian leaseholds, Commissioner Lurton went counter to it in the case of the Japanese leasehold of Port Arthur and Dairen. In one case, a transfer of jurisdiction took place; in the other, it did not.

But although the two are widely different in effect, in fact diametrically opposed, the later opinion, it must be pointed out, does not necessarily overrule the earlier, because in principle either is strictly complementary to the other. Both of them recognize the explicit retention of China's sovereignty in the leaseholds, and both of them uphold the treaty rights of the United States. The only respect in which the Commissioner goes a step beyond the opinion of the Solicitor of the State Department is in declaring that where complete jurisdiction is not ceded to a lessee Power, extraterritoriality does not cease. This is clearly a logical deduction from the Solicitor's opinion, for if the cessation of extraterritoriality in a leasehold depends on the transfer of jurisdiction, there is hardly any room for doubt that no right need be waived by a third Power if no such transfer of jurisdiction is made.

Perhaps it may be added that due to the fact that the Solicitor and the Commissioner were concerned with the in-

terpretation of two different groups of treaties, it is not
necessary to reconcile their opinions. But in comparing the
latter, it should not be overlooked that they were based on
essentially identical reasoning and that neither was inconsistent with the other.

III. THE A MANDATES

In this connection, the suspension of the capitulatory
régime in the A Mandates may be discussed. The legal
status of these areas is still undecided,[1] but without enter-
ing into the juristic niceties involved in the determination
of the sovereignty of Palestine, Iraq, and Syria and the
Lebanon, we may well consider them as instances at least
of a temporary transfer of jurisdiction by the Principal
Allied Powers [2] to the Mandatories concerned, after Turkey
had lost control over the several areas.[3]

In the case of Palestine, the intention of the Principal
Allied Powers to transfer the administration of the mandated area to Great Britain was explicit. In the articles
of the mandate it was expressly laid down that " the Manda-

---

[1] See Wright, "Sovereignty of the Mandates," *A. J. I. L.*, vol. xvii, pp.
691-703; Rougier, " *La Première Assemblée de la Société des Nations*,"
(ch. x, *Les Mandats*), *Révue générale de droit international public*
(hereafter referred to as *R. G. D. I. P.*), vol. xxviii, p. 333; Pic, " *Le
Régime du Mandat d'après le Traité de Versailles*," (ii, *Caractères
Juridiques du Mandat*), ibid., vol. xxx, p. 330.

[2] See the preambles to the articles of the mandates, League of Nations,
Official Journal, 1922, no. 8, pt. ii, pp. 1007, 1013; 1924, no. 10, p. 1346.

[3] Before the conclusion of the unratified Treaty of Sèvres, Aug. 10,
1920, these areas were conquered territories under the *de facto* control of Great Britain and France. The Treaty of Sèvres recognized
the provisional independence of Syria and Mesopotamia, but entrusted
the selection of the Mandatories over them as well as over Palestine
to the Principal Allied Powers. Arts. 94 and 95, Great Britain, *Treaty
Series*, no. 11 (1920), p. 26. By the Treaty of Lausanne, July 24, 1923,
Turkey renounced " all rights and title whatsoever over or respecting
the territories " situated outside her frontiers. Art. 16, *ibid.*, no. 16
(1923), p. 21.

tory shall have full powers of legislation and of administration save as they may be limited by the terms of this mandate." [1]   Moreover, in connection with the judicial system of Palestine, Great Britain was entrusted with the responsibility for its establishment in such a way as might assure complete security to foreigners and natives alike. [2]

As to Syria and the Lebanon, the Mandatory, France, was charged with the framing of an organic law in agreement with the native authorities, but " pending the coming into effect of the organic law, the Government of Syria and the Lebanon shall be conducted in accordance with the spirit of this mandate," [3] one of whose provisions was that the Mandatory should establish in the mandated areas a judicial régime compatible with the guarantee of the rights of natives and foreigners. [4]   Thus, like Palestine, Syria and the Lebanon were placed under the temporary administration of France, at least as far as the judicial department was concerned.

Finally, in regard to Iraq, although it was recognized as an independent country by Great Britain in virtue of the Treaty of Alliance dated October 10, 1922, [5] it was agreed in this same treaty that " His Majesty the King of Iraq undertakes that he will accept and give effect to such reasonable provisions as His Britannic Majesty may consider necessary in judicial matters to safeguard the interests of foreigners." [6]   This shows that Great Britain exercises in Iraq a considerable share of the judicial power of the so-called independent government.

[1] Art. 1, League of Nations, *Official Journal*, 1922, no. 8, pt. ii, p. 1007.

[2] Art. 9, *ibid.*, p. 1008.

[3] Art. 1, *ibid.*, p. 1013.

[4] Art. 6, *ibid.*, p. 1014.

[5] Great Britain, *Parliamentary Papers*, 1922 [Cmd. 1757], Iraq, Treaty with King Feisal.

[6] Art. 9, *ibid.*, p. 4.

All in all, we may say that the A Mandates constitute instances at least of a temporary transfer of jurisdiction to the Mandatories by the principal Allied Powers. The temporary nature of the mandatory system is indicated by the principle set forth in article 22 of the Covenant of the League of Nations with respect to the A Mandates, that " certain communities formerly belonging to the Turkish Empire have reached a stage of development where their existence as independent nations can be provisionally recognized subject to the rendering of administrative advice and assistance by a Mandatory until such time as they are able to stand alone."

The articles of the mandates for Palestine and Syria and the Lebanon were approved by the Council of the League of Nations on July 24, 1922,[1] and came into effect on September 29, 1923.[2] The articles of the mandate for Iraq were not approved until September 27, 1924.[3] By these articles, the capitulatory system was suspended, and foreigners were subjected, during the continuance of the mandates, to the judicial régimes established by the respective Mandatories.[4]

[1] League of Nations, *Official Journal*, 1922, no. 8, pt. ii, p. 825.

[2] *Ibid.*, 1923, no. 10, p. 1217.

[3] *Ibid.*, 1924, no. 10, pp. 1346-1347.

[4] Palestine, art. 8, " The privileges and immunities of foreigners, including the benefit of consular jurisdiction and protection as formerly enjoyed by Capitulation or usage in the Ottoman Empire, shall not be applicable in Palestine. Unless the Powers whose nationals enjoyed the aforementioned privileges and immunities on August first, 1914, shall have previously renounced the right to their re-establishment, or shall have agreed to their non-application for a specific period, these privileges and immunities shall, at the expiration of the mandate, be immediately reestablished in their entirety or with such modifications as may have been agreed upon between the Powers concerned." *Ibid.*, 1922, no. 8, pt. ii, p. 1008. Art. 5 of the mandate for Syria and the Lebanon was to the same effect, *ibid.*, p. 1014. The Council of the League, in approving the articles of the mandate for Iraq, decided upon the non-application of the Capitulations in that country " as long as the Treaty of Alliance [between Great Britain and Iraq] is in force." *Ibid.*, 1924, no. 10, p. 1347.

In Palestine, after the articles of the mandate were approved, Great Britain issued an Order in Council, dated August 10, 1922, providing for the judicial régime to be established in the mandated territory. It gave the Civil Courts jurisdicton over foreigners, subject to the following provisos. In offenses punishable with imprisonment for a term exceeding fifteen days or a fine exceeding £E.5, foreigners might claim to be tried by a British magistrate; in offenses not triable by a magistrate, foreigners might claim that their interrogation during the preliminary investigation should be undertaken by a British magistrate; and foreigners committed for trial before the District Court or the Court of Criminal Assize might claim that the Court sholud contain a majority of British judges. In civil cases, they might claim that at least one member of the Court should be a British judge. In civil and criminal cases heard by the Supreme Court in its appellate capacity, a foreigner might claim that the Court should contain a majority of British judges. Matters of personal status affecting foreigners other than Moslems should be decided by the District Court according to the personal law of the parties concerned. The District Court, in trying matters of this nature, should be constituted by the British president sitting alone. Where persons other than British subjects were involved, the president might invite the consul or a representative of the consulate of the foreigner concerned to sit as an assessor for the purpose of advising upon the personal law in question. In case of appeals, the consul or his representative should sit in the same capacity in the Court of Appeal.[1] Up to 1923, all the Powers, except the United States, had ceased to exercise their consular jurisdiction in Palestine.[2]

[1] Great Britain, *Statutory Rules and Orders,* 1922, no. 1282, art. 58, 60, 61, 62, 63, 64.

[2] See *Report on Palestine Administration,* 1923, p. 19.

Following the conclusion of the Treaty of Alliance between Great Britain and Iraq, a number of subsidiary agreements were entered into, one of which, dated March 25, 1924, dealt with jurisdiction over foreigners. In this agreement, substantially the same provisions were made as in the Palestine Order in Council of 1922, with a view to the guarantee of the rights of foreigners in Iraq.[1]

By way of summary, it may be said that in all these cases, according to the terms of the mandates, the Capitulations were merely suspended and that as a condition of this suspension, the Mandatories were charged with the duty of establishing in the respective areas a judicial system calculated to protect the rights of foreigners as well as of natives.

[1] Arts. 2 & 4, Great Britain, *Parl. Pap.*, 1924 [Cmd. 2120], Iraq.

CHAPTER VII

SEPARATION

THE third way in which extraterritorial rights are brought or tend to be brought to an end is by the separation from the parent State of a part of an Oriental country in which the system exists. Here the abolition of consular jurisdiction has not always followed immediately upon the separation, but the tendency has been in the direction of abolition whenever a portion of a Power whose jurisdiction is impaired by treaty is able to assert its independence.

I. GREECE

The independence of Greece in 1830 ended the régime of extraterritoriality in that country, although there was no express provision to that effect in the main acts relating to the establishment of the independent government in Greece. The régime was discontinued, " for the reason, apparently, that the new kingdom was placed under the protection of Great Britain, France, and Russia." [1]

II. ROUMANIA

In Roumania, the foreign Powers began to enjoy the privileges accorded to them by the Turkish Capitulations in the eighteenth century. Russia was the first Power to secure the right to establish a consulate in Moldavia and Wallachia. The treaty of Kutschuk Kaïnardji, July 10/21, 1774, recognized the special interest of Russia in the Danubian Principalities by allowing her to address representa-

---

[1] Hinckley, *American Consular Jurisdiction in the Orient* (Washington, 1906), p. 183.

tions to the Porte on their behalf.[1]   This treaty paved the
way for the assumption by Russia of consular jurisdiction
in Roumania, which dated from the unpublished treaty of
1781.[2]   The other Powers, including Austria, Prussia,
France and England, established their consulates in the
Danubian Principalities toward the end of the eighteenth
century and at the beginning of the nineteenth.[3]

In the nineteenth century, before the independence of
Roumania was recognized, she made several endeavors to
secure the abrogation of foreign jurisdiction within her
confines.   In September, 1857, the Divan of Moldavia discussed the question, and, in the *projet* which was drawn up,
after demonstrating the illegality of applying the Turkish
Capitulations in the Principalities, the Divan contended for
the discontinuance of the foreign rights of extraterritoriality, inasmuch as they had been granted by Turkey under
conditions peculiar to herself and as the laws and judicial
system of Roumania gave sufficient security to the life and
property of her foreign residents.   Upon these considerations it was concluded that " the Christian States can have
no interest in maintaining in the Principalities the Capitulations which are not applicable at all and which are the cause
of confusion and of innumerable conflicts," and the wish
(*voeu*) was expressed " that the foreigners who inhabit the
Principalities submit to the jurisdiction of the country." [4]
No action was taken by the Powers.

After the Paris Conference, the treaty of March 30,

---

[1] Art. 16, Noradounghian, *Recueil*, vol. i, p. 327.

[2] Schoell, *Histoire abrégée des traités de paix* (Paris, 1817-18), vol.
xiv, p. 444. *Cf.* Boéresco, " *La Situation politique des anciennes Prin-
cipautés du Danube avant 1878*," R. G. D. I .P., vol. iv, pp. 349-350.

[3] *Ibid.*, pp. 351, 352, 354, 356.

[4] *Ibid.*, pp. 369-370.

1856, provided for the meeting of a Special Commission at Bucharest "to inquire into the actual state of the Principalities and to propose the bases for their future organization." [1]   The Commission met at Bucharest the following year and rendered a report, which declared: "Consular jurisdiction having been established originally in the Orient only to protect the Christian foreigners against the Mussulman legislation, its application appears to be an anomaly in a State where there are no Mussulmans and where the legislation is Christian."   The Russian Consul added, besides, that this jurisdiction had undergone such an extension that, on the one hand, it assimilated to the status of foreigners and extraterritorialized thousands of working families in the Principalities, and that, on the other, it arrogated to itself the right of deciding cases which, according to the treaties, were within the exclusive competence of the local courts. [2] It was, perhaps, in response to this report that the Russian Government entered into a treaty with the Principalities on November 22, 1869, giving up her extraterritorial rights there. [3]

In 1869, B. Boéresco, then Minister of Justice, published his *Mémoire* on consular jurisdiction in Roumania.   He advanced the theory, as had been done before, that the Capitulations did not apply to the Principalities and that the privileges guaranteed by them should not be maintained by the European Powers.   The arguments on which this theory was based were, briefly, that the sole intention of the negotiators of the Capitulations was to apply them to Mussulman countries; that Roumania, being a Christian country, was not within their purview; that in spite of the suzerainty of Turkey over the Principalities, Roumania had always re-

[1] Art. 23, *State Papers*, vol. xlvi, p. 15.

[2] Boéresco, *loc. cit.*, pp. 372-373.

[3] Art. 18, *Archives diplomatiques*, 1874, vol. iv, p. 105.

tained its sovereign rights; that the Sublime Porte having
no judicial power in Roumania, could not confer it upon
foreign Powers; that Roumania having retained its treaty-
making power, the Ottoman Empire could not exercise it
on Roumania's behalf; that the Capitulations had never
been promulgated or published in Roumania, and therefore
were not in force there; that the stipulations of the Capitulations were in conflict with the laws of the Principalities, which
measured up to the standard of those of the other Christian
Powers and which, therefore, excluded the operation of
consular jurisdiction in Roumania; that there were in force
in Roumania a Civil Code, a Penal Code, a Code of Criminal Procedure, a Code of Civil Procedure, and a Commercial Code, all of which were modeled on the best systems
of European jurisprudence; and that although the judicial
officers of Roumania were by no means perfect, measures
were adopted to ensure a stable, independent and efficient
judiciary.[1]

At the end of the Congress of Berlin, in 1878, the privileges of extraterritoriality enjoyed by the Powers in Roumania were retained,[2] although the independence of the
latter was formally recognized.[3] As a matter of fact, however, the system of extraterritoriality in Roumania has long
since fallen into desuetude. Thus, it is said by a German
authority:

Ever since the beginning of their national regeneration, the
Roumanian authorities have refused to enforce the judgments of
the foreign consuls and to lend assistance to the execution of the
judicial acts of the same [consuls], and since the declaration
of independence of March 14/26, 1877, the jurisdiction of the

[1] B. Boéresco, *Mémoire sur la jurisdiction consulaire en Roumanie*
(Bucharest, 1869).

[2] Art. 49, *State Papers*, vol. lxix, p. 764.

[3] Art. 43, *ibid.*, p. 763.

foreign consuls has actually been put an end to, for the idea of
national judicial sovereignty [*Justizhoheit*], which was guaranteed to the Roumanians by article 7 of the Treaty of Paris of
March 18/30, 1856, does not permit a foreign jurisdiction in
their own country.[1]

To-day, a number of treaties are in existence, which
pledge the Roumanian Government to accord " the most
complete protection " to the person and property of their
foreign residents, who, in turn, are held to the same " conditions and formalities " as are prescribed for the natives.[2]
The British treaty of October 31, 1905, is even more explicit. It provides: " They [subjects of either country in
the other] shall, on compliance with the laws of the country, have free access to the Courts of Justice, either for the
prosecution or for the defence of their rights, and in this
respect they shall enjoy all privileges and immunities of
native subjects." [3]   No special privileges are given to the
foreigners by these treaties, and during their sojourn in
Roumania they are simply placed on the same footing as the
natives.

III. SERBIA

Before Serbia attained her independence in 1878, attempts
had been made by her to throw off the yoke of extraterritoriality. In 1862, from January 25 to February 5, a conference was held in Belgrade by the foreign Consular Body
to discuss the maintenance of consular jurisdiction in Serbia. At the conference the British, French, Italian, Russian, Prussian and Austrian consuls were present. Although

---

[1] Leske und Loewenfeld, *Die Rechtsverfolgung im internationalen
Verkehr* (Berlin, 1895-1904), vol. ii, p. 192.

[2] Art. 5, Italian treaty of Aug. 5/17, 1880, *State Papers*, vol. lxxi,
p. 165.

[3] Art. 3, *State Papers*, vol. xcviii, p. 88. *Cf.* art. 2 of French treaty of
March 6, 1907, *ibid.*, vol. ci, p. 319.

some of the members referred to the improved system of law in Serbia, others stressed the insufficiency of a mere improvement of the letter of the law and the necessity of having an impartial judiciary, of whose existence in Serbia they were uncertain.

On the other hand, the Serbian Government contended that legislation in Serbia had reached a high stage of development, that a criminal procedure had long been in force, which afforded the necessary guarantees to the accused, and that the project of a formal code of criminal procedure had been drawn up and was being submitted to the deliberation of the Senate. In view of the development of the Serbian State, the hope was entertained that " the Powers would cease to assert in a Christian country, provided with a European legislation and organization, the privileges adapted to non-Christian countries, in order that in this manner the letter of the Capitulations may hereafter cease to be in opposition to their spirit." [1]

The conference adjourned without doing anything in the interest of the Serbian aspirations. Even after the Berlin Congress of 1878, when the Powers recognized the independence of Serbia,[2] their rights of extraterritoriality remained intact. " The immunities and privileges of the foreign subjects," article 37 of the treaty of July 13, 1878, provided, " as well as the rights of Consular jurisdiction and protection, such as they exist to-day, shall remain in full force so long as they are not modified by common accord between the Principality and the interested Powers." [3]

Soon after the conclusion of the Treaty of Berlin, however, the Powers vied with each other in giving up their

---

[1] *Archives diplomatiques,* 1863, vol. ii, pp. 94-114.

[2] Art. 34, Treaty of Berlin, July 13, 1878, *State Papers,* vol. lxix, p. 761.

[3] *Ibid.,* p. 762.

extraterritorial rights in Serbia. On October 20/November 9, 1879, Italy entered into a convention with Serbia, which recognized the principle that subjects of either party should enjoy " the most constant and complete protection for their person and property " and that, in this regard, they should simply enjoy the same privileges as the natives.[1] In 1880, Great Britain consented " to surrender the privileges and immunities hitherto enjoyed by her subjects in Serbia, in virtue of the Capitulations between Great Britain and the Ottoman Empire." The surrender was made on the specific proviso, " that the said Capitulations shall, as regards all judicial matters, except those affecting real estate in Servia, remain in full force as far as they concern the mutual relations between Britis subjects and the subjects of those other Powers, which, having a right to the privileges and immunities accorded by the aforesaid Capitulations, shall not have surrendered them." [2] This condition was fulfilled when all the important Powers later made treaties with Serbia, abandoning their jurisdiction in that country. The list includes Austria-Hungary,[3] the United States,[4] Germany [5] and France.[6]

IV. MONTENEGRO

Montenegro was the third of the Balkan triumvirate which gained complete independence after the Congress of Berlin.[7] No disposition was made of the status of the Capitulations in Montenegro, but the Powers had ceased to

---

[1] Art. 2, *State Papers*, vol. lxx, p. 574.

[2] Art. 13, treaty of Jan. 26/Feb. 7, 1880, *ibid.,* vol. lxxi, p. 19.

[3] April 24/May 6, 1881, art. 13, *ibid.,* vol. lxxii, p. 940.

[4] Oct. 14, 1881, art. 12, Malloy, vol. ii, p. 1621.

[5] Jan. 6, 1883, art. 25, *State Papers,* vol. lxxix, p. 541.

[6] Jan. 18, 1883, art. 66, *ibid.,* vol. lxiv, p. 138.

[7] Art. 26, *ibid.,* Treaty of Berlin, July 13, 1878, vol. lxix, p. 758.

exercise their consular jurisdiction there long before Montenegro was merged in the newly established Serb-Croat-
Slovene State.[1]

V. BULGARIA

Up to 1878, Bulgaria had been a province of the Ottoman Empire, to which all the Capitulations applied. By the
Treaty of Berlin, July 13, 1878, she was constituted into
an autonomous tributary principality of the Sultan.[2] The
change of the status of Bulgaria, however, did not affect
the existence and operation of the Capitulations in that
country.[3]

Since the proclamation of her independence in 1908, Bulgaria has entered into consular treaties with Italy,[4] Austria-
Hungary[5] and Russia,[6] and also extradition treaties with
Austria-Hungary[7] and Russia,[8] all of which omit mention
of the status of the Capitulations. Whether it was intended
thus to do away permanently with the right of extraterritoriality enjoyed by these powers in Bulgaria may be a moot
question. At the Paris Peace Conference of 1919, when
the Bulgarian delegation was apprised of the terms of the
peace, it raised the point that the above-mentioned treaties
actually had the effect of excluding the system of the Capitu-

[1] Leske und Loewenfeld, *op. cit.*, p. 343.

[2] Art. 1, *State Papers*, vol. lxix, p. 751.

[3] Art. 8 of the Treaty of Berlin provides: " The immunities and privileges of the foreign subjects, as well as the rights of consular jurisdiction and protection, such as have been established by the Capitulations
and usages, shall remain in full force as long as they are not modified by
consent of the interested parties." *Ibid.*, p. 754.

[4] March 10, 1910, *ibid.*, vol. ciii, p. 389.

[5] May 18, 1911, *ibid.*, vol. civ, p. 695.

[6] Oct. 29, 1911, *ibid.*, vol. cvii, p. 693.

[7] May 18, 1911, *ibid.*, vol. civ, p. 720.

Oct. 29, 1911, *ibid.*, vol. cvii, p. 700.

lations and lodged a strong protest against article 175 of the draft treaty,[1] which, as signed at Neuilly on November 27, 1919, provided: " The immunities and privileges of foreigners as well as the rights of jurisdiction and of consular protection enjoyed by the Allied and Associated Powers in Bulgaria by virtue of the Capitulations, usages, and treaties, may form the subject of special conventions between the Powers concerned and Bulgaria." [2]   At the time of writing, no conventions of this sort appear to have been made.

The latest published expression of American policy on the status of the Capitulations in Bulgaria is contained in a note of the Department of State to its representative at Sofia, dated February 12, 1913, which declared:

You are authorized to bring to the knowledge of the Foreign Office, in whatever manner you may deem expedient, the fact that this Government, recognizing that it has no intrinsic right to the benefit of the Capitulations as established by the Treaty of Berlin, stands ready to facilitate the negotiations in which the Bulgarian Government is engaged, by assenting in advance to the relinquishment of such rights as it now enjoys in this respect, at such time as the signatory Powers shall all have consented to the discontinuance of the Capitulatory régime.[3]

The United States Government, however, did not ratify the Treaty of Neuilly of November 27, 1919, and, according to a letter from the Department of State, in answer to the author's inquiry, " no convention of the character contemplated in Article 175 of that treaty has been concluded between the United States and Bulgaria."

---

[1] *Observations of the Bulgarian Delegation on the Conditions of Peace with Bulgaria* (Paris, 1919), pp. 123-124.

[2] Great Britain, *Treaty Series,* 1920, no. 5, p. [127].

[3] U. S. *Foreign Relations,* 1913, p. 77.

CHAPTER VIII

Protection

THE fourth method whereby extraterritoriality is sometimes abrogated is by the passing of a Power in which such a system exists under the protection of another in which it does not. The form of protection varies according as the treaties which bring it about vary in providing for it. It never involves any change of sovereignty and does not always entail a transfer of jurisdiction. We shall find further on that protection in itself does not *ipso facto* abrogate extraterritoriality. As a rule, the abandonment of foreign jurisdiction in a protectorate is conditioned upon an improvement of the judicial system there consistent with the principles of modern jurisprudence.

I. MADAGASCAR

In Madagascar, as we have seen, extraterritoriality was abolished only after France annexed the island in 1896. While it was under the protection of France, the latter's attempts to seek the consent of Great Britain to the discontinuance of her consular jurisdiction in Madagascar were unfruitful. One of the reasons for the British refusal to comply with the request of France was that the status of the island was not changed by the forcible annexation on the part of France and remained to be that of a protectorate, which should not involve the abrogation of all treaties between Madagascar and other Powers. The United States, likewise, insisted upon a " categorical statement " regarding the effect of the annexation, before she would give up her extraterritorial rights in the island. All this goes to show that the establishment of a protectorate does not necessarily put an end to extraterritoriality in the protected State.[1]

II. ZANZIBAR

Zanzibar became a British protectorate by the treaty of June 14, 1890,[2] and notification was sent out by the British Foreign Office to this effect on November 4.[3] On May 11, 1906, an Order in Council was made public, which established the British judicial system in Zanzibar. According to this Order, the jurisdiction of the British Court " extends to British subjects, to British protected persons, to foreigners with respect to whom the Sultan of Zanzibar has decreed, or the Sovereign or Government whose subjects or citizens they are or are claimed as being, has, by Treaty or otherwise, agreed with His Majesty for, or consented to the exercise of jurisdiction by His Majesty, and to Zanzibar subjects in the regular service of such foreigners." [4] This Order took effect on November 4, 1908,[5] on which date the sultan issued a decree to the same effect.[6]

After the establishment of the British protectorate over Zanzibar, France by a declaration exchanged with the British Government on August 5, 1890, engaged to recognize it as soon as she should receive notification of the same. But it was understood on either side that the establishment of the protectorate would not affect the rights and immunities enjoyed by French citizens in the territory in question.[7] In

[1] *Cf. supra*, pp. 104 *et seq.*

[2] *State Papers*, vol lxxxii, p. 653.

[3] *Ibid.*, p. 654; U. S. *Foreign Relations*, 1890, p. 476.

[4] *State Papers*, vol. xcix, p. 461.

[5] *Ibid.*, vol. ci, p. 78.

[6] *Ibid.*, p. 649.

[7] *Parliamentary Papers*, 1890 [C. 6130], Africa, no. 9 (1890), p. 2.

1897, in compliance with a British request in connection with the British rights in Madagascar, France gave the British Government the assurance that she would abandon her extraterritorial jurisdiction in Zanzibar, as soon as regularly constituted judicial authorities should be set up there.[1] This promise was fulfilled in 1904, when France formally gave up her rights of jurisdiction in Zanzibar.[2]

On November 14, 1899, a convention was concluded between Germany and Great Britain, by which the former renounced her rights of extraterritoriality in Zanzibar, the renunciation being understood, however, to take effect only when the other nations had also given up their rights.[3] The condition was deemed by the German Government to have been fulfilled in 1907, when Portugal abandoned her jurisdiction in Zanzibar. Consequently, an exchange of notes was effected on February 25/March 15, 1907, between Germany and Great Britain, giving effect to the renunciation of 1899, and on June 1, 1907, the German emperor issued a decree announcing the abolition of German jurisdiction in Zanzibar.[4]

The United States made a treaty with Great Britain on February 25, 1905, which contained a conditional renunciation of her extraterritorial rights in Zanzibar, similar to that embodied in the German treaty of 1899.[5] After Portugal and Germany definitely gave up their rights, the United States followed suit in 1907.[6]

---

[1] *Supra*, p. 107.

[2] Exchange of Notes, March 13/18, 1904, *State Papers,* vol. xcix, pp. 357 *et seq.*

[3] *Ibid.,* vol. ci, p. 234.

[4] *Ibid.,* p. 235.

[5] Malloy, vol. i, p. 795.

U. S. *Foreign Relations,* 1907, pt. i, p. 574.

Similar renunciations were made by Italy in 1905,[1] and by Portugal,[2] Belgium,[3] Austria-Hungary[4] and Russia[5] in 1907.

III. TONGA

The German Empire concluded a treaty with Great Britain on November 14, 1899, by which the former renounced in favor of the latter all her rights in Tonga, including those of extraterritoriality.[6] In 1900, Tonga was placed under British protection. The treaty which established the protectorate provided also that " Her Majesty shall have and exercise jurisdiction . . . in the case of the subjects or citizens of all foreign Powers in Tonga."[7] The German renunciation took effect on September 1, 1902, by the Imperial Order of June 26, 1902.[8] The United States was deprived of her jurisdictional rights in Tonga on July 28, 1919, when Lord Curzon, British Foreign Secretary, notified the American Government of the denunciation by Great Britain on behalf of the Queen of Tonga of the treaty of October 2, 1886.[9]

IV. TUNIS

In 1881, Tunis was placed under the protection of France.[10] On March 27, 1883, the French president promulgated a law, passed by Parliament, establishing a French tribunal and six magistrates' courts in Tunis, to take cog-

---

[1] *State Papers,* vol. xcix, p. 375.

[2] *Ibid.,* vol. ci, p. 237.

[3] *Ibid.,* p. 233.

[4] *Ibid.* p. 232.

[5] *Ibid.,* p. 237.

[6] *Ibid.,* vol. xci, p. 71.

[7] Treaty of May 18, 1900, *State Papers,* vol. cvi, pp. 521, 522.

[8] *Ibid.,* vol. ci, p. 656.

[9] *Ibid.,* vol. cxii, p. 580.

[10] Treaty of May 12, 1881, Rouard de Card, *op. cit.,* p. 232.

nizance of all civil and commercial questions between
Frenchmen and French-protected subjects and of all criminal
cases in which Frenchmen and French-protected subjects are
defendants, and authorizing His Highness the Bey to extend
the jurisdiction of these courts by edicts or decrees with the
assent of the French Government.[1] By virtue of this
authority, the Bey of Tunis issued a decree on May 5, 1883,
to the effect that " the subjects of the friendly Powers whose
Consular Tribunals shall be suppressed shall become amenable to the jurisdiction of the French Tribunals under the
same conditions as the French themselves." [2]

On September 13, 1882, the French Ambassador at London, M. Tissot, spoke informally to Earl Granville, British
Foreign Secretary, on the subject of a proposed judicial reform in Tunis, saying that the French Government intended
to establish in Tunis on January 1, 1883, tribunals which
would render useless the exercise of the rights then existing
under the Capitulations. " There would be no inconveni-
ence," he said, " in the change to foreigners, because the
object of the Capitulations was to defend foreigners from
the injustice to which they would have been exposed by recourse to the Native Courts." The French Government
proposed to do in Tunis, he added, what England had done
in Cyprus. Earl Granville thanked him for the information, but said that the matter required his careful consideration before he could express an opinion.[3]

In his conversation with Sir Julian Pauncefote, British
Under Secretary for Foreign Affairs, on October 4, 1882,
M. Tissot again alluded to the subject of consular jurisdic-
tion in Tunis. In the course of discussion, Sir Julian

[1] *Parliamentary Papers*, 1884 [C. 3843)], Tunis. no. 1 (1884), p. 15.
[2] *Ibid.*, p. 18.
[3] Earl Granville to Mr. Plunkett, Sep. 13, 1882, *Parliamentary Papers*, 1884 [C. 3843], Tunis, no. 1 (1884).

stressed the importance of British interests in Tunis and expressed the desire to know what guarantees the French Government was prepared to offer to these interests. In reply, M. Tissot assured Sir Julian that the judicial institutions which the French Government proposed to establish in Tunis would leave nothing to be desired and that the foreigners in Tunis would find the same security as was afforded to them by the judiciary in France.[1]

The British attitude toward the question of extraterritoriality in Tunis was from the outset favorable to the French point of view. Early in the negotiations, Lord Granville said:

Her Majesty's Government are willing to recognize the justice of the contention that there would be no sufficient reason for maintaining Consular jurisdiction in Tunis when the Native Courts are superseded by French Tribunals. The institutions which have grown up under the Capitulations with Turkey have been found essential for the protection of foreigners under the peculiar circumstances of the Ottoman Empire, and the necessity for them disappears when Tribunals organized and controlled by an European Government take the place of the Mussulman Courts.

Concluding this correspondence, Lord Granville evinced on behalf of his government the readiness to entertain any proposals on the subject the French Government might make, with the proviso that Great Britain would reserve all other rights and privileges, commercial or otherwise, guaranteed to her subjects by treaties.[2]

---

[1] M. Tissot to M. le Président du Conseil, Ministre des Affaires Étrangères, Oct. 5, 1882, *Publications of the Permanent Court of International Justice* (hereafter referred to as *P. P. C. I. J.*), series c, no. 2, add. vol., p. 287.

[2] Earl Granville to Mr. Plunkett, Oct. 16, 1882, *Parliamentary Paper* cited.

On May 10, 1883, Count d'Aunay left with the British Foreign Office a *note verbale,* together with copies of the laws providing for the organization of French jurisdiction in Tunis. The note adverted once more to the precedent of England's assumption of jurisdiction over foreigners in Cyprus, and to the belief on the part of France that England would accord to the French proposal the same reception as France had accorded to the British régime in Cyprus. It took occasion also to reiterate the judicial guarantees offered by the laws establishing the French régime in Tunis, with a view of convincing the British Government of the acceptability of the French request.[1]

Having taken cognizance of the French note and laws, Earl Granville expressed his willingness to accede to the French proposal in the following terms:

As I have had occasion to inform Your Excellency in the course of conversation on this subject, Her Majesty's Government are quite disposed to waive the rights of this country, under the Capitulations and Treaties, to the extent which may be required to give full scope to the exercise of civil and criminal jurisdiction over British subjects by the new French tribunals.

In a separate Memorandum, inquiries were made as to certain technical details, which do not need to detain us here.[2] To this Memorandum a reply was made also in the form of a Memorandum.[3] While this communication was regarded by the British Government as on the whole satisfactory, there still remained some points as to which the British Government considered that it was called upon to make

[1] *Ibid. Cf.* Le Ministre des Affaires Étrangères à M. Tissot, May 8, 1883, *P. P. C. I. J., loc. cit.,* p. 289.

[2] Earl Granville to M. Tissot, June 20, 1883, *Parliamentary Paper* cited.

[3] Reply to Memorandum annexed to the Letter from the Foreign Office of June 20, 1883, *ibid.*

reservations before surrendering British consular jurisdiction in Tunis. These reservations were:

1. The right of British subjects to challenge assessors in the new Courts.

2. The admission of duly qualified British advocates to practice before the Courts, without this privilege being limited, as at present proposed, to those only who are now established in Tunis.

3. The extension to Great Britain of all privileges reserved to any other Power in connection with the new system of jurisdiction in Tunis.

4. The immediate settlement by arbitration, or otherwise, of outstanding claims of British subjects in Tunis.

5. The cesser of military jurisdiction over British subjects in cases cognizable by the Civil Tribunals.[1]

These reservations were agreed to by the French Government without difficulty.[2]

In the meantime, the British consular authorities in Tunis were informed of the passing of an Order in Council, regarding the cessation of British extraterritoriality there, and they were instructed to take cognizance of no new cases after December 31, 1883.[3] The Order in Council referred to was issued on December 31, 1883, providing for the cessation of British jurisdiction on January 1, 1884.[4]

On September 18, 1897, an arrangement was entered into between Great Britain and France to the following effect:

Art. 1. The treaties and conventions of every kind in force between the United Kingdom of Great Britain and Ireland and France are extended to the Regency of Tunis.

The Government of Her Britannic Majesty will abstain from

---

[1] Earl Granville to M. Waddington, Nov. 16, 1883, *Parliamentary Paper* cited.

[2] M. Waddington to Earl Granville, Dec. 29, 1883, *ibid.*

[3] Earl Granville to Dr. Arpa, Dec. 28, 1883, *ibid.*

[4] *State Papers,* vol. lxxiv, p. 695.

claiming for its consuls, its subjects and its establishments in
the Regency of Tunis other rights and privileges than those
secured for it in France.[1]

Cognizance was taken of this arrangement by the Bey of
Tunis, who, on October 16, 1897, decreed the abrogation
of all earlier treaties with foreign Powers relative to Tunis.[2]

In a recent case, the British Government took occasion to
remind the French Government that what the former had
engaged to do in 1883 and 1897 was simply to delegate the
exercise of British jurisdiction in Tunis to French tribunals,
and not to abolish it irrevocably. The arguments advanced
on both sides in connection with this case, so far as they
relate to the question of extraterritoriality in Tunis, are
essentially a part of our study. Let us first examine briefly
the facts of the case.

On November 8, 1921, the French Government published
in Tunis and Morocco (French zone) under the sovereignty
of the Bey of Tunis and the Sultan of Morocco respectively,
certain national decrees, the effect of which was shortly
to confer French nationality on persons born in those countries of parents also born there and justiciable before French
tribunals.[3] In virtue of these decrees, the French Government claimed to impose the obligations of French nationality on British subjects in Tunis and Morocco (French zone)
in such a manner as to override their status as British subjects and render them liable to French military service.

Upon being informed by Consul-General Sarell that the
French authorities in Tunis had ordered the enlistment of
all British subjects born there in 1902 of parents also born

---

[1] *Documents diplomatiques, revision des traités tunisiens, 1881-1897*,
p. 87.

[2] *Documents diplomatiques, Afrique, 1881-1898*, p. 88.

[3] See *P. P. C. I. J.*, series c, no. 2, add. vol., pp. 120, 121, 158, 159

in Tunis,[1] Lord Hardinge, British Ambassador at Paris, lodged a protest with the French Foreign Office, on January 3, 1922, which contained, among other things, the following statement:

English law provides that persons born of British parents of whatever generation in countries where His Majesty's Government possesses extraterritorial rights, are deemed to have been born within British allegiance and so placed on the same footing as persons who derive British nationality in virtue of birth within the British dominions. In foreign countries where His Majesty's Government do not possess extraterritorial rights, children of British parents of the first generation are British subjects in contemplation of British law. It was not till September 18th, 1897, that His Majesty's Government finally gave up British capitulatory rights in the Regency. It follows, therefore, that in contemplation of English law, all persons born of British parents in Tunis before the 18th September, 1897, and all children of such parents, are British subjects.[2]

In his reply, dated January 10, 1922, M. Poincaré wrote to Lord Hardinge, in answer to the British argument based on the capitulatory rights of Great Britain, that the provision of the English law under which the children of British subjects born in countries where His Majesty has capitulatory rights of jurisdiction are deemed to be born within His Majesty's allegiance dates only from the passing of the British Nationality and Status of Aliens Act of 1914, and cannot, therefore, apply to Tunis, where British capitulatory rights had already ceased; that the capitulatory rights of jurisdiction possessed by Great Britain in Tunis came to a definite end in 1884; that in so far as the Anglo-French arrangement of September 18, 1897, relative to Tunis,

[1] *P. P. C. I. J., loc. cit.,* p. 160.
[2] *Ibid.,* p. 164.

might be held to apply to the question at issue, there was entire similarity in the treatment of British subjects in that protectorate and those born in France, inasmuch as the children born in France of foreign parents also born there were in French law deemed to be French citizens.[1]

On February 6, 1922, Lord Hardinge replied to M. Poincaré on the above points as follows: That the principle of English law embodied in section (i) of the British Nationality and Status of Aliens Act of 1914 was not of recent origin but was declaratory of a long-established usage; that the British extraterritorial rights did not come to an end in 1884, but that the change effected between Lord Granville and M. Tissot on June 20, 1883, amounted to no more than the consent of His Majesty's Government to the exercise by the French Government in their behalf of the capitulatory rights of jurisdiction which the British Government still maintained *vis-à-vis* his Highness the Bey of Tunis; and that the treatment accorded to British subjects in Tunis and that accorded to those in France were not similar, since the latter were given the right to opt against French nationality. In conclusion, the British Government offered to submit the dispute to the Permanent Court of International Justice at the Hague.[2]

M. Poincaré, on the contrary, contended that the principle of the English law referred to above was unknown to common law, which recognized only the principle of *jus soli*, whereas the principle of *jus sanguinis* was introduced by statute law, which made its first appearance in 1914. Regarding the cessation of the British capitulatory rights in Tunis in 1884, it was pointed out once more that such was the case and that, furthermore, in the correspondence between Lord Granville and M. Tissot, in 1883, no mention

[1] *Ibid.*, pp. 167-168.
[2] *Ibid.*, pp. 170-173.

was made of the delegation to France of the rights enjoyed
by Great Britain, which had been suggested in Lord Hardinge's note of February 6. Moreover, the British Order in
Council of December 31, 1883, had expressly provided for
the termination of these rights in Tunis. As to the similarity of treatment accorded to British subjects in Tunis
and in France, the French Government admitted that the
British observation relative to the right of option was true
of the law of 1874, but added that the right was taken away
in 1889 from foreigners born in France of parents also born
there and that if it was restored by the law of July 22, 1893,
it was only in the case where one of the parents who was
born in France would not give his or her nationality to the
child. Finally, M. Poincaré insisted on treating the question as one of domestic jurisdiction and not subject to arbitration.[1]

On July 14, 1922, a Memorandum prepared by the British
Government was communicated by Sir Milne Cheetham,
British Chargé d'Affaires at Paris, to the French Government. The arguments stated above were summarized and
re-emphasized in the Memorandum, which closed with the
wish that the French Government might consent to the submission of the dispute to arbitration and the determined
announcement that " should they nevertheless persist in their
decision to refuse arbitration, His Majesty's Government
will, in this event, have no alternative but to place the whole
question before the Council of the League of Nations in
accordance with the terms of the Covenant of the League.[2]

In the midst of these negotiations, a report was received
at the British Foreign Office that ten British subjects had
been arrested by the *gendarmerie* in Tunis and forcibly put

[1] *P. P. C. I. J., loc. cit.,* pp. 178-184.
[2] *Ibid.,* p. 189.

into military uniform.[1] Protests were lodged by Mr. Andrews with the French Resident-General, and the immediate release of the British subjects arrested was demanded.[2] At the same time, Sir Milne Cheetham protested to M. Poincaré against the proceedings of the French authorities at Tunis and repeated the declaration that " His Majesty's Government must hold the French Government responsible for any losses or damage consequent upon the action taken by their officials." [3]

In the meantime, the French Government refused its consent to the submission of the case either to the Permanent Court of International Justice or to the Council of the League of Nations.[4] On August 14, Sir Milne Cheetham informed M. Poincaré of the fact " that, in view of the attitude displayed by the French Government, His Majesty's Government have now no alternative but to submit the dispute which has arisen to the Council of the League of Nations; and that they are taking steps with a view to this question being placed upon the agenda for the Council of the League at its forthcoming meeting." [5]

Accordingly, the question was submitted by the British Government to the Council of the League.[6] On October 4, 1922, the Council adopted a resolution, referring to the Permanent Court of International Justice the question as to whether the dispute between Great Britain and France " is or is not by international law solely a matter of domestic

---

[1] Acting Consul-General Andrews to the Earl of Balfour, July 22, 1922, ibid., p. 192.

[2] Ibid., pp. 198, 199.

[3] Sir Milne Cheetham to M. Poincaré, Aug. 1, 1922, ibid., pp. 200-201.

[4] M. Poincaré to Sir Milne Cheetham, Aug. 5, 1922, ibid., p. 204.

[5] Ibid., p. 205.

[6] League of Nations, Official Journal, 3rd. yr., no. ii (pt. ii), p. 1206.

jurisdiction." [1]   After seven sittings, one private and six public, the Court answered the question in the negative. [2]

During the preliminary hearings at the Hague, the French Government submitted its Case, which argued, as in the previous correspondence, that British jurisdiction in Tunis had been terminated since 1884. [3] The British Case, after referring to the treaty of May 12, 1881, which established the French protectorate over Tunis and to the treaty of July 19, 1875, which regulated the relations of Great Britain to Tunis, reviewed the negotiations between France and Great Britain between 1882 and 1883 regarding the cessation of British extraterritoriality in Tunis.   The note of Lord Granville to M. Tissot, June 20, 1883, was cited to show " that it merely amounts to a consent on the part of Great Britain to allow French tribunals to exercise on its behalf capitulatory rights of jurisdiction, which it still maintained *vis-à-vis* the Bey of Tunis."   Then, the Order in Council of December 31, 1883, was quoted, and commenting on this Order, the British Case said:

It will be observed that by the terms of this Order in Council, the jurisdiction which Her Majesty abandoned was expressly limited to " such matters and cases as come within the jurisdiction of the said French tribunals," and further, that it is only " the operation of the Orders in Council regulating Her Majesty's Consular Jurisdiction in Tunis," which is determined and not the convention with the Bey of Tunis whereby capitulatory rights of jurisdiction were conferred upon Her Majesty.

The arrangement of September 18, 1897, was likewise referred to and quoted, and certain modifications of it agreed upon in 1919 between the British and French Governments were taken note of.   In conclusion, the British Case declared:

[1] *P. P. C. I. J.*, series b, no. 4, p. 8.

[2] *Ibid.*, p. 32.

[3] *Ibid.*, ser. c, no. 2, add. vol., p. 30.

It is desired to be pointed out that (in the submission of His Majesty's Government) neither by the Convention of 1897, nor by the modifications introduced by the aforesaid notes were the rights of Great Britain as against the Bey of Tunis under the Convention of 1875 between Great Britain and Tunis affected.[1]

In reply to the British Case, the French Government submitted its Counter-Case, wherein they reviewed the diplomatic correspondence had with England on the subject and reasserted that the renunciation of British jurisdiction in Tunis took place. in 1883 with the issuance of the Order in Council of December 31, and not in 1897. The Counter-Case further stated:

Even if the Note of June 20, 1883, and the Order in Council of December 31 of the same year, were not to be considered as a complete abandonment of the Capitulations, it seems difficult [to maintain] that after the Arrangement of September 18, 1897, Great Britain could still affirm that her relations with Tunis continue to be regulated by the general Anglo-Tunisian Treaty of July 19, 1875.

Referring to the British argument that the British rights of extraterritoriality in Tunis were simply delegated to the French tribunals there and were not definitively abandoned, the French Counter-Case observed:

This allegation is materially inexact. France, the protector of Tunis, renders justice in Tunis, not in the name of the foreign Powers, but in her own name. The suppression of foreign consular jurisdiction has been effected, not by delegation to France of the exercise of rights whose enjoyment belonged to the Powers and which they might still revive, but by extinction, to the benefit of the Bey of Tunis, of rights retransferred by the latter to France. This is so true that the Bey of Tunis himself,

[1] *Ibid.,* pp. 41-44.

by a decree of May 5, 1883, declared that in case of the renunciation by the Powers of their privileges of jurisdiction, he would
renounce the exercise of the right of jurisdiction which he
would then recover, normally, in full. From the legal analysis
of the extinction of the Capitulations in Tunis, it follows that
it is not each of the Treaty Powers that transmits to France
its rights of consular jurisdiction, but it is Tunis that transmits
to France the exercise of a right of jurisdiction, the enjoyment of which she [Tunis] has, under the condition of the
exercise, recovered.

Finally, the French advanced the argument that all the
treaties and conventions between Tunis and foreign Powers
had been definitely abrogated by decrees of the Bey of Tunis
at one time or other,[1] and that they had been superseded by
arrangements of a different nature, entitling the Powers to
no greater privileges in Tunis than were granted to them in
France, so that the rights of consular jurisdiction were abolished once and for all and could not be revived.[2]

To the French Case the British Government submitted a
reply in the form of a Counter-Case, which asserted:

It is the contention of His Majesty's Government, as explained in the British Case, that the convention of 1875 between
Great Britain and Tunis, under which capitulatory rights were
conferred upon Great Britain, was, on November 8th, 1921, and
still is, in force as between Great Britain and Tunis. . . . By
the delegation to France in 1883 of the exercise of British rights
and the Convention of 1897, both of which were a consequence
of the recognition of the French régime of Protection, Great
Britain did not forego its capitulatory rights as against the Bey.
There is no basis either in Lord Granville's note of June 20th,
1883, or the Convention for such a result, which would be

[1] See the Decrees of Feb. 1, Aug. 30 and Oct. 16, 1897, *ibid.*, pp. 333,
337, 338.
[2] *Ibid.*, pp. 234-250.

clearly contrary to the intention of the parties concerned, having regard to the safeguards consistently demanded and obtained by European States in Mussulman countries.[1]

To sum up the arguments of both sides before the Permanent Court of International Justice at the Hague, in so far as they related to the status of British extraterritoriality in Tunis: The British Government contended that the note of Lord Granville of June 20, 1883, merely signified the consent of the British Government to the exercise by the French tribunals on behalf of the British Government of rights which were maintained *vis-à-vis* the Bey of Tunis; that the Order in Council of December 31, 1883, instead of abrogating the British treaty of 1875 with Tunis, terminated only the operation of the Orders in Council regulating British jurisdiction in Tunis and limited the British renunciation to " such matters and cases as come within the jurisdiction of the said French tribunals "; that neither by the convention of September 18, 1897, nor by the modifications introduced by the notes of 1919, did the British Government forego its rights as against the Bey of Tunis; and that, therefore, the convention of July 19, 1875, between Great Britain and Tunis " was, on November 8th, 1921, and still is, in force as between Great Britain and Tunis."   On the other hand, the French Government took the position that the note of June 20, 1883, and the Order in Council of December 31 of the same year, amounted to a complete abandonment of British jurisdiction in Tunis; that even if these documents could not be so regarded, the arrangement of September 18, 1897, must be construed to mean such a renunciation; that the rights of jurisdiction exercised by France in Tunis were not delegated by the Powers but expressly by the Bey of Tunis himself by virtue of his Decree of May 5, 1883; that successive Decrees of the Bey in 1897

[1] *Ibid.*, p. 459.

had announced the definite abrogation of all the treaties with foreign Powers which contained extraterritorial provisions; and that, therefore, the treaty of July 19, 1875, between Great Britain and Tunis had become null and void.

In the question referred to the Permanent Court of International Justice, the latter was not called upon to pass on the merits of the case; what it was requested to do was only to decide whether the question at issue between France and Great Britain " is or is not by international law solely a matter of domestic jurisdiction." Consequently, in the opinion rendered by the Court, it merely took note of the " different views " taken by the two Governments " with regard to the scope of the declarations made by Great Britain in this respect and also with regard to the construction to be placed upon the Arrangement of 1897," [1] without taking upon itself to pass upon these views; and with respect to the main question submitted to it, the Court ruled that it should be answered in the negative, that is to say, that the dispute " is not by international law solely a matter of domestic jurisdiction." [2]

By an exchange of notes effected between the Marquess Curzon of Kedleston and Count de Saint-Aulaire on May 24, 1923, at London, it was agreed, on certain conditions, to discontinue the proceedings relative to the French Nationality Decrees, but " it is of course understood that in agreeing to discontinue the proceedings at the Hague, neither His Majesty's Government nor the French Government abandon the point of view which they have maintained in the diplomatic correspondence and in the preliminary hearings at the Hague." [3]

Thus, the question is still an open one, for definite settle-

[1] *P. P. C. I. J.*, series b, no. 4, p. 29.

[2] *Ibid.*, p. 32.

[3] Great Britain, *Treaty Series*, no. 11 (1923).

ment has been avoided. Leaving aside the technical bearings of the rights of extraterritoriality on the question of nationality, one may well conjecture that so long as France maintains regularly constituted judicial authorities in Tunis, it is quite unlikely that Great Britain will ever reassert its extraterritorial jurisdiction in the Regency on the basis of the treaty of July 19, 1875, which is claimed by the British Government still to be in force. However, the mere fact that Great Britain takes issue with the view that she abandoned her capitulary rights as against the bey of Tunis and maintains that she delegated the rights to be exercised by France in her behalf leads to two inevitable conclusions: (1) That the establishment of a protectorate does not *ipso facto* terminate existing treaty rights enjoyed by third parties in the protectorate, including those of extraterritoriality; and (2) that wherever these rights of jurisdiction are given up, they are abandoned because of a general improvement of the native judicial system brought about by the protecting State. This is assuming that the British view is the correct one.

The negotiations between France and Italy for the suspension of the latter's capitulatory rights in Tunis are equally suggestive of these views. It was on February 8, 1883, that the formal opening of the conversations on the subject in question took place between France and Italy. In discussing the question, the Italian Minister, Mancini, emphasized the guarantees to be offered by the new French judicial system, and inquired as to what was precisely proposed to be done in this respect.[1] After a number of conditions were laid down by the one party and fulfilled by the other,[2] the Italian Government finally agreed to the suspen-

[1] Minister of Foreign Affairs to the Italian Ambassador at Paris, Feb. 9, 1883, *Archives diplomatiques*, 1884, vol. iv, pp. 263, 264.

[2] *Ibid.*, p. 282; 1885, vol. i, pp. 65, 69, 72-74, 74-77, 80, 84-88.

sion of Italy's consular jurisdiction in Tunis. The protocol of suspension was signed on January 25, 1884, and by it the Italian Government agreed to " suspend in Tunis the exercise of the jurisdiction of the Italian Consular Courts," this jurisdiction to be " transferred to the Courts recently instituted in Tunis, whose competence His Highness the Bey, by a Decree of May 5, 1883, extended to the nationals of the States which should consent to cause their own Consular Courts to cease functioning." [1]

Before this agreement was reached, however, it had been expressly declared by the Italian Government (1) that what was abandoned by the latter was merely its judicial competence in Tunis, all other immunities and guarantees flowing from the Capitulations, usages and treaties, remaining in full force; (2) that the Italian Government, in view of the substitution of the Tunisian Courts by a French régime, agreed merely to a suspension of their extraterritorial rights; and (3) that this suspension was conditioned on the equal adhesion of all the other Powers, and that whatever privileges and immunities were extended to them should equally be extended to Italy.[2]

Other Powers have followed in the footsteps of England and Italy in suspending or abandoning their extraterritorial rights. According to the language of the declarations made by these Powers, these documents may be divided into two categories. Some of them provide for the renunciation of the right of invoking the Capitulations, while others merely express the intention to abstain from claiming any more privileges in Tunis than are accorded to them in France.

[1] *State Papers,* vol. lxxv, p. 469.

[2] *Aide-Mémoire* of the Minister of Foreign Aaffairs to the Ambassador of France, July 13, 1883, *Archives diplomatiques,* 1884, vol. iv, p. 281; also The Minister of Foreign Affairs to the Italian Consul-General at Tunis, *ibid.,* 1885, vol. i, pp. 83-84.

An example of the first group is the declaration between Austria-Hungary and France, dated July 20, 1896, which stipulated:

Austria-Hungary declares that it renounces the right of invoking in Tunis the régime of the Capitulations and that it will refrain from claiming there for its Consuls and its Nationals other rights than those acquired for them in France in virtue of the treaties existing between Austria-Hungary and France.[1]

Declarations similar to this were made by Germany, November 18, 1896,[2] Belgium, January 2, 1897,[3] and the United States, March 15, 1904.[4]

Examples of the second group are more numerous than of the first. Their language is similar, save in the former the engagement to " renounce the right of invoking the régime of the Capitulations " is conspicuously absent. To this group belong the declarations of Russia, October 2/14, 1896,[5] Switzerland, October 14, 1896,[6] Spain, January 12, 1897,[7] Denmark, January 26, 1897,[8] the Netherlands, April 3, 1897,[9] Sweden and Norway, May 5, 1897,[10] and the arrangement between France and Great Britain, September 18, 1897.[11]

[1] *Documents diplomatiques, revision des traités tunisiens, 1881-1897,* p. 47.
[2] *Ibid.,* p. 74.
[3] *Ibid.*
[4] Malloy, vol. i, p. 545.
[5] *Doc. dip. cited,* p. 73.
[6] *Ibid.*
[7] *Ibid.,* p. 75.
[8] *Ibid.,* p. 76.
[9] *Ibid.*
[10] *Ibid.,* p. 77.
[11] *Ibid.,* p. 78.

In all these cases, some difficulty may be encountered in ascertaining the precise extent of the abstention. If we take the British view as a standard, which is, at least as far as France is concerned, open to question, the second group of declarations must be construed to mean that the Capitulations were not abrogated, although the exercise of the rights conferred by them was suspended by these declarations. Whether any difference of interpretation was intended by the insertion, in the first group of declarations, of the engagement " to renounce the right of invoking the régime of the Capitulations," and whether an abstention greater in extent than was embodied in the second group of arrangements was intended, are disputable questions. But it appears from the absence, in either group, of any specific renunciation of the Capitulations that both may be regarded as connoting the same thing. Although it is not expressly so stated in the declarations of the second group, what is terminated by them is, as by those of the first group, the right of invoking the Capitulations and not the Capitulations themselves. This is again taking it for granted that the British view is the correct one.

As has been mentioned above, all the treaties and conventions between Tunis and the foreign Powers were declared to be and to remain " definitely abrogated " by decrees of the bey, dated respectively February 1, August 30 and October 16, 1897.[1] Whether the action of the bey is tantamount to the intended nullification is a question still unanswered.

V. MOROCCO

On March 30, 1912, Morocco was by treaty placed under the protection of France.[2] Eight months later, on Novem-

[1] *Documents diplomatiques, Afrique, 1881-1898*, pp. 85, 87, 88.

[2] *State Papers*, vol. cvi, p. 1023.

ber 27, by a treaty concluded with Spain, France recognized the latter's interests in the Spanish " zone of influence " in the Shereefian Empire.[1]

In both the French and Spanish zones, steps have been taken by the majority of the Powers to renounce their extraterritorial rights, but there are some exceptions to the rule.

One of the Powers which has not yet given up its extraterritorial jurisdiction in Morocco (French zone) is Great Britain. Although the secret articles annexed to the Anglo-French declaration of April 8, 1904, expressed the willingness of the British Government to entertain any suggestions that the French Government might make with regard to judicial reforms in Morocco,[2] Great Britain has shown no sign of transferring her rights of jurisdiction in the Shereefian Empire to the established French courts. On the contrary, she has insisted on their maintenance by the British authorities. An occasion for the unmistakable reaffirmation of the British policy relating to this question in Morocco, as in Tunis, was furnished by the case of the French Nationality Decrees.

The facts of the case have been related above.[3] After the French Government sought to apply to the British subjects in Morocco the decrees in question, Lord Hardinge,

[1] Art. 1, *ibid.*, p. 1025.

[2] " Article 2. His Britannic Majesty's Government have no present intention of proposing to the Powers any changes in the system of the Capitulations, or in the judicial organization of Egypt. In the event of their considering it desirable to introduce in Egypt reforms tending to assimilate the Egyptian legislative system to that in force in other civilized countries, the Government of the French Republic will not refuse to entertain any such proposals, on the understanding that His Britannic Majesty's Government will agree to entertain the suggestions that the Government of the French Republic may have to make to them with a view of introducing similar reforms in Morocco." *P. P. C. I. J.*, ser. c, no. 2, add. vol., p. 501.

[3] *Supra*, pp. 147 *et seq.*

British Ambassador at Paris, protested that such a position was untenable on account of the capitulatory rights still enjoyed by the British subjects in Morocco.[1] In a later despatch, the British Government further contended that the Nationality Act of 1914, which regarded as British subjects those who were born of British parents in countries where Great Britain enjoyed extraterritorial rights, was merely declaratory of existing practice, and that France could not establish the principle of *jus soli* in a country over which it had no sovereign rights, but exercised only the powers of a protectorate. The note suggested that unless the French Government withdrew the decrees from application to British subjects, His Majesty's Government could only reiterate the demand that the question be referred to arbitration.[2]

In reply, M. Poincaré, in addition to denying the existence in English law of the principle of the Act of 1914, claimed that " responsible for the order and reforms in the French zone of the Shereefian Empire, the French Government has, conjointly with the Sultan, the sovereign right to legislate on the nationality of the descendants of foreigners, in virtue of their birth on the territory, from the moment the foreign Powers which claim them have, in accepting the protectorate, abdicated all title to the maintenance of the prolongation of their jurisdictional privileges." The exercise of this sovereign right, it was argued, was not a subject for arbitration.[3]

The British Memorandum of July 14, 1922, referring to Morocco, merely stated that " the question does not indeed, at present, arise so far as concerns British subjects, seeing that British capitulatory rights exist, and the British com-

[1] Lord Hardinge to M. Poincaré, Jan. 10, 1922. *P. P. C. I. J.*, series c, no. 2, add vol. p. 165.

[2] Same to Same, Feb. 28, 1922, *ibid.*, pp. 176-178.

[3] M. Poincaré to Lord Hardinge, April 7, 1922, *ibid.*, pp. 185, 186.

munity in Morocco are therefore [subject?] neither to native nor to French legislation." [1]

Finally, as has been seen, the question was submitted by the British Government to the Council of the League of Nations, and by the latter it was referred to the Permanent Court of International Justice, which was requested to decide whether the dispute between France and Great Britain was or was not by international law solely a matter of domestic jurisdiction.

Before the Permanent Court of International Justice, the French Government admitted in their Case that the British Government still exercised capitulatory rights in Morocco, but contended that the refusal of Great Britain to close her consular courts in Morocco was illegitimate and in contravention of the engagement which she had made in adhering to the Franco-German convention of November 4, 1911,[2] to recognize the French tribunals when they should be constituted and then to renounce, in concert with the other Powers, her judicial régime in Morocco.[3]

After referring to the French treaty of 1912 establishing the protectorate over Morocco, and the British treaty of 1856 regulating the relations between Great Britain and Morocco, the British Case went on to say:

[1] *Ibid.*, p. 191.

[2] "Art. 9. In order to avoid, as far as possible, diplomatic representations, the French Government will urge the Moorish Government to refer to an arbitrator, nominated *ad hoc* in each case by agreement between the French consul and the consul of the Power interested, or, failing them, by the two Governments, such complaints brought by foreign subjects against the Moorish authorities or agents acting in the capacity of Moorish authorities as shall not have been found capable of adjustment through the intermediary of the French consul and the consul of the Power interested. This mode of procedure shall remain in force until such time as a judicial system, founded on the general principles embodied in the legislation of the Powers interested, shall have been introduced, which shall ultimately, by agreement between those Powers, replace the consular courts." *Ibid.*, p. 508.

[3] *Ibid.*, p. 30.

The capitulatory rights of jurisdiction conferred upon His Britannic Majesty by the above treaty are still being exercised by His Majesty's Consular Courts in Morocco, there has been no delegation of those rights to the French tribunals, as in the case of Tunis, nor have those rights been waived, abandoned, or modified in any way.[1]

The Counter-Case of the French Government again relied upon the British adhesion to the Franco-German convention of 1911 as a ground for holding that " Great Britain is not free to delay indefinitely the recognition of the French courts " in Morocco, and added that " the same effects which are deduced in Tunis from the creation of the French courts of the Protectorate, should be deduced in Morocco from the same creation." [2]

In the British Counter-Case, it was reiterated that " in Morocco His Majesty's capitulatory rights were, on November 8th, 1921, and still are, indisputably, in full vigour, and in direct exercise by the British Authorities." [3]

To the French argument that the British Government should put an end to their extraterritorial rights in Morocco on account of their adhesion to the Franco-German convention of 1911, the British Counter-Case devoted an extended refutation. In the first place, it was declared, the Franco-German convention of 1911 was not an agreement for the suppression of the Capitulations; what it did was to provide a means of dealing with the claims by foreigners against the Moorish authorities prior to the establishment of the new French judicial system. The wording of article 9 clearly contemplated that the replacement of the consular courts by the new régime could only be effected by agreement between the Powers concerned. Moreover, as between

[1] *P. P. C. I. J., loc. cit.*, p. 54.
[2] *Ibid.*, p. 252.
[3] *Ibid.*, p. 464.

France and Great Britain, the question of the Capitulations
in Egypt and Morocco was already regulated by article 2 of
the Anglo-French declaration of 1904, in which the British
Government agreed to " entertain proposals " for the abolition of the Capitulations in Morocco on condition that the
French Government would do the same in Egypt, and the
British Government, by acceding to the Franco-German convention of 1911, had no intention of substituting " the introduction of the new judicial system in Morocco for the
abolition of Capitulations in Egypt as the date on which
His Majesty's Government were pledged to abandon their
rights." Article 2 of the Anglo-French declaration of 1904
still held good, and article 9 of the 1911 convention could
only be regarded as subordinate thereto. Furthermore, the
French assumption that the British accession to the convention of 1911 was unconditional was shown to be incompatible with the facts, as the accession was explicitly declared
to be conditional on the internationalization of Tangier, " a
condition which has not yet been fulfilled." Finally, it was
asserted by the British Counter-Case that after the British
accession to the convention of 1911, negotiations were
opened between Great Britain and France for the reciprocal
abrogation of the Capitulations in Egypt and Morocco, but
that it was due to the refusal of the French Government to
sign the draft convention that the British consular tribunals
still remained in existence in Morocco.[1]

To sum up, the position taken respectively by the British
and French Governments is perfectly simple and intelligible.
The French Government held Great Britain to the engagement of 1911, which, according to the latter, could not be
brought into effect, so long as the French Government failed
and refused to live up to the conditions on which the adhesion of Great Britain had been made. It was contended

[1] *Ibid.*, pp. 471-473. Draft convention referred to given on p. 518.

by the British, and admitted by the French Government, that the capitulatory rights enjoyed by Great Britain in Morocco had never been given up and were still in force.

By a convention signed at Paris, on December 18, 1923,[1] by Great Britain, France and Spain, regarding the organization of the statute of the Tangier Zone, it was agreed that the Capitulations should be abolished in the Zone and that a Mixed Court should be established to replace the existing consular jurisdictions.[2] The details of the new Mixed Court of Tangier were regulated by a special *dahir* annexed to the convention. According to the *dahir,* the Mixed Court should be composed of four titular members, including one French, one Spanish, and two British magistrates, and of a number of deputy members (*membres adjoints*), including subjects or citizens of each of the Powers signatory to the Act of Algeciras, except Germany, Austria and Hungary.[3]

In 1913, the French Government requested the United States Secretary of State to recognize the French protectorate over Morocco and to renounce American consular jurisdiction in the Shereefian Empire.[4] In his reply, dated February 13, 1914, Mr. John Bassett Moore, Acting Secretary of State, conditioned the recognition of the reforms adopted by the French Government in Morocco on the settlement of certain pending issues regarding American interests in Morocco.[5] The negotiations went on until the War intervened. In 1915, the attention of the United States Government was called to the decision of the French Resident-General that pending the duration of a state of siege which

---

[1] Great Britain, *Treaty Series,* no. 23 (1924). Ratifications were deposited May 14, 1924, *ibid.,* p. 3.

[2] Arts. 13, 48, *ibid.,* pp. 9, 41.

[3] Art. 1, *ibid.,* p. 64.

[4] U. S. *Foreign Relations,* 1914, pp. 905, 906.

[5] *Ibid.,* pp. 907-914.

had been declared, certain cases hitherto tried before the civil courts should be transferred to the French military courts, even if the offenders were citizens of a country enjoying capitulatory rights.[1] Thereupon, Mr. F. L. Polk, Acting Secretary of State, took occasion to reassert the rights of the United States and instructed the American Ambassador at Paris to bring to the notice of the French Government the action of the French Resident-General in Morocco and " to protest against it in so far as it affects citizens of the United States." [2] Since that date, nothing further has been published as to the progress of the negotiations for the abrogation of American extraterritorial rights in Morocco.[3]

The majority of the Powers have, however, relinquished their extraterritoriality in Morocco (French zone). These include Russia, January 15 (18), 1914;[4] Spain, March 7, 1914;[5] Norway, May 5, 1914;[6] Greece, May 8 (21), 1914;[7] Sweden, June 4, 1914;[8] Switzerland, June 11,

[1] Chargé Blake to the Secretary of State, Dec. 8, 1915, U. S. *Foreign Relations,* 1915, p. 1097.

[2] The Acting Secretary of State to Ambassador Sharp, Dec. 29, 1915, *ibid.,* p. 1098.

[3] In reply to an inquiry addressed by the author, the Department of State informs him that the judicial status of American citizens in Morocco has not changed since 1913. "The recognition of the French protectorate," says the Department's letter, " by a note of January 15, 1917, from the Secretary of State to the French Ambassador at Washington was given upon the understanding that the question of the recognition of the protectorate was distinct from that of the modification of extraterritorial rights." The American Government, moreover, has not adhered to the Tangier Convention of Dec. 18, 1923.

[4] *State Papers,* vol. cvii, p. 821.

[5] *Ibid.,* vol. cix, p. 939.

[6] *Ibid.,* vol. cvii, p. 818.

[7] *Ibid.,* vol. cviii, p. 876.

[8] *Ibid.,* p. 877.

1914;[1] Denmark, May 12, 1915;[2] Bolivia, June 21, 1915;[3] Japan, July 14, 1915;[4] Belgium, September 22, 1915;[5] Italy, March 9, 1916;[6] Portugal, April 6, 1916;[7] the Netherlands, May 26, 1916;[8] and Costa Rica, May 31, 1916.[9] All the declarations made by these Powers with France give as the ground for relinquishing their extra-territorial jurisdiction in Morocco (French zone) the improved judicial system in the Shereefian Empire under French protection; they all begin with the statement, "Taking into consideration the guarantees of judicial equality offered to foreigners by the French Tribunals of the protectorate, etc."

By the Treaty of Versailles, June 28, 1919, Germany, having recognized the French protectorate in Morocco, agreed to accept all the consequences of its establishment, and thereby renounced the régime of Capitulations therein, such renunciation taking effect from August 3, 1914.[10] A similar renunciation was made by Austria in the Treaty of St. Germain, September 10, 1919,[11] and by Hungary in the Treaty of Trianon, June 4, 1920.[12]

In the Spanish, as in the French zone of Morocco, Great

[1] *State Papers*, vol. cxiii, p. 1042.

[2] *Ibid.*, vol. cix, p. 913.

[3] *Ibid.*, p. 872.

[4] *Ibid.*, p. 939.

[5] *Ibid.*, p. 871.

[6] *Ibid.*, vol. cxiv, p. 767.

[7] *Ibid.*, vol. cx, p. 878.

[8] *Ibid.*, p. 875.

[9] *Ibid.*, p. 835.

[10] Art. 142, *Treaty of Peace between the Allied and Associated Powers and Germany* (London, 1919), p. 73.

[11] Art. 97, *Treaty of Peace between the Allied and Associated Powers and Austria* (London, 1921), p. 41.

[12] Art. 81, Great Britain, *Treaty Series*, no. 10 (1920), p. 23.

Britain and the United States do not seem to have made any express renunciation of their extraterritorial rights. All the other Powers, however, have definitely given up their privileges of jurisdiction there. These include France, November 17, 1914;[1] Norway, March 9, 1915;[2] Russia, May 4 (17), 1915;[3] Sweden, May 5, 1915;[4] Belgium, December 29, 1915;[5] Denmark, January 29, 1916;[6] Italy, November 28, 1916;[7] Greece, May 17 (30), 1917;[8] and Portugal, July 20, 1918.[9] The declarations made by these Powers with Spain, as in the case of the French zone, all mention the fact of the guarantees of judicial equality offered to foreigners by the Spanish tribunals in Morocco as justifying the abandonment of consular jurisdiction.

VI. EGYPT

In Egypt, under Mehemet Ali and his successors, the privileges of the Capitulations received such an extension that they constituted a total departure from the terms of the Capitulations themselves, and, in effect, a gross violation of these treaties. The foreign consuls usurped power which was not conferred upon them, and altogether the situation presented a spectacle of an unfounded invasion of the sovereignty of the territorial power.[10]

[1] *State Papers,* vol. cviii, p. 470.

[2] *Ibid.,* vol. civ, p. 986.

[3] *Ibid.,* p. 1011.

[4] *Ibid.,* vol. cxii, p. 1165.

[5] *Ibid.,* vol. cix, p. 871.

[6] *Ibid.,* vol. cx, p. 842.

[7] *Ibid.,* p. 915.

[8] *Ibid.,* vol. cxii, p. 1108.

[9] *Ibid.,* vol. cxiv, p. 950.

[10] Scott, *The Law Affecting Foreigners in Egypt* (rev. ed., Edinburgh, 1908), pp. 196-200.

The abuses indulged in by the foreign consuls called forth the report of Nubar Pasha, Minister of Foreign Affairs, to the Khedive Ismail, appealing for the speedy amelioration of the situation.[1] This report was transmitted to the Powers, and after eight years of protracted negotiation, the régime of the Mixed Courts was established in 1875 and went into operation on February 1, 1876. "The privilege of jurisdiction," says Scott, " was very considerably modified by the institution of the Egyptian Mixed Tribunals in 1876. The principal result of the reform was to reduce the competence of the Consular Courts; but, although greatly restricted, the jurisdiction of the consuls was not abolished. They still retained their competence in questions of personal status, in actions where both parties were their nationals, and in cases of crime and delict where the accused was their fellow-subject." [2]

The régime set up in 1876 consists of three courts of first instance, which have their seats respectively in Alexandria, Cairo and Mansourah, and a court of appeal at Alexandria.[3] "The Court of First Instance at Alexandria has a Bench of eighteen judges, twelve of whom are foreigners and six natives; the court of Cairo has thirteen foreign and six native judges; the Mansourah court has six foreign and three native judges; while the Court of Appeal has a Bench of fifteen judges, ten of whom are foreign and five native." [4] All these judges are appointed by the Egyptian Government, but to assure the competence of the foreign judges, the latter must be nominated by their own governments.[5] These

---

[1] *Documents diplomatiques*, no. xiii, Nov. 1869, p. 77.

[2] Scott, *op cit.*, p. 209.

[3] *Réglement d'Organisation Judiciaire pour les Procès Mixtes en Égypte*, tit. i, ch. i, arts. 1, 3, *State Papers*, vol. lxvi, p. 593.

[4] Scott, *op. cit.*, p. 210.

[5] *Réglement*, tit. i, ch. 1, art. 5, *State Papers*, vol. lxvi, p. 593.

judges, whether native or foreign, are all declared to be irremovable, thus guaranteeing their absolute independence.[1]

The civil jurisdiction of the Mixed Courts extends to all cases, except those of personal status, between foreigners and natives and between foreigners of different nationalities; to all cases of immovable property between natives and foreigners or between foreigners of the same nationality or of different nationalities.[2] Owing to the incompetence of the native courts during the early days of the Mixed Court régime, the jurisdiction of the Mixed Tribunals has been considerably extended by judicial interpretation, so as to cover cases which would not come under their competence, if strict regard were had to the original articles of the *Réglement*. Thus, by applying the theory of " mixed interest," it has been held that cases involving the interest of a third party, even if they may be between persons of the same nationality, are cognizable by the Mixed Courts.[3] The penal jurisdiction of the Mixed Courts embraces police contraventions committed by one foreigner against another or a native, and certain delicts and crimes committed by or against the judges and officials of the Mixed Courts.[4]

In civil matters, the First Instance Courts are divided into (1) the Summary Court, (2) the Civil Court, (3) the Commercial Court, and (4) the *Tribunal des Référés*. The Summary Court consists of one judge, whose duty is first to conciliate parties in dispute, and, in case this is impossible, to decide some civil cases of a certain value in first instance and others in last resort. The Civil Court is composed of five judges, three of whom are foreign and two native, and

---

[1] *Réglement*, tit. i, ch. i, art. 19, *ibid.*, p. 595.

[2] *Réglement*, tit. i, ch. i, art. 19, as modified by Decree (1) of March 26, 1900, art. 1, *ibid.*, p. 594; vol. xciv, p. 882.

[3] Scott, *op. cit.*, pp. 219 *et seq.*

[4] *Réglement*, tit. ii, ch. i, arts. 6-9, *State Papers*, vol. lxiv, pp. 598-9.

takes cognizance, in first instance, of all civil cases not deferred to the Summary Court, and, on appeal, of all judgments rendered by the last court in all matters other than
possessory actions and actions of restoration (*reintégrande*)
and actions respecting leases of wakf lands, which are taken
before the Court of Appeal. The Commercial Court is made
up of five judges, three foreign and two native, and decides,
in first instance, all cases which are considered as commercial by the rules of the Commercial Code, other than those
which are deferred to the Summary Court. The *Tribunal
des Référés* is held by one judge, who shall decide after
hearing both parties, in civil as well as commercial matters,
what summary measures are to be taken without prejudice
to the question at issue, and on the execution of judgments
without prejudice to questions of interpretation.[1]

Penal matters are of three kinds, police contraventions,
delicts and crimes. The court for the contraventions consists of a single foreign judge. For the delicts, a Correc-
tional Court is created, of which two judges are foreign
and one native, assisted by four assessors. The latter should
all be of foreign nationality, if the defendant is a foreigner.
If the defendant is native, half of the assessors should be
native. Finally, the Court of Assizes, which is competent
to try crimes, consists of three judges of the Court of Appeal, of whom two are foreign and one native. The Court
of Assizes is assisted by twelve jurymen, half of whom
should be of the nationality of the defendant.[2]

[1] *Code de Procédure Civile et Commerciale Mixte,* tit. i, ch. i, arts. 26,
29, 32, 33, 34, Wathelet et Brunton, *Codes Egyptiens* (Brussels, 1919-
20), vol. i, pp. 338-340; *Réglement,* tit. i, ch. i, art. 14, *State Papers,*
vol. lxvi, p. 594; Decree (11) of March 26, 1900, art. 33, *ibid.,* vol. xcii,
p. 898. *Cf.* Scott, *op. cit.,* pp. 213-214.

[2] *Réglement,* tit. ii, ch. i, § 1, *State Papers,* vol. lxvi, pp. 597-8; Decree
(3) of March 26, 1900, art. 3, *ibid.,* vol. xcii, p. 884. *Cf.* Scott, *op. cit.,*
p. 215.

By a notification of the British Foreign Office, December 18, 1914, Egypt was placed under British protection, and it was declared that " His Majesty's Government will adopt all measures necessary for the defense of Egypt and the protection of its inhabitants and interests." [1] Since that date, a number of Powers have relinquished their consular jurisdiction in Egypt. These include Greece,[2] Portugal,[3] Norway,[4] Sweden[5] and Denmark.[6] According to the Treaty of Versailles, June 28, 1919, Germany recognized the British protectorate over Egypt and renounced her extra-territorial rights therein, the renunciation taking effect from August 4, 1914.[7] A similar renunciation was made by Austria in the Treaty of St. Germain, September 10, 1919.[8]

At the beginning of 1922, the British Government declared the termination of the British protectorate over Egypt and granted its independence.[9] By taking this action, the British Government did not intend to alter the *status quo* with regard to the protection of foreign interests in Egypt pending the conclusion of a formal agreement between the British and Egyptian Governments.[10] Under these circum-

[1] *State Papers*, vol. xviii, p. 185.

[2] Sep. 4, 1920, *ibid.*, vol. cxiii, p. 367.

[3] Dec. 9, 1920, *ibid.*, p. 424.

[4] April 22, 1921, *ibid.*, vol. cxiv, p. 350.

[5] July 28, 1921, *ibid.*, p. 390.

[6] July 14, 1921, *ibid.*, p. 199.

[7] Art. 147, *The Treaty of Peace between the Allied and Associated Powers and Germany* (London, 1919), p. 74.

[8] Art. 102, *The Treaty of Peace between the Allied and Associated Powers and Austria* (London, 1921), p. 42.

[9] See Declaration to Egypt, Feb. 21, 1922, *Parl. Pap.*, 1922 [Cmd. 1592], Egypt, no. 1 (1922), p. 29; Circular Despatch to His Majesty's Representatives Abroad, March 15, 1922, *ibid.* [Cmd. 1617], Egypt, no. 2 (1922).

[10] In the Declaration to Egypt, it was stated that "the protection of foreign interests in Egypt and the protection of minorities" was one

stances, the régime of extraterritoriality in its modified form is retained by those Powers which have not expressly renounced it.[1]

of the matters absolutely reserved to the discretion of the British Government pending the conclusion of an agreement with Egypt, but that until then the *status quo* should remain intact. The Circular Despatch of March 15 announced that "the termination of the British protectorate over Egypt involves, however, no change in the *status quo* as regards the position of other Powers in Egypt itself." See *Parl. Pap.* cited.

[1] So far as the United States Government is concerned, it still maintains its extraterritorial rights in Egypt. In reply to a letter of inquiry addressed by the author, the Department of State informs him that "in recognizing the British protectorate over Egypt in April, 1919, this Government reserved for further discussion the question of the modification of any rights belonging to the United States which might be deemed to be affected by the recognition," and that "this Government's recognition of the independence of Egypt in April, 1922, was made subject to the maintenance of the rights which had theretofore existed."

CHAPTER IX

Unilateral Cancellation

THE fifth method of procedure in discontinuing the system of extraterritoriality is by unilateral cancellation. This method was resorted to by Turkey more than once, always eliciting loud protests from the Powers. On October 11, 1881, a circular was sent out to the effect that certain rights accorded to the consuls by virtue of a long established usage was thenceforth to be abolished. In reply, the Powers declared by their joint notes of December 25, 1881, and February 25, 1882, that the sultan had no authority to annul the existing usages without previous consultation and agreement with the Powers concerned.[1]

At the beginning of the World War, Turkey endeavored once more to abrogate the extraterritorial system by unilateral action. On September 10, 1914, the foreign embassies at Constantinople received a note from the Turkish Ministry for Foreign Affairs, to the effect that on and after the first of October, the Ottoman Empire would abolish the Capitulations which restricted the sovereignty of Turkey in her relations with certain Powers. It was stated that owing to the improved state of Ottoman jurisprudence and to the interference entailed by the Capitulations with the legislative and administrative autonomy of the Ottoman Empire, the decision had been taken to abrogate, from the above-stated date, the Capitulations, " as well as all privileges and toleration accessory to these Capitulations or resulting from

[1] Rivier, *Principes du droit des gens* (Paris, 1896), vol. i, p. 544.

them, and to adopt as the basis of relations with all States the general principles of international law." [1]

The United States Government lodged its protest by sending, on September 16, 1914, the following telegram to the American Ambassador at Constantinople:

You are instructed to notify the Ottoman Government that this Government does not acquiesce in the attempt of the Ottoman Government to abrogate the Capitulations, and does not recognize that it has a right to do so or that its action, being unilateral, has any effect upon the rights and privileges enjoyed under those conventions. You will further state that this Government reserves for the present the consideration of the grounds for its refusal to acquiesce in the action of the Ottoman Government and the right to make further representations later. [2]

A copy of this telegram was also sent to the Turkish Ambassador at Washington on the same day. [3] On September 10, all the other embassies at Constantinople, including the German and Austrian, sent identic notes to the Sublime Porte, stating that while communicating to their respective governments the note respecting the abolition of the Capitulations, they must point out that the capitulatory régime was not an autonomous institution of the Empire but the resultant of international treaties, which could not be abolished either wholly or in part without the consent of the contracting parties. It was, therefore, declared that in the absence of an understandng arrived at before the first of October between the Ottoman Porte and the foreign governments concerned, the ambassadors could not recognize the executory force after that date of a unilateral decision of the Turkish Government. [4]

[1] U. S. *Foreign Relations*, 1914, p. 1092.

[2] *Ibid.*, p. 1093.

[3] *Ibid.*, p. 1094.

[4] Sir L. Mallet to Sir Edward Grey, Sept. 10, 1914, *Parl. Pap.*, 1914-16 [Cd. 7628], Miscellaneous, no. 13 (1914), p. 23.

Later, the protest of the British Ambassador was confirmed by his Government, which instructed him to reiterate to the Ottoman Government the binding nature of the Capitulations and the invalidity of the unilateral action of the Porte in abrogating them.   He was also authorized to say to the Turkish Government that the British Government would reserve their liberty of action in regard to any Turkish violation of the Capitulations and would demand due reparation for any prejudice to the British subjects resulting therefrom.[1]

To the American contention that the Capitulations were bilateral agreements and could not be abrogated by unilateral action, the Turkish Ministry for Foreign Affairs answered that "the Sublime Porte had, like every State, the right to denounce, at any time, international acts concluded without stipulations of duration."   It was maintained that the change of conditions justified the action of the Turkish Government, "since the régime of the Capitulations, obsolete and no longer responding to modern needs, even when it is confined within its true contractual limits, threatens its own existence, and renders very difficult the conduct of Ottoman public affairs."[2]   As we shall see presently, this point of view is open to serious question.

On September 4, 1915, the Turkish Foreign Office communicated to the American Ambassador a *note verbale,* which insisted that the Capitulations had been definitively abrogated and that "since October 1, 1914, the European international public law must govern the relations of the states and foreign subjects with the Imperial authorities and Ottoman subjects."   It was added that if the Imperial Ministry re-

---

[1] *Note Verbale* communicated to the Sublime Porte, Oct. 1, 1914, *ibid.,* p. 53.

[2] The Minister for Foreign Affairs to Ambassador Morgenthau, Dec. 5, 1914, U. S. *Foreign Relations,* 1915, p. 1302.

ceived any further communication on the subject, it would, to its regret, " find itself in the painful necessity not to give it any effect and to pay no attention to the matter to which it refers." [1]   The United States Government, however, was in total disagreement with the Porte as to the effect of this declaration.   It insisted on the continued validity of the Capitulations, although it indicated its willingness to consider the abandonment of its extraterritorial rights in Turkey whenever the state of Turkish justice warranted such a measure.   Ambassador Morgenthau was instructed to notify the Ottoman Government that the United States would hold it responsible for any injury which might be occasioned to the United States or to its citizens by a failure to observe the Capitulations.[2]

At the First Lausanne Conference on Near Eastern Affairs, held November 22, 1922–February 4, 1923, the Turkish delegation defended the cancellation of the Capitulations by their government in 1914.   One of the arguments advanced was that the Capitulations were unilateral in nature and could be revoked at the will of the Sublime Porte.   " It is an undoubted fact," said the Memorandum of the Turkish delegation, " that in taking such a decision Turkey merely exercised a legitimate right.   As a matter of fact, the Capitulations are essentially unilateral acts.   In order that an act may be regarded as reciprocal, it must above all contain reciprocal engagements.   From an examination of the texts, the evidence shows that in granting the privileges in question to foreigners in Turkey, the Ottoman emperors had no thought of obtaining similar privileges in favor of their subjects traveling or trading in Europe."   It was further contended that the Capitulations were voidable on the prin-

[1] U. S. *Foreign Relations*, 1915, p. 1304.
[2] The Secretary of State to Ambassador Morgenthau, Nov. 4, 1915, *ibid.*, p. 1305.

ciple of *rebus sic stantibus.* " Even supposing that the
Capitulations were bilateral conventions," the Turkish statement asserted, " it would be unjust to infer from that that
they are unchangeable and must remain everlastingly irre-
vocable. Treaties whose duration is not fixed imply the
clause *rebus sic stantibus,* in virtue of which a change in
the circumstances which have given rise to the conclusion
of a treaty may bring about its cancellation by one of the
contracting parties, if it is not possible to cancel it by mutual
agreement." [1]

That the Capitulations were at first unilateral in form
there can be no question. This is admitted by the author
ities who have examined the matter.[2] But to say that they
have remained unilateral acts would be incorrect. In every
case, as we know, the Capitulations were at one time or
other converted into treaties consistent with the forms laid
down by international law and binding on each contracting
party. Indeed, the Sublime Porte itself admitted, on one occasion, the validity of these agreements as mutually binding
treaties. In a *Mémoire* addressed by the Porte to the representatives of the foreign Powers, in May, 1869, it was declared in unequivocal terms:

The Capitulations having been consecrated by treaties subse-

[1] Great Britain, *Parl. Pap.,* 1923 [Cmd. 1814], Turkey, no. 1 (1923),
p. 478; France, *Documents diplomatiques, Conférence de Lausanne,* vol.
i, pp. 450-451.

[2] " The Capitulations were, in principle, gracious concessions (*concessions gracieuses*)." Pradier-Fodéré, " *La Question des Capitulations,*"
R. D. I., vol. i, p. 119. According to another writer, it is a mistake to
give to the Capitulations the name of treaties, which presuppose two
contracting parties stipulating for their interests. " Here [in the Capi-
tulations] one finds only concessions and privileges and exemptions of pure
liberality given by the Porte to France." Lawrence, *Commentaire sur les
éléments du droit international et sur l'histoire des progrès du droit des
gens de Henry Wheaton* (Leipzig, 1868-80), vol. iv, p. 123; *cf.* Ancien
Diplomate, *Le Régime des Capitulations,* p. 9.

quently concluded between the Sublime Porte and the foreign Powers, should, so long as they are in force, be scrupulously respected in the same manner as these treaties.[1]

It is certainly unthinkable that the Turkish delegation to the Lausanne Conference should have taken upon themselves to contradict a solemn engagement of their own government made over half a century before.

As to the statement that treaties, in order to be reciprocal, must contain reciprocal engagements, one would look in vain for a sound basis of this contention. To give one instance, treaties of peace concluded at the end of a war have never been reciprocal in nature. Does this mean that all such treaties are of no effect and can be annulled at the will of the vanquished? Nothing of the sort is sanctioned by international law.

In regard to the second contention of the Turkish delegation, it is admitted that the principle *rebus sic stantibus* is recognized by the majority of publicists to be an implied clause of all unnotifiable treaties.[2] But, taking it for granted that the change of the circumstances which had led to the conclusion of the Capitulations had, in 1914, reached such a stage as to justify the demand for their abrogation, we cannot absolve the Sublime Porte from the responsibility for a breach of good faith. For while the rule *rebus sic stantibus* is recognized by a vast number of writers, it is also their opinion that the clause " ought not to give a State

[1] *Archives diplomatiques*, 1870, vol. i, p. 249.

[2] " For it is an almost universally recognized fact that vital changes of circumstances may be of such a kind as to justify a party in demanding to be released from the obligations of an unnotifiable treaty. The vast majority of publicists, as well as the Governments of the Civilized States, defend the principle *conventio omnis intelligitur rebus sic stantibus*, and they agree, therefore, that all treaties are concluded under the tacit condition *rebus sic stantibus*." Oppenheim, *International Law* (3rd ed., London, 1920), vol. i, pp. 688-9.

the right, immediately upon the happening of a vital change of circumstances, to declare itself free from the obligations of a treaty, but should only entitle it to claim to be released from them by the other party or parties to the treaty." [1] In other words, before a State can release itself from the obligations of a treaty on the principle *rebus sic stantibus,* it must first enter into negotiations with the other contracting party or parties to that effect,[2] with a view of examining the reasons for the proposed cancellation or modification of the obligations in question and reaching a common accord on the subject.[3]

In the case of Turkey, there is all the more reason for such a common accord. Ever since the admission of the Ottoman Empire in 1856 " to participate in the advantages of the European public law and concert," [4] every important question of Turkish foreign relations has been a concern of the general European polity. Far more than ordinary synallagmatic agreements, therefore, the Capitulations had a binding force which should not be lightly brushed aside.

Contrary to established principle, the Sublime Porte, without making any earnest attempt to reach a satisfactory agreement with the Powers, announced by unilateral action the end of all the Capitulations, and when the United States Government protested against it, the Turkish Foreign Office categorically replied that the abrogation had become a *fait accompli* and that no further discussion of the question would be engaged in. This shows that while the Turkish Government intended to make use of the clause *rebus sic*

<hr>

[1] *Ibid.,* p. 692.

[2] *Ibid., cf.* Phillimore, *Three Centuries of Treaties of Peace* (London, 1919), p. 138.

[3] Pouritch, *De la clause " rebus sic stantibus " en droit international public* (Paris, 1918), p. 81.

[4] Art. 7, Treaty of Paris, Mar. 30, 1856, *State Papers,* vol. xlvi, p. 12.

stantibus, it refused to enter into negotiations the which are recognized to be a necessary part of the procedure laid down by international law for the application of that principle.

In fine, it may be reiterated that the measure taken by the Turkish Government in 1914 to abrogate its treaty obligations by unilateral action is wholly unfounded in law and has been vigorously opposed by the Powers. The policy has failed of its desired end, and, as will be seen,[1] the Ottoman Empire was finally compelled to seek the restoration of its judicial autonomy by means of bilateral or rather multi-lateral negotiations instead of unilateral cancellation.[2]

[1] *Cf. infra,* pp. 185 *et seq.*

[2] It is interesting to note that even before the Lausanne Conference of 1922-1923, the Turkish Government had consented in the suspension of the unilateral cancellation of the Capitulations. Russian Ambassador at Constantinople to Russian Minister of For. Aff., Sep. 18 (Oct. 1), 1914, Scott, *Dip. Doc. relating to the Outbreak of the European War* (New York, 1916), pt. ii, pp. 1422-3.

CHAPTER X

Diplomatic Negotiation

The last method of procedure in attempting to secure the modification or abrogation of extraterritoriality is by diplomatic negotiation, which usually results in an agreement of one sort or another. In classifying this method as distinct from the above-mentioned, the fact is not lost sight of that in all the other methods described, a larger or smaller measure of diplomatic negotiation is also involved. But in all of them, except in the case of unilateral cancellation, which is an illegal method, the negotiation is carried on between the foreign Powers on the one side and, on the other, Powers other than those which originally granted the extraterritorial rights. In this chapter, we shall deal with the negotiations in which the States granting these rights have engaged with the foreign Powers to get rid of the same.

I. TURKEY

Turkey availed herself of this method at the Congress of Paris in 1856. During the session of March 25, the question of abolition was brought up for discussion. Ali Pasha argued that the Capitulations were disadvantageous alike to the foreigner and to the Ottoman Government; that they created " a multiplicity of governments in the Government;" and that they were an insuperable obstacle to all reform. Count Clarendon, Count Walewski and Count Cavour expressed themselves very sympathetically and were favorably inclined to the Turkish point of view. On the

other hand, Count de Buol and Baron de Burquency hesi-
tated to grant to Turkey her judicial autonomy at once.
While agreeing that the Capitulations needed modification,
Baron de Burquency deemed it important that the modification should be proportionate to the judicial reforms inaugurated by the Ottoman Empire. A protocol was drawn up
and signed, embodying the wish (*voeu*) that a conference
should be assembled at Constantinople, after the conclusion
of peace, to deliberate upon the matter.[1] The promised
conference was, however, never held.

After the failure of 1856, Turkey was for a long time
unable to shake off completely the restrictions on her judicial autonomy. It was only recently that some Powers
evinced a readiness to assist Turkey in recovering her independence in the realm of justice. By the treaty of February 26, 1909, Austria-Hungary engaged to give " her full
and sincere support " to the Turkish negotiations for the
abolition of the capitulatory régime.[2] In 1912, Italy made
an identical promise.[3]

More recently, the Ottoman Empire has succeeded in concluding treaties with certain Powers, recognizing the cessation of the capitulatory régime in Turkey. At the beginning
of the European War, Germany and Austria-Hungary
offered as the price of Turkish assistance in the conflict their
consent to abrogate the Capitulations. This was later confirmed by Germany in a treaty of January 11, 1917, which
provided that Germans in Turkey and Turks in Germany
should enjoy the same treatment as the natives in respect
of the legal and judicial protection of their persons and
property and that to this end they should have free access
to the courts and be subjected to the same conditions as the

---

[1] *State Papers*, vol. xlvi, pp. 100-101.

[2] Art. 8, *ibid.*, vol. cii, p. 182.

[3] Treaty of Lausanne, Oct. 18, 1912, art. 8, *ibid.*, vol. cvi, p. 1102.

natives.[1] On August 6, 1917, a law was promulgated by
the German Emperor for the execution of the treaties of
January 11, 1917. It laid down that by imperial order it
could be determined (*bestimmt*) to abolish the rights of
jurisdiction enjoyed by the German consuls in Turkey.[2]
Austria abolished her extraterritorial rights in Turkey by
the treaty of March 12, 1918.[3]

On January 6, 1921, a treaty was concluded with the
Soviet Government in Russia, which declared:

> The Government of the R. S. F. S. R. considers the Capitu-
> latory régime to be incompatible with the free national develop-
> ment and with the sovereignty of any country; and it regards
> all the rights and acts relating in any way to this régime as
> annulled and abrogated.[4]

At the Conference of Lausanne, November 22, 1922–
February 4, 1923, a Commission headed by Marquis Garroni
of Italy was charged with the examination of questions relating to the régime of foreigners in Turkey. The Commission held its first meeting on December 2, 1922, at the
opening of which Marquis Garroni recognized " that according to present-day ideas of law the capitulatory régime
is regarded as liable to diminish the sovereign powers of an
independent State; and it is intelligible," he added, " that
Turkey should demand the abolition of this régime, which
has had its day." He desired, however, that the Turkish
Government would " substitute for it such guarantees as
regards legislation and administration of justice as will inspire confidence in all those who will be obliged to have re-

---

[1] Art. 1, Martens, *N. R. G.*, 3rd ser., vol. ix, p. 709.

[2] *Reichsgesetzblatt*, 1918, p. 355.

[3] The text of this treaty is not available; it is referred to by Hamid,
Das Fremdenrecht in der Türkei (Berlin, 1919), p. 22.

[4] Art. 7, *Current History*, vol. xvii, p. 278.

course thereto." Three Sub-Commissions were created, the first of which was to deal with the legal position of foreign persons in Turkey.[1]

At this same meeting a memorandum was read by the Turkish delegation. It began by explaining the origin of the Capitulations and after reviewing what was promised by the Powers in 1856, continued thus:

This shows that as long as sixty-six years ago the representatives of England, France and Italy recognized in so solemn a Congress as the one described, the necessity of terminating the Capitulations because of their incompatibility with modern conceptions of law, and because of the manner in which they infringed the sovereignty of the State.

During the period subsequent to the conclusion of the Treaty of Paris, Turkey has worked feverishly at the perfection of her judicial system, which she had already taken in hand.

The commercial code, the penal code, the codes of civil and penal procedure, as well as the laws regarding the " Tribunaux de Paix," and also all the administrative laws and regulations, have been established on the model of codes and laws in force in European countries.

Above all, it has quite recently been possible to carry out a very important reform in the civil law, by which our judicial institutions have been completely secularized; the free will of the parties in the matter of contracts and agreements has been recognized as paramount, and the principle of the freedom of the will has been accorded the same place as in Europe; further, while these laws were being elaborated and promulgated, a faculty of law was instituted at Constantinople, whose programme is more or less identical with that of the corresponding faculties in Europe. This situation has produced during forty years a body of distinguished judges and advocates who possess all the necessary qualifications, and it is to them that at the

[1] *Parliamentary Papers*, 1923 [*Cmd.* 1814], Turkey, no. 1 (1923), p. 467; *Documents diplomatiques, Conférence de Lausanne*, vol. i, p. 443.

present time the important task of administering justice is
assigned.

A considerable number of young men have since the change
of régime in 1908 studied in the various faculties of law of
the Empire, and are now appointed to various posts in the
magistracy.

After mentioning the treaties which the Turkish Government concluded with Austria-Hungary, Italy, Germany and
Russia in the present century,[1] the Turkish statement went
on to enumerate the defects of the capitulatory régime.

With regard to civil matters, the Turkish statement alluded to the unsavory effects of the existence of a multiplicity of laws and jurisdictions. The parties to a contract
had to be familiar with the laws of each foreign country,
in order to live up to their requirements, and in case of an
appeal, application had to be made to a court of appeal of
the country whose nationals the foreigners concerned were.
Even in the mixed tribunals, difficulties of procedure were
not wanting. The judges were not men of legal training;
they were as a rule partial to their compatriots; and they
had so many other duties to perform that interminable de-
lays were caused in the administration of justice.

The attitude of the foreign members (who supported the foreigner with great partiality as though they were his advocates),
and especially that of the dragomans, caused regrettable misun-
derstandings which caused the matter to be transferred from the
judicial domain to that of diplomacy. This state of affairs
caused the suits to drag on for a very long time and made it
impossible for the Commercial Court to bring them to an end.

Even after the judgment had been pronounced, there were
numerous obstacles to its execution. "Indeed, it was no
rare thing to see judgments given against foreigners remain
unexecuted."

[1] *Supra*, p. 185.

On the penal side, the hands of the Turkish authorities were tied by the treaty restrictions, of which the consular officers made the widest use, " in order to withhold deliberately from justice offenders who had infringed the public order and security of the country." When a criminal took refuge in the abode of a foreigner, the police could not lay its hands upon him in the absence of the dragoman, and in the meantime the criminal found a means of escaping. Besides, owing to the requirement of hearing a foreign witness in the presence of the dragoman, either or both could exercise an influence on the progress of the prosecution " by answering the summons or by refusing to appear." The statement ended the enumeration of the defects of the capitulatory régime with the assertion that " similarly, difficulties arose in connection with the execution of sentences in criminal cases," and that " the sovereignty of the state and the prestige of the judicial authority were as gravely prejudiced." Then the statement went on to cite authorities in substantiation of the defects and disadvantages mentioned, and sought to justify the cancellation of the Capitulations by the Porte in 1914, on the ground that they were originally unilateral acts subject to revocation, and that a treaty is voidable on the principle of *rebus sic stantibus*.[1] Finally, after summing up the arguments advanced, the Turkish delegation concluded their memorandum by saying:

In view of the foregoing, the Government of the Grand National Assembly of Turkey can in no wise agree to the reestablishment of the Capitulations, which are in direct conflict with the modern conception of a State and with the principles of public law.[2]

[1] For a criticism of this view, *vide supra*, pp. 180 *et seq.*
[2] *Parliamentary Papers*, 1923 [*Cmd.* 1814], Turkey, no. 1 (1923), pp. 471-479; *Documents diplomatiques, Conférence de Lausanne*, vol. i, pp. 446-451.

At the second meeting of the Commission on the Régime of Foreigners in Turkey, held on December 28, 1922, Marquis Garroni told the delegates that the sub-commission dealing with the judicial régime of foreigners in Turkey, under the presidency of Sir Horace Rumbold, had found it impossible to continue its labors in consequence of differences of view between the Allies and Turkey.[1] A report rendered by Sir Horace was read, telling of what had transpired at the meetings of the sub-commission. According to this report, the Allied and Turkish delegates exchanged questionnaires and answers, proposals and counter-proposals, on the various questions discussed. From the very beginning, the discussion revealed a considerable, though not fundamental divergence of view—a divergence which was fortunately narrowed by concessions made on either side. One of the concessions made by the Turkish delegation was that all questions of personal status affecting foreigners were to be subject to the exclusive jurisdiction of the national tribunals or other competent national authorities in the country to which the foreigners belonged. As the discussion proceeded further, the divergence of view increased, especially when it was proposed that Turkey should admit foreign judges to its magistracy and permit them to participate in its legal reform. Regarding these two questions

the Turkish delegation strongly maintained that any introduction into the Turkish judicature of a special element, even in the conditions suggested in the questionnaire, would constitute an encroachment on the sovereignty and independence of Turkey. The Turkish delegation maintained with no less insistence that existing Turkish legislation amply met the requirements of modern life; that one could without any apprehension leave to the Grand National Assembly the duty of applying to this legislation such modifications as might seem

[1] *Parliamentary Paper* cited, p. 481.

necessary from time to time; that the Turkish judicature, which had been recruited for over forty years from among the graduates of the faculty of law [in Constantinople], was fully qualified for its task, and that foreigners no less than Turkish nationals would find in the legislative and judicial system of Turkey all the guarantees required for the safety of their persons and their interests.

At the end of this dscussion of the sub-commission, a draft containing the detailed proposals of the Allies was handed by the president to the Turkish delegation, inviting the latter to entrust its legal adviser with the examination of this draft, in consultation with the Allied legal advisers, with a view to the satisfactory settlement of the question. Finally, the Allied legal advisers had to inform the sub-commission of their failure to reach an agreement with the Turkish adviser, and after a fruitless attempt to secure from the Turkish delegation any counter-proposals which they might desire to make, the sub-commission had to report to Marquis Garroni that it was unable to continue its work.[1]

At the second meeting of the Commission on the Régime of Foreigners, Ismet Pasha once more objected strenuously to the imposition of foreign judges on the Turkish magistracy. "The Turkish delegation were greatly astonished," he declared, " to find themselves confronted with such a proposal, the purpose of which is to institute a régime clearly incompatible with the independence and sovereignty of Turkey." He emphasized and re-emphasized the progress which Turkey had made in her judicial reform and the sufficiency of the guarantees offered by it in place of the Capitulations. As evidence of this fact, he testified that

the régime of general international law which has been operative in Turkey since 1914, without the conclusion of any con-

[1] *Parliamentary Paper* cited, pp. 500-508.

vention whatever, has never given rise to any complaint on the part of the very numerous nationals of neutral States, or on that of the Allied nationals who remained in Turkey. The experience acquired during this long period of eight years has proved that Turkish institutions are entirely adequate and contain all the guarantees necessary for safeguarding the interests in question.

On the other hand, it was asserted that of the new countries no such guarantee as it was sought to impose on Turkey were required. The address of the Turkish delegate ended with the challenge that

the Turkish Government have no fear in calling upon the public opinion of the world to judge and compare the treatment accorded to foreigners in Turkey by the Turks, both in the past and at present, and the cruel and arbitrary treatment to which the Turks have been subjected by foreigners at Constantinople and elsewhere at the same time and under the same conditions.

In the discussion that followed, the Allied delegations showed their dissatisfaction with the position taken by Turkey. M. Barrère was the first to speak, and he found it impossible for the French delegation to accept the blank refusal meted out by the Turkish delegation to the Allied proposals. It would be impossible, he said, for the French delegation to consent to the suppression of the Capitulations, were sufficient guarantees not offered by the Turkish Government. Baron Hayashi dwelt upon the experience of Japan with regard to the abolition of extraterritoriality, and urged the Turkish delegation to adopt a conciliatory attitude. Mr. Child, the American unofficial " observer," discoursed on the sanctity of international obligations and the fundamental equity which foreigners might expect from the Turkish Government, pointing out " that treaties which give foreigners a status of security in Turkey can deprive Turkey of nothing, and indeed would be the very foundation of her economic future." Lord Curzon, after alluding to the remarks that had been made by his colleagues, openly declared himself to be in accord with what the French delegate had said. He then reviewed the arguments of Ismet Pasha, showing their invalidity, and ended with the plea that the Turkish Government consider very carefully what had been said and perhaps at a later date give the Allies an opportunity of hearing their revised views on the subject.[1]

The third meeting of the Commission on the Régime of Foreigners was held on January 6, 1923. In reply to the speeches made by the Allied representatives at the previous meeting, Ismet Pasha read a long statement, adhering to the decision that the Turkish Government had already come to. Comments were made by the various delegations on the substance of the speech, the general hope being that the Turkish delegation would formulate counter-proposals, which would make it possible to find some common ground of agreement. But Ismet Pasha insisted that he was not in a position to make further concessions.[2]

At the fourth meeting of the Second Commission, held on January 27, 1923, Marquis Garroni reported on the suggestions that had been made to the Turkish delegation regarding the judicial guarantees to be offered to the foreigners. What had been suggested was the attachment of certain European legal advisers to the Turkish Ministry of Justice and judicial régime.[3]

In the draft terms of the treaty of peace presented to the Turkish delegation on January 31, 1923, it was provided that " the High Contracting Parties agree to abrogate the Capitulations relating to the régime of foreigners in Turkey

[1] *Parl. Pap.* cited, pp. 488-498; *Doc. dip.* cited, pp. 459-467.

[2] *Parl. Pap.* cited, pp. 509-519; *Doc. dip.* cited, pp. 469-476.

[3] *Parl. Pap.* cited, p. 523; *Doc. dip.* cited, p. 479.

both as regards conditions of entry and residence and as regards fiscal and judicial questions." [1] Together with the draft treaty was sent a draft convention, in pursuance of which the foreigners were to have free access to the Turkish courts; actions in real property, as well as in civil, commercial and criminal matters, were placed under the jurisdiction of the Turkish courts; questions of personal status, under that of the national tribunals or other national authorities established in the country of which the parties were nationals; and the Turkish Government was obliged to ensure to foreigners in Turkey, both as regards person and property, protection in accordance with international law. [2] To this draft convention a draft declaration was attached, whereby Turkey was to engage that foreign legal counsellors would be chosen to assist in the administration of justice in Turkey in accordance with the latest proposals of the Allied delegations. [3]

Subsequent to the meetings of the Commission on January 31 and February 1, informal conversations between Ismet Pasha and the plenipotentiaries of the three inviting Powers took place, as a result of which further concessions were offered to Ismet Pasha on February 3 and 4. Regarding the draft declaration relative to the administration of justice in Turkey, the inviting Powers offered to replace it by another, under which the legal advisers were to possess no judicial functions and were to have merely general powers of observing the working of the Turkish courts, ensuring appeals against improper decisions and bringing complaints to the notice of the proper Turkish authorities. [4]

[1] Art. 26, *Parl. Pap.* cited, p. 695.

[2] Ch. iii, Draft Convention respecting the Régime Applicable to Foreigners in Turkey, *ibid.*, pp. 798-780.

[3] *Ibid.*, pp. 801-803.

[4] *Ibid.*, pp. 834-836; *Doc. dip.* cited, vol. ii, Feb. 1, 1923-Feb. 4, 1923, pp. 11-12.

In his reply to the Allied offers, dated February 4, 1923, Ismet Pasha, expressing the hope that there would be no longer any difficulty in settling the small differences which had arisen regarding the judicial guarantees to be offered by Turkey, attached a revised draft of the declaration, which tended to curtail the powers of the legal counsellors.[1]

On this same day, a last-minute effort was made by Lord Curzon and his French and Italian colleagues, in an informal meeting in the British delegate's room, to arrive at a final settlement, but owing to the Turkish delegation's insistence on their point of view with regard to the economic and judicial issues, the conference was broken up without accomplishing its desired end.[2]

The Lausanne Conference was resumed on April 23, 1923,[3] when three committees were created, the first of which was designated as the General Committee, to deal with the outstanding political questions and the judicial part of the draft convention respecting the régime of foreigners in Turkey.[4] At a meeting of this Committee, on May 1, the Turkish delegation took exception to any specific provision for the abrogation of the Capitulations in Turkey, as, in their view, the latter had become a *fait accompli* since 1914. The Allies, supported by the Americans, held that bilateral treaties could not be abolished by a unilateral act, but they accepted the Turkish point of view in principle, subject to the discovery of a satisfactory formula for article 26 of the draft treaty. This article, as has been seen, provided

[1] *Parl. Pap.* cited, pp. 840, 852-853; *Doc. dip.* cited, vol. ii, pp. 19, 21.

[2] *Parl. Pap.* cited, pp. 842-851. See also M. Bompard's report to M. Poincaré, *Doc. dip.* cited, vol. ii, pp. 126-9.

[3] The official proceedings of the conference have not yet been made public. What is given below is gathered from the despatches to the London *Times*, which are necessarily incomplete.

[4] London *Times*, Apr. 24, 1923, 14c.

that the High Contracting Parties " agree to abrogate " the Capitulations, while the Turkish delegation desired it to read " declare completely abrogated." [1]

The discussion with regard to the judicial status of foreigners in Turkey came to a head at the meeting of the first committee on May 4. The point at issue was a provision in the draft declaration to the effect that domiciliary visits, searches or arrests of persons other than those taken in *flagrante delicto* could be carried out in the judicial areas of Constantinople, Smyrna, Samsoun and Adana only with the previous consent of one of the foreign legal counsellors.[2] The Turks claimed that the Allies had accepted a counter-draft presented by the Turkish delegation on February 4, which omitted this provision,[3] while the Allies denied it. After a prolonged debate, Sir Horace Rumbold proposed that the Allies' counter-draft and the old draft would be examined by the drafting committee. Ismet Pasha still persisted, and finally Sir Horace said that the Allies would circulate their counter-draft and, waiving its proposed examination by the drafting committee, reserved the right to discuss it again in committee.[4]

On June 4, the Allied and Turkish delegations smoothed over their difficulty by reaching a compromise on the disputed point. Instead of requiring the previous consent of the legal counsellors to the domiciliary visits, searches and arrests in the four judicial areas, all such measures taken in Constantinople and Smyrna should be brought without delay to the notice of the legal counsellors.[5]

The Treaty of Peace, together with the subsidiary agree-

[1] *Ibid.*, May 2, 1923, 13c.
[2] *Cf. Parl. Pap.* cited, p. 835.
[3] *Ibid.*, p. 852.
[4] London *Times*, May 5, 1923, 12e.
[5] *Ibid.*, June 5, 1923, 13a.

ments, was signed on July 24, 1923. Article 28 of the Treaty of Peace provided: "Each of the High Contracting Parties accepts, in so far as it is concerned, the complete abolition of the Capitulations in Turkey in every respect." [1] The Convention (IV) respecting Conditions of Residence and Business and Jurisdiction recognized the application of the principles of international law in all questions of jurisdiction.[2] The much-debated declaration was also signed in the form accepted on June 4 by the Turkish delegation. By this declaration, the Turkish Government proposed to engage for a period of not less than five years a number of European legal counsellors, to be selected from a list prepared by the Permanent Court of International Justice from among jurists nationals of countries which did not take part in the World War. These legal counsellors were to serve as Turkish officials under the Minister of Justice, some of them being posted in Constantinople and others in Smyrna. Their duties were specified as follows: to take part in the work of the legislative commissions; to observe the working of the Turkish courts and to forward such reports to the Minister of Justice as were deemed by them necessary; to receive all complaints regarding the administration of justice, with a view of bringing them to the notice of the Minister of Justice in order to ensure the strict observance of law; and to receive all complaints caused by domiciliary visits, perquisitions or arrests, which should, in Constantinople and Smyrna, be brought immediately after their execution to the notice of the legal counsellor by the local representative of the Minister of Justice.[3]

[1] Great Britain, *Treaty Series*, 1923, no. 16, p. 25.

[2] "Art. 15. Subject to the provisions of Article 16, all questions of jurisdiction shall, as between Turkey and the other Contracting Powers, be decided in accordance with the principles of international law." Art. 16 provides for the adjudication of questions of personal status involving non-Moslem foreigners by their home authorities. *Ibid.*, p. 201.

[3] *Ibid.*, pp. 201-203.

Article ii of the as yet unratified Turco-American treaty of August 6, 1923, also provides for the termination of the extraterritorial rights of the United States in Turkey.[1]

II. PERSIA

At the Paris Peace Conference, the Persian, delegation presented three groups of claims, the first group containing their case for the abolition of extraterritoriality. After reciting briefly the facts involved, the statement of the Persian delegation went on to say:

Meanwhile, for a number of years, the Persian Government have entered resolutely in the path of judicial reforms, with the aid of foreign advisers, taking France as a model. The work of codification is being actively pursued and Persian justice will shortly offer all the guarantees of justice as in the European States. Consequently, there is no reason to continue indefinitely the peculiar situation created in favor of foreigners in Persia and the time has come to terminate it.[2]

Therefore, the Persian Government claimed " that the treaties made between Persia and foreign countries be subjected to a revision, to the end that all clauses contravening the political, judicial, and economic independence of Persia be eliminated." [3] But due to the inability of the Persian Government to " organize, administer, or control the Kingdom of Persia within the pre-war boundaries," the Persian delegation did not get a chance to state their case.[4]

The only European Power which has abandoned its rights of jurisdiction in Persia is Russia. By the treaty of Feb-

---

[1] *Current History,* vol. xix, p. 100.

[2] *Claims of Persia before the Conference of the Preliminaries of Peace at Paris,* p. 4.

[3] *Ibid.,* p. 6.

[4] Temperley, *A History of the Paris Peace Conference* (London, 1920-24), vol. vi, p. 211.

ruary 26, 1921, it was agreed by Persia and Russia " that Russian subjects in Persia and Persian subjects in Russia shall, as from the date of the present Treaty, be placed upon the same footing as the inhabitants of the towns in which they reside; they shall be subject to the laws of their country of residence, and shall submit their complaints to the local courts." [1] The reason for the action of the Soviet Government is plainly stated in the opening article of the treaty:

In order to confirm its declarations regarding Russian policy towards the Persian nation, . . . the R. S. F. S. R. formally affirms once again that it definitely renounces the tyrannical policy carried out by the colonizing governments of Russia which has been overthrown by the will of the workers and peasants of Russia.

Inspired by this principle and desiring that the Persian people should be happy and independent and should be able to dispose freely of its patrimony, the Russian Republic declares the whole body of treaties and conventions concluded with Persia by the Tsarist Government, which crushed the rights of the Persian people, to be null and void.[2]

Thus, the relinquishment by Russia of extraterritoriality in Persia represents partly an attempt to atone for the injustices inflicted by Czarist Russia on Persia, and partly an endeavor to restore the administrative autonomy of the latter country.[3]

[1] Art. 16, *State Papers*, vol. cxiv, p. 905. *Cf.* League of Nations, *Treaty Series*, no. 268.

[2] Art. 1, *State Papers*, vol. cxiv, p. 901.

[3] The Soviet Civil Code, moreover, contains some extraordinary provisions, so that the Soviet Government may be regarded as having been so generous with malice prepense. See *Columbia Law Review*, vol. xxiv, p. 689.

III. JAPAN

After the disturbances incident to the overthrow of the Shogunate and the restoration of the Mikado, Japanese statesmen addressed themselves seriously to a movement for reform, which was destined to startle the world. They saw that two of the sovereign rights of their country—tariff and jurisdiction—had been sadly impaired, and that in order to take her place among the Great Powers of the world, it was imperative for Japan to regain her autonomy in these particulars. They took advantage of the provision made in various treaties for their general revision in 1872, and a commission headed by Prince Iwakura, and including Kido, Okuba, Ito, Yamagutsi, was sent out in 1871, to negotiate for the revision and to study institutions abroad. The Commissioners were heartily received by the people and government of the United States. The American Government promised to treat with Japan most liberally, but it was found that the Commissioners were not clothed with the authority to conclude and sign a treaty. Their mission to Europe proved to be a complete failure. The Powers were unwilling to relinquish their extraterritorial rights before Japan could show an improved system of law and judicial administration.[1]

In the meantime, the Minister of Italy at Yedo proposed, in 1873, a special convention with Japan relative to the travel of foreigners in the interior. The draft convention contained a provision which required the foreigners traveling beyond the limits of the jurisdiction of their consuls to submit to the protection and jurisdiction of the territorial authorities, " according to the usages which prevail in the countries of Europe and America." [2]

[1] Foster, *American Diplomacy in the Orient* (Boston & New York, 1903), pp. 345-348.

[2] U. S. *Foreign Relations*, 1873, pt. i, p. 270.

Taking cognizance of this draft treaty, the French Government instructed its representative at Washington to sound the American Government on its opinion regarding the Italian proposal.[1] On June 21, 1873, Mr. Hamilton Fish, American Secretary of State, wrote to Mr. Schenck, American Minister at London, to seek an interview with Earl Granville and to communicate to him the views of the American Government. Mr. Fish declared:

Japan has no firmer friend than the United States; no one more ready than we to recognize her rightful autonomy. But on a candid review of the situation, the President is forced to the conclusion that it is not yet safe to surrender to the local authorities the guaranteed rights of ex-territoriality. We have not such knowledge of the administration of justice in that kingdom, and of the means for the protection of the liberty and rights of foreigners, as would justify such surrender at this time.[2]

Similar instructions were sent out to the American Ministers at Paris, Berlin and the Hague.[3] Due to the disapproval of the Powers,[4] the Italian Government was obliged to " refuse to accept the conditions proposed by the projected convention as a basis of free travel in the interior of Japan." [5]

The importance of this episode lies in the fact that from the very outset, the Powers have conditioned their consent to the modification of extraterritoriality in Japan on a commensurate amelioration of the judicial system in that country. As the following account of the Japanese negotiations

[1] U. S. *Foreign Relations*, 1873, pt. i, p. 169.

[2] *Ibid.*, p. 383.

[3] *Ibid.*, p. 383.

[4] For the French and German attitude, see *ibid.*, pp. 261, 296.

[5] *Ibid.*, p. 272.

with the Powers will show, this fact was ever present in the minds of the negotiators on both sides.

Impressed with the failure of the mission of 1871, and with the need of speedy reform in her judicial system as well as in other matters, Japan plunged into a vigorous attempt to improve her internal conditions. Students were sent abroad to imbibe the spirit of Western civilization, at the same time that foreigners of distinction were called to Japan to help and advise in this general reform movement.[1] In 1875, an imperial decree was issued, convoking the provincial assemblies, in order that the emperor might " govern in harmony with public opinion." In the same year, British and French troops stationed in Yokohama for the protection of their respective nationals were withdrawn, the first manifestation on the part of the European nations of a disposition to respect the sovereignty of Japan. Edicts followed in rapid succession, which provided for the compilation of a constitution after Western models, enacted and put into force a penal code and a code of procedure, and announced the convocation of a national parliament.[2]

With this program of reform under way, the Japanese Government, in 1878, approached the Diplomatic Corps at Tokio for a revision of the treaties. The Foreign Minister of Japan pointed out to the foreign Powers concerned the abuses of the extraterritorial system [3] and asked for its modification. To this, the Powers, except the United States, again turned a deaf ear, Great Britain being the leading

[1] Notably M. Boissonade, of the University of Paris, whose assistance in compiling the Japanese codes has made his name immortal in the annals of Japan's legal reform.

[2] U. S. *Foreign Relations,* 1875, pt. ii, pp. 787, 794; 1876, p. 381; 1881, pp. 658, 692, 728.

[3] For a contemporary account of these abuses see D. C. Greene, *Extraterritoriality in Japan* (an essay read before the Kobe and Osaka Missionary Conference in April, 1884), pp. 2-11.

obstructionist. The United States dissented from the general attitude of the Powers by concluding with Japan a treaty giving the latter full right over her tariff.[1] This treaty was of no significance except as a specimen of American sympathy with the Japanese aspirations, as its validity was conditioned on the conclusion of similar treaties with other Powers, which was not done.[2]

On February 25, 1882, a conference was opened at Tokio, to consider the question of treaty revision. Count Inouye, representing Japan, told the foreign representatives of the efforts made by his country to reform her internal administration in every respect. " I may call your attention," he said, " especially to the reforms brought into our laws and our judicial procedure, which assure the security of person and property by the introduction of codes of law and of criminal procedure in conformity with modern ideas." He believed that the moment had come when all the obstacles to the free intercourse between Japan and the Powers should be removed. The Japanese Government, he declared, " proposes now to open the whole country to foreigners and to accord to them access to all parts of the Empire, on condition that they submit to Japanese law." [3] Due to a disagreement on the permanency of treaties, however, Japan was unable to reap anything out of the conference.[4]

A more formal effort was made in 1886, when a diplomatic conference was called at Tokio. At this conference, Count Inouye, the Foreign Minister, again took an active part. The deliberations were extended to the following year, when Japan agreed that in addition to the native

[1] Art. 1, Malloy, vol. i, p. 1022.

[2] Art. 10, *ibid.*, p. 1024.

[3] *Archives diplomatiques*, 1897, vol, iv, pp. 213-214.

[4] Japan was willing to sign only temporary treaties, while the Powers insisted on permanent agreements. *Ibid.*, p. 345.

judges there should be a body of European and American experts, who should constitute a majority in every court before which aliens might be required to appear. When this important concession was obtained, the Europeans went further and insisted that the judges should be nominated by the Diplomatic Corps and that the latter should control the laws, rules of procedure, and details of the administration of justice. Upon receiving news of these exorbitant demands, the Japanese public was greatly excited, and a wave of indignation swept over the whole country. Count Inouye was forced to give up his portfolio, and in July, 1887, the Foreign Office notified the foreign representatives that the treaty negotiations were to be adjourned till the completion of the new codes under preparation.[1] During the conference, the United States showed a friendly attitude to the Japanese point of view and concluded with Japan a treaty of extradition on April 29, 1886.[2] In submitting the treaty to the Senate, President Cleveland declared that it had been made partly because of the support which its conclusion would give to Japan in her efforts towards judicial autonomy and complete sovereignty.[3]

Count Inouye was succeeded by Count Okuma in the Foreign Office. The new Minister changed his tactics, and instead of seeking for the collective support of all the Powers, he endeavored to enter into separate agreements with each one of them. On November 30, 1888, a treaty was concluded with Mexico, which fully recognized Japan's judicial control over Mexican citizens and vessels within the territorial limits of Japan.[4] Meanwhile, negotiations

---

[1] *Archives diplomatiques,* 1897, vol. iv, p. 346. *Cf.* Foster, *op. cit.,* pp. 357-358.

[2] Malloy, vol. i, p. 1025.

[3] U. S. *Sen. Ex. Journal,* vol. xxv, p. 495.

[4] Art. 8, *State Papers,* vol. lxxix, p. 131.

were resumed with Great Britain. On January 19, 1889, a draft treaty and two draft notes were transmitted to the British Government by the Japanese Minister at London. The terms contained in these drafts pertaining to extraterritoriality were briefly: that for five years after the coming into force of the proposed treaty, British consular jurisdiction in Japan should be limited to a restricted number of ports; that outside of these limits Japanese courts should have exclusive jurisdiction; that British consular jurisdiction should " wholly cease and determine " at the expiration of the five-year period; that the Government of Japan should strive to complete the elaboration of Japan's law codes within the following year; that in case such elaboration should be delayed beyond two years after the proposed treaty was concluded, the Japanese Government should then ask for the postponement of the date of totally abolishing British consular jurisdiction until at least three years after the codes in question should have been promulgated; and that the Japanese Government should engage a number of foreign judges in the Supreme Court, to constitute a majority in cases involving foreigners as defendants.[1] In their counterdrafts, the British Government accepted the Japanese terms with slight modifications.[2] But the offers made by Japan were again resented by the Japanese public, and the party in opposition to Count Okuma declared his treaty measure to be unconstitutional. The popular indignation became so intense that on October 19, 1889, a fanatic threw a bomb at Count Okuma, and the work of treaty revision was again suspended.[3]

After these failures, the Japanese Government abandoned

---

[1] *Parliamentahy Papers,* 1894 [C. 7548], *Japan,* no. 1 (1894), pp. 7, 10, 11.

[2] *Ibid.,* pp. 19, 20, 23.

[3] Hishida, *International Position of Japan,* pp. 142-143.

the hope of success in diplomatic negotiations. Efforts were exerted to push on the reform movement, with a view of winning over foreign sentiment by means of visible signs of progress. In this, the Japanese were much more successful than in their previous resort to diplomacy. The reforms culminated in the promulgation of the imperial constitution in 1889.[1] In 1891, the Civil Code, the Code of Civil Procedure, the Commercial Code, and the Code of the Constitution of Courts were promulgated, thus completing the entire Japanese legal system.[2]

Viscount Aoki, who succeeded Count Okuma as Foreign Minister, again took up the negotiations for treaty revision. He insisted on the judicial autonomy of Japan. His correspondence with the British Government on the employment of foreign judges and the completion of Japan's legal codes, gives additional evidence of the importance of the legal argument in every attempt at the modification of the extra-territorial régime.

With reference to the improvement of the Japanese judiciary, Viscount Aoki enumerated the specific reforms brought about since 1872, viz.: the creation of a separate and independent system of courts; the promulgation of various codes of law and the imperial constitution; the introduction of a system of competitive examinations for appointments to the judgeships; and the promulgation of a new law providing for a comprehensive and complete reorganization of the imperial courts of justice. Having dwelt upon the above-mentioned reforms, Viscount Aoki declared:

In the light of these important facts, it may be asserted, without fear of contradition, that when Japanese Tribunals supersede Consular Courts, no case in which a foreigner is

[1] U. S. *Foreign Relations*, 1889, p. 536.

[2] Okamura, " The Progress of the Judicial System in Japan," *Journal of the Society of Comparative Legislation,* new series, vol. i, p. 51.

interested will ever be tried in Last Instance, except by a Court composed, at least, of a majority of Judges, who have submitted to the test of a severe competitive examination, and are, consequently, well grounded in the principles of Western jurisprudence, besides being thoroughly conversant with the laws of Japan.

In addition to the improvement of the Japanese courts, Viscount Aoki attempted also to show the progress which the Japanese Government had made in bringing the work of codification to its completion. He said:

Nearly ten years have elapsed since the Criminal Code and the Code of Criminal Procedure were promulgated, and the time can now only be reckoned by months before the Constitution which was prumulgated a year ago will come into force. The Imperial Government have for years been engaged in the labor of elaborating Civil and Commercial Codes, and it is a matter of public notoriety that these great works are nearly completed, and will ere long be proclaimed. And the fact that they have not already been promulgated, in the presence of so many inducements connected with Treaty revision, betrays the solicitude of the Imperial Government that, when issued, they shall be complete.[1]

The British Government proposed a new draft treaty, which provided that British consular jurisdiction should continue to be exercised for five years and that if at the end of this period the new codes of Japan should have been in actual and satisfactory operation for twelve months, Great Britain would relinquish her extraterritorial jurisdiction.[2] This draft treaty was accepted by Viscount Aoki as a basis for further negotiation.[3]

[1] *Parl. Pap.*, 1894 [C. 7548], Japan, no. 1 (1894), p. 51.
[2] *Ibid.*, p. 63.
[3] Viscount Aoki to Mr. Fraser, Sep. 12, 1890, *ibid.*, p. 65.

Viscount Aoki was succeeded by Viscount Enomotto, who shared the view that before the abolition of extraterritoriality could be expected, there should exist in Japan in actual operation a satisfactory system of jurisprudence. Although the new codes had been promulgated in 1891, the civil and commercial codes were not immediately put into force. When the Upper House was deliberating on the question, on May 26, 1892, Viscount Enomotto appeared on the scene and made a speech, in which he openly disabused the minds of those who dreamed of securing judicial autonomy without offering adequate guarantees to foreign life and property. He said:

In considering the clauses in need of revision as a whole, our motto must be simply the protection of our ancient national rights and national interests, and for the accomplishment of this purpose there is one method, and one only, that of enacting and carrying into effect a Code of Laws fit to be accepted by the civilized nations of the world.

However eagerly all classes of Japanese may desire to possess a Treaty free from all imperfections and defects, it admits of no manner of doubt that until such a Code of Laws shall be in operation friendly countries will withhold their consent to revision. . . . Those persons who descant upon the shortcomings of the present Treaties are in the habit of looking back to the time of their inception, and attributing their defects to the limited knowledge of foreign affairs possessed by the Ministers of the day. But the Ministers of thirty years ago could not possibly be intimately acquainted with the circumstances of foreign countries, and even granting the necessary experience in exceptional instances, the Treaty Powers could not have been induced to subject the precious lives and property of their subjects to the laws of Japan, and that for the very good reason that there were at that time no laws fit to be enforced in a civilized society, to whose protection their lives and property could have been committed.[1]

[1] *Ibid.,* p. 71.

In spite of Viscount Enomotto's eloquent plea, the imperial diet passed a law, which was sanctioned by imperial decree on November 24, 1892, postponing the operation of the Civil and Commercial Codes.[1]

In 1892, the Japanese Government took advantage of the withdrawal of consuls by Portugal, and issued an ordinance putting an end to the consular jurisdiction hitherto enjoyed by Portugal in Japan.[2] Between January 18, 1893, and April 10, 1894, notes were exchanged with the Hawaiian Government, by which the latter abandoned their rights of jurisdiction in Japan.[3]

Meanwhile, negotiations had once more been resumed with Great Britain and other Powers for the revision of their treaties with Japan.   In 1894, the conversations with Great Britain were transferred from Tokio to London.   Viscount Aoki, who was then Japanese Minister at Berlin, was instructed to go over to London to carry on and finish the work of treaty revision.   Finally, after assuring the British Government of the actual reforms introduced by Japan into her judicial system,[4] Viscount Aoki succeeded in obtaining from Great Britain a new treaty, which was signed on July 16, 1894.   Article 20 provides for the abrogation of all existing treaties and of the extraterritorial rights enjoyed by Great Britain under them.   Article 21 stipulates that " the present Treaty shall not take effect until at least five years after its signature." [5]   The intent of the latter provision is clearly explained by the note of Viscount Aoki to Earl Kimberley, July 16, 1894, which announced:

---

[1] *Parl. Pap.*, cited, p. 74.

[2] Hishida, *op. cit.*, p. 143. Presumably with Portugal's consent, but no information is available on this point.

[3] *State Papers,* vol. lxxxvi, p. 1185.

[4] *Parl. Pap.*, cited, pp. 94-95.

[5] *State Papers,* vol. lxxxvi, pp. 46, 47.

That the Imperial Japanese Government, recognizing the advantage of having the Codes of the Empire which have already been promulgated in actual operation when the Treaty stipulations at present subsisting between the Government of Japan and that of Great Britain cease to be binding, engage not to give the notice provided for by the first paragraph of Article XXI of the Treaty of Commerce and Navigation, signed this day, until those portions of said Codes which are now in abeyance are brought into actual force.[1]

Treaties were also entered into with the United States, November 22, 1894,[2] Italy, December 1, 1894,[3] Peru, March 20, 1895,[4] Russia, May 27/June 8, 1895,[5] Denmark, October 19, 1895,[6] Brazil, November 5, 1895,[7] Germany, April 4, 1896,[8] Sweden and Norway, May 2, 1896,[9] Belgium, June 22, 1896,[10] France, August 4, 1896,[11] the Netherlands, September 8, 1896,[12] Switzerland, November 10, 1896,[13] Spain, January 2, 1897,[14] Portugal, January 26, 1897,[15] Chile, September 25, 1897,[16] Austria-Hungary, December 5, 1897,[17] Argentina, February 3, 1898,[18] and Greece, May 20/

[1] *Ibid.*, p. 52.
[2] Art. 18, Malloy, vol. i, p. 1035.
[3] Art. 19, *State Papers*, vol. lxxxvi, p. 1194.
[4] Art. 17, *ibid.*, vol. lxxxvii, p. 1223.
[5] Art. 18, *ibid.*, p. 862.
[6] Art. 18, *ibid.*, p. 694.
[7] Art. 10, *ibid.*, p. 1194.
[8] Art. 20, *ibid.*, vol. lxxxviii, p. 588.
[9] Art. 17, *ibid.*, p. 458.
[10] Art. 18, *ibid.*, p. 404.
[11] Art. 23, *ibid.*, p. 536.
[12] Art. 18, *ibid.*, p. 547.
[13] Art. 14, *ibid.*, p. 490.
[14] Art. 19, *ibid.*, vol. lxxxix, p. 965.
[15] Art. 18, *ibid.*, p. 976.
[16] Art. 11, *ibid.*, vol. xcix, p. 936.
[17] Art. 22, *ibid.*, vol. lxxxix, p. 987.
[18] Art. 10, *ibid.*, vol. xcii, p. 226.

June 1, 1899.[1] These treaties put an end to consular jurisdiction in Japan; they all took effect in July and August,
1899.

The close proximity of the dates of these negotiations and of the Sino-Japanese War has led to the conception or misconception that Japan's success in that conflict
was mainly responsible for the restoration of her judicial
autonomy and her other rights of sovereignty. To cite a
typically inaccurate statement,

Prior to her victory over China, she [Japan] was subject to
foreign aggression as much as China, but subsequent to the
Chino-Japanese War, when she had demonstrated her prowess
and ability, her sovereignty remained intact and immune from
all external aggressions; what is more, she recovered her lost,
or delegated rights of sovereignty.[2]

For the sake of scientific accuracy, the author deems it
necessary to devote a few words to the refutation of this
widely held belief.

At the very outset, it may be admitted that the victory of
Japan over China in the war of 1894-95 had much to do
with the increase of Japan's prestige in the world. To the
political ascendancy of the island empire, the Sino-Japanese
War doubtless contributed signally. But to say that the
recovery of Japan's sovereign rights was due to her defeat
of China and especially to ascribe the abolition of extraterritoriality in Japan to that event would be to ignore many
other important considerations.

In the first place, it must be pointed out that if we compare the dates more carefully than is usually done, we will
find that the most important treaty abolishing extraterri-

[1] Art. 11, *ibid.*, p. 369.
[2] Bau, *Foreign Relations of China* (rev. and enl. ed., New York,
Chicago, etc., 1923), p. 494.

toriality in Japan was concluded prior to the opening of the
Sino-Japanese War; to say nothing of the treaty of November 30, 1888, with Mexico, and the exchange of notes
of January 13, 1893/April 10, 1894, with the Hawaiian
Islands, the British treaty was concluded on July 16, 1894.
Owing to the predominant interest of Great Britain in Japan,
her treaty was by far the most important, and its importance
is indicated by the fact that all the later agreements of the
same nature were largely modeled after it. Contrary to
the popular belief, this treaty was concluded before instead
of after the outbreak of the Sino-Japanese War.[1]   When
we recall that negotiations for the revision of her treaties
had been embarked upon by Japan since 1871, twenty-three
years before the war with China took place, and that the
main lines of the British treaty had been fairly settled by the
end of 1890, it is impossible to establish any causal relationship between the war and the abolition of extraterritoriality
in Japan.

True, the American and other treaties were concluded
after the opening of hostilities between China and Japan,
and, in fact, the majority of them were signed and ratified
after the Peace of Shimonoseki, which bears the date of
April 17, 1895. Had the Japanese success in the late war
exerted any influence on the consummation of the protracted
negotiations in these cases, it could not have been an important, much less a controlling, one. As has been mentioned, the provisions of the later treaties were but verbal
reproductions of the terms of the British treaty, which, it
must have been thought, if they could regulate the rights
and obligations of the nationals of the country with the

---

[1] Actual hostilities began on July 25, 1894, when two Chinese vessels,
the *Kuang-yi* and the *Tsi-yuen*, opened fire on the Japanese naval forces
off the islands of Phung and Shapain. A declaration of war was
issued by both governments simultaneously on August first. See Vladimir, *The China-Japan War* (New York, 1896), pp. 95-96, 113.

greatest commercial interest in Japan, could do the same thing
with regard to the nationals of all the other Treaty Powers.

In the case of the United States particularly, little importance need be attached to the outcome of the Sino-Japanese War and its effect on the abolition of extraterritoriality
in Japan. It is to be borne in mind that of all the Powers
which had treaty relations with Japan, the United States
was the earliest to evince a willingness to respond to Japan's
appeal for treaty revision. The support of the American
Government and people was pledged as early as 1871 to the
efforts of Japan, while successively in 1878 and 1886, the
United States Government displayed its friendship by concluding extradition and tariff conventions with Japan. This
background of sincere support was a natural prelude to the
final promise for the abolition of American extraterritoriality in Japan, and even if the Sino-Japanese War had not
occurred, it is unlikely that the United States would have
delayed its action much longer. Moreover, if the United
States Government had chosen to procrastinate, the progress
of the war would have furnished the best pretext. On the
contrary, however, that government made its treaty for the
abolition of extraterritoriality in Japan while the storm was
still raging.

As a matter of fact, the most important consideration
which prompted the Powers to agree to the restoration of
Japan's judicial autonomy was the progress which Japan
had achieved in the way of judicial reform. Had the war
been the controlling factor and had Japan's military success
alone been regarded as sufficient to entitle her to complete
judicial rights, the Powers would logically have had to give
up their extraterritoriality without imposing any other conditions. But this was not what happened. All the treaties
were to take effect in 1899, although some of them had been
concluded as early as 1894, the intervening period being in-

tended for the coming into force of the Japanese Codes;
and as has been stated above, the Japanese Government
agreed to refrain from giving notice of the cessation of the
old treaties, " until those portions of said Codes which are
now in abeyance are brought into actual operation." It is evident, therefore, that glamorous as it was, Japan's successful
emergence from the war with China did not of itself lead
to the abolition of extraterritoriality. Any attempt simply
to explain the situation on this score and to ignore the more
important considerations altogether, is an unfounded conjecture and should be discredited by any student of the history of international relations.

IV. SIAM

Ever since the extraterritorial system was formally introduced into Siam, this State has been undergoing a series of
judicial reforms.   The fruit of these reforms was the formal
renunciation or promise of renunciation on the part of the
foreign Powers of their consular jurisdiction in Siam.   In
1883, Great Britain entered into a treaty with Siam which
granted to the Siamese Government the right to establish
an " International Court " composed of Siamese judges and
administering Siamese law, to decide disputes between
British subjects in Chiengmai, Lakon and Lampoonchi, the
right of the British consul to intervene in such cases being
reserved.[1] The International Court system was extended
in 1884-1885 and 1896 to other Siamese provinces.[2]   On
February 13, 1904, France made a similar agreement with
Siam, the operation of the Siamese International Court being extended to cases arising in Chiengmai, Lakon, Lampoonchi and Nan.[3]   Denmark on March 24, 1905, and Italy

[1] *State Papers*, vol. lxxiv, p. 81.
[2] Great Britain, *Treaty Series*, no. 9 (1897), pp. 2, 3.
[3] *State Papers*, vol. xcvii, p. 964.

on April 8, 1905, concluded treaties with Siam to identically
the same effect.[1]   By her treaty of March 23, 1907, France
agreed to the extension of the system to all her Asiatic subjects and protégés, and to the abolition of the International
Court régime after the promulgation and putting into effect
of the Siamese codes.[2]   On March 10, 1909, Great Britain
agreed by a new treaty to extend the jurisdiction of the
International Courts to " all British subjects in Siam regis-
tered at the British consulate after the date of the present
Treaty." The transfer of the jurisdiction of the International Courts to the ordinary Siamese courts was also
promised on the same conditions as were laid down by the
French treaty of 1907.   All other British subjects in Siam
not belonging to the class mentioned above were subjected
to the jurisdiction of the ordinary Siamese courts.[3]   The
right of evocation was maintained, but it should " cease to
be exercised in all matters coming within the scope of codes
of laws regularly promulgated." [4]   Denmark agreed, on
March 15, 1913, to submit all Danish subjects coming to
Siam after the ratification of the treaty of that date to the
jurisdiction of the ordinary Siamese courts.[5]   In 1916, the
Russian Government, upon its own initiative, entered into
negotiations for a treaty similar to the British treaty of
1909, but the outbreak of the revolution in Russia cut the
matter short.[6]

In explaining the conclusion of the treaty of 1909, the
British Minister at Bangkok, besides alluding to the admin-

---

[1] *State Papers*, vol. ci, pp. 290-409.

[2] *Ibid.*, vol. c, p. 1029.

[3] *Ibid.*, vol. cii, p. 127.

[4] Sec. 3 of the protocol annexed to the treaty of March 10, 1909,
ibid., p. 130.

[5] *Ibid.*, vol. cvii, p. 751.

[6] *Siam's Case for Revision of Obsolete Treaty Obligations* (1919), p. 11.

istrative inconveniences occasioned by the partial cessation of extraterritoriality in one section of Siam and its maintenance in another, mentioned " various additional factors, such as the desire of British subjects to acquire the right to hold land . . . , the codification of Siamese law, and the very creditable and successful efforts made by the Siamese Government to improve the standard of their judicial administration." [1]   This is cited to show that here, as in every other case, a preponderating amount of importance is attached to the improvement of the judicial régime as a prerequisite for the restoration, partial or complete, of judicial autonomy.

At the Paris Peace Conference of 1919, Siam prepared a *Case* for the revision of her treaty obligations. One of the latter which Siam sought to get rid of completely was that of extraterritoriality. After presenting briefly the history of extraterritoriality in Siam,[2] the *Case* of Siam gave the following as reasons for requesting its abolition: (1) that it invaded the sovereignty of Siam, a free nation; (2) that it made the administration of impartial justice difficult, if not impossible; (3) that it put obstacles in the way of the maintenance of order, being a continual affront to Siam's dignity and a fruitful source of irritation; (4) that it was expensive—involving, as it did, the maintenance of European judges and advisers; and (5) that it tended to discourage the completion of the Siamese codes of laws then in progress, since there was nowhere even in the British or Danish treaty any assurance that once these codes were completed and promulgated, the requirement that European judges and advisers assist in the Siamese courts would be

[1] Memorandum explanatory of the circumstances which render the modification of the present system of British extraterritorial jurisdiction in Siam desirable. *Parliamentary Papers*, 1909 [Cd. 4646], Siam, no. 1 (1909).

[2] *Siam's Case*, pp. 7-13.

yielded and these courts restored to their full measure of authority, as recognized by the treaties previous to 1855.

Under these circumstances, a transfer of jurisdiction from the international to the ordinary Siamese courts would be in name only, even with the obliteration of the privilege of evocation, which was rarely exercised. For these reasons, it was declared " that this oppressive scheme of exterritoriality must be removed in its entirety, both because it works practical and unnecessary hardship to Siam and because it is unjust." [1]

All Siam succeeded in doing at Paris was to secure from the defeated Powers the abrogation of their extraterritorial rights in Siam. By the Treaty of Versailles, June 28, 1919, Germany made such a renunciation as from June 22, 1917.[2] Similar renunciations were made by Austria in the Treaty of St. Germain, September 10, 1919,[3] and by Hungary in the Treaty of Trianon, June 4, 1920.[4]

On December 16, 1920, the United States entered into a treaty with Siam, containing a protocol, article 1 of which announced that the system of extraterritorial jurisdiction established in Siam for citizens of the United States and " the privileges, exemptions, and immunities " now enjoyed by them as a part of or appurtenant to the system " shall absolutely cease and determine on the date of the exchange of ratifications " and that thereafter all citizens of the United States, and persons, corporations, companies and associations entitled to its protection in Siam should be subjected to the jurisdiction of the Siamese courts. However, until

---

[1] *Siam's Case*, pp. 17-20.

[2] Art. 135, *The Treaty of Peace between the Allied and Associated Powers and Germany* (London, 1919), p. 71.

[3] Art. 110, *The Treaty of Peace between the Allied and Associated Powers and Austria* (London, 1921), p. 43.

[4] Art. 94, Great Britain, *Treaty Series,* no. 10 (1920), p. 25.

the promulgation and putting into force of all the Siamese codes, and for a period of five years thereafter, but no longer, the United States, through its diplomatic and consular agents in Siam, whenever in its discretion it deems proper so to do in the interests of justice, may evoke any case pending before any Siamese court, except the Supreme or Dika Court, in which an American citizen, or a person, etc., entitled to its protection, is defendant or accused.[1] This is the most important concession obtained by Siam after the treaties of peace with Germany, Austria and Hungary, so far as extraterritorial jurisdiction in Siam is concerned. The protocol subjects American citizens in Siam to the jurisdiction of the ordinary Siamese courts without the intermediary stage of the " International Courts." The only guarantee the United States has deemed it necessary to impose on Siam is that of evocation, which can take place only in the rarest cases of miscarriage of justice.[2]

V. CHINA

Ever since the opening of the present century, China has made repeated attempts to secure the modification of the extraterritorial régime. Up to the present time, no less than six Powers have promised the ultimate abolition of extraterritoriality in China in addition to a number of others, which have been deprived of their judicial rights. The first treaty embodying a promise for the abolition was that of September 5, 1902, with Great Britain, article 12 of which provides:

China having expressed a strong desire to reform her judicial

---

[1] Malloy, vol. iii (1923), p. 2835.

[2] See art. 2 of the protocol. According to a recent press despatch, a new commercial treaty was concluded between France and Siam on February 14, 1925, by which the former, subject to certain conditions, engaged to abolish her extraterritorial rights in Siam. London *Times,* February, 16, 1925, 11 c.

system and to bring it into accord with that of Western nations, Great Britain agrees to give every assistance to such reform, and she will also be prepared to relinquish her extra-territorial rights when she is satisfied that the state of Chinese laws, the arrangement for their administration, and other considerations warrant her in so doing.[1]

Similar provisions were contained in the treaties with Japan [2] and the United States,[3] signed separately on October 8, 1903.[4] Article 10 of the treaty with Sweden, dated July 2, 1908, provides that " as soon as all the Treaty Powers have agreed to relinquish their extraterritorial rights, Sweden will also be prepared to do so." [5]   By a declaration annexed to the treaty of June 13, 1918, the Swiss Government made the same promise.[6]   Finally, by an exchange of notes between China and Mexico, September 26, 1921, embodying an agreement for the provisional modification of the Sino-Mexican treaty of December 14, 1899, which had been denounced by Mexico on November 11, 1920,[7] the Mexican Government engaged to " express on one of the amendments of the above-mentioned Treaty the renouncement that will be made to the consular jurisdiction in China." [8]

With the declaration of war on Germany and Austria-Hungary, on August 14, 1917, China abrogated all her treaties with these countries and put an end to their extra-

---

[1] MacMurray, *Treaties*, vol. i, 1902/7, p. 351.

[2] *Ibid.*, 1903/4, p. 414.

[3] *Ibid.*, 1903/5, p. 431.

[4] Art. 16 of the unratified treaty with Portugal of November 11, 1904, had an identical provision. *Ibid.*, 1902/9, p. 374.

[5] *Ibid.*, 1908/11, p. 745.

[6] *Ibid.*, vol. ii, 1918/8, p. 1430.

[7] *Cf. supra*, p. 91, n. 1.

[8] League of Nations, *Treaty Series*, vol. xiii, p. 208.

territorial privileges.[1]   A circular note was sent on the same
day to the Diplomatic Corps, stating:

Now that China has declared that a state of war exists with
Germany and Austria-Hungary, as regards all civil and criminal
cases involving Germans and Austrians in China, a set of provisional regulations governing the trial of civil and criminal
cases of enemy subjects has been drawn up, which were promulgated and put into effect on the 14th instant.

The first article of these regulations provided: " Civil and
criminal cases of enemy subjects will be tried during the
period of the War by the Chinese courts." [2]

At the Paris Peace Conference of 1919, China made another attempt to secure the abolition of extraterritoriality.
A statement was made and presented by the Chinese delegation, which set forth the Chinese claim to territorial jurisdiction.   After reviewing briefly the basis of extraterritorial
rights enjoyed by foreigners in China, and the successive
promises made by the Powers to relinquish them, the statement declares:

While we do not claim that the Chinese laws and their administration have reached such a state as has been attained by the
most advanced nations, we do feel confident to assert that China
has made very considerable progress in the administration of
justice and in all matters pertaining thereto since the signing of
the above-mentioned Commercial Treaties.

The evidences of this progress are given as follows: (1)
adoption of a National Constitution; (2) preparation of
Civil, Criminal, and Commercial Codes, and Codes of Civil
and Criminal Procedure; (3) establishment of new Courts,
viz., District Courts, High Courts or Courts of Appeal, and

[1] *Presidential Mandate*, Aug. 14, 1917, *ibid.*, 1917/7, pp. 1361-2.
[2] *Ibid.*, pp. 1372-3.

the *Taliyuan* or Supreme Court; (4) improvements in legal procedure, such as the separation of civil and criminal cases, publicity of trial and judgments; etc.; (5) careful training of judicial officers; and (6) reform of prison and police systems.

Furthermore, the maintenance of the system of extraterritoriality in China appears to be still less justifiable, if we look at the serious defects in its operation. Among these defects the statement mentions (1) diversity of laws applied; (2) lack of effective control over witnesses or plaintiffs of another nationality; (3) difficulty in obtaining evidence where a foreigner commits a crime in the interior; and (4) conflict of consular and judicial functions. These defects, it is contended, have led to the total abolition of the system in Japan by all the Powers, and to its partial abolition in Siam by certain Powers. "China, therefore, asks that the system will also disappear in China at the expiration of a definite period and upon the fulfilment of the following conditions:" (1) promulgation of a Criminal, a Civil, and a Commercial Code, a Code of Civil Procedure, and a Code of Criminal Procedure; and (2) establishment of new courts in all the localities where foreigners reside. China undertakes to fulfil these conditions by the end of 1924. But before the actual abolition of extraterritoriality, China requests the Powers (1) to submit every mixed case where the defendant is a Chinese to Chinese courts without interference on the part of the foreigners, and (2) to allow the execution of warrants issued or judgments delivered by Chinese courts within the Concessions or within the precincts of any foreign building without any previous examination by any consular or foreign judicial officer.

Finally, the statement asserts that the abolition of extraterritoriality in China would be of benefit to the foreign Powers as well as to China, in that it would tend to remove the many inconveniences involved in cases between foreigners of different nationalities, and to develop international commerce, possibly to open the whole country to the trade and residence of foreigners.[1] No action seems to have been taken by the Conference on the question, and the *status quo* was maintained.

In 1919, China concluded a treaty with Bolivia, article 2 of which contained a most-favored-nation clause. In an exchange of notes between the two governments, Bolivia has agreed to refrain from interpreting the inclusion of this clause in the treaty as an admission of the Bolivians in China to extraterritorial rights.[2]

On June 1, 1920, a treaty was entered into by China with Persia, which provided expressly that " in all civil and criminal cases to which Persian subjects are parties, they shall be subject to Chinese law and jurisdiction." [3]

China severed her treaty relations with Russia in 1920, because of her indisposition to recognize the Soviet régime in that country. At the instance of the Minister of Foreign Affairs, a Presidential Mandate was issued on September 23, 1920, declaring " the suspension of the recognition of the Russian Minister and Consuls in China." Following this, Prince Koudacheff, then Minister of Russia to China, addressed a note to the Doyen of the Dipomatic Corps at Peking, requesting the heads of the missions in China to examine into the status of Russians resident there. In a note, dated October 11, 1920, the Doyen inquired the Chinese Foreign Office on the subject. In reply, the Minister of Foreign Affairs said, in his note of October 22, " Russian citizens in China will continue to enjoy the rights secured

[1] *Questions for Readjustment submitted by China to the Peace Conference* (Paris, 1919), pp. 14-18.

[2] *China Year Book*, 1921-22, p. 371.

[3] Art. 4, *State Papers*, vol. cxiv, p. 677; *cf.* League of Nations, *Treaty Series*, vol. ix, p. 21.

to them by treaties." But " Russian consular jurisdiction must, of course, cease. In the trying of cases in which foreigners are plaintiffs and Russians defendants, the Chinese courts may apply Russian laws, but only those which do not conflict with Chinese legal rights. Possibly persons, well versed in Russian law, may be employed as advisers to the Chinese law courts." Desiring further elucidation, the Diplomatic Corps addressed another note on November 18, which was replied on November 29 to the following effect: " Both civil and criminal cases in which Russians are involved undoubtedly come, by treaty, under the jurisdiction of Consular Courts. But China has at present ceased to recognize the Russian Consuls in their official capacity and, as a result of this measure, there are now no persons capable of exercising this function. China could therefore not do otherwise than assume jurisdiction over the civil and criminal cases in which Russians resident in China are involved. This measure naturally results from the present situation." [1] The abolition of Russian extraterritorial rights was confirmed by the new treaty between China and Russia, signed on May 31, 1924.[2]

By the treaty of May 20, 1921, Germany renounced her extraterritorial privileges in China and consented to the proposition that thereafter her nationals in China should be subjected to Chinese local jurisdiction.[3]

---

[1] *China Year Book,* 1921-22, pp. 626-632. Quotations are from the unofficial translation of the *Year Book.*

[2] Art. 12, *Chinese Social and Political Science Review,* vol. viii, p. 224.

[3] On May 20, 1921, H. von Borch, " authorized representative of the Government of the Republic of Germany," made a written declaration to Dr. W. W. Yen, Chinese Minister of Foreign Affairs, in which he " formally declares to consent to the abrogation of the consular jurisdiction in China." The declaration was embodied in the Sino-German Commercial Treaty of even date, article 3 of which reads: " They [nationals of each country in the other] shall be placed, their persons

The most recent attempt on the part of China to obtain the consent of the Powers to the abolition of extraterritoriality was made at the Conference on the Limitation of Armament opened in Washington on November 12, 1921. On November 25 of that year, Dr. Chung Hui Wang, representing the Chinese delegation, presented to the Committee on Pacific and Far Eastern Affairs a statement, setting forth China's wishes with regard to the modification and ultimate abolition of consular jurisdiction. Dr. Wang pointed out the following as some of the serious objections to the system of extraterritoriality in China:

(*a*) In the first place, it is in derogation of China's sovereign rights, and is regarded by the Chinese people as a national humiliation.

(*b*) There is a multiplicity of courts in one and the same locality, and the interrelation of such courts has given rise to a legal situation perplexing both to the trained lawyer and to the layman.

(*c*) Disadvantages arise from the uncertainty of the law. The general rule is that the law to be applied in a given case is the law of the defendant's nationality, and so, in a commercial transaction between, say, X and Y of different nationalities, the rights and liabilities of the parties vary according as to whether X sued Y first, or Y sued X first.

(*d*) When causes of action, civil or criminal, arise in which foreigners are defendants, it is necessary for adjudication that they should be carried to the nearest Consular Court, which might be many miles away; and so it often happens that it is practically impossible to obtain the attendance of the necessary witnesses, or to produce other necessary evidence.

(*e*) Finally, it is a further disadvantage to the Chinese that

as well as their properties, under the jurisdiction of the local courts; they shall conform themselves to the laws of the country where they reside." The treaty was ratified by China on July 1, 1921. *China Year Book,* 1921-22, pp. 738 *et seq.*

foreigners in China, under cover of extraterritoriality, claim immunity from local taxes and excises which the Chinese themselves are required to pay.

Dr. Wang then dwelt upon the progress made by China in her judicial reform. He enumerated (1) the Civil Code, still in course of revision; (2) the Criminal Code, in force since 1912; (3) the Code of Civil Procedure; (4) the Code of Criminal Procedure, both of which had just been promulgated; and (5) the Commercial Code, part of which had been put into force. "Then there is a new system of law courts established in 1910. The judges are all modern, trained lawyers, and no one could be appointed a judge unless he had attained the requisite legal training." Dr. Wang declared that the China of today was not like the China of twenty years ago, when Great Britain encouraged her to reform her judicial system, and that, *a fortiori,* she was not the China of eighty years ago, when the system of extraterritoriality was first imposed on her. This, Dr. Wang continued, warranted the wish of China for the progressive modification and ultimate abolition of the system.[1]

A sub-committee was appointed to consider the proposals submitted by China. At the ninth meeting of the Committee of the Whole, November 29, 1921, the Sub-Committee on Extraterritoriality submitted some draft resolutions, which were unanimously adopted by the Committee without further discussion, and later approved, also without discussion, by the Conference at its fourth Plenary Session, held on December 10, 1921. One of the resolutions adopted was:

That the Governments of the Powers above named shall establish a Commission (to which each of such Governments shall appoint one member) to inquire into the present practice of

[1] *Conference on the Limitation of Armament* (Washington, 1922), pp. 932-936.

extraterritorial jurisdiction in China, and into the laws and judicial system and methods of judicial administration in China, and to assist and further the efforts of the Chinese Government to effect such legislation and judicial reforms as would warrant the several Powers in relinquishing, either progressively or otherwise, their respective rights of extraterritoriality.[1]

The resolutions provided that "the Commission herein contemplated shall be constituted within three months after the adjournment of the Conference;" but due to the unsettled conditions in China, the Chinese Government requested and the Powers agreed that the investigation by the Commission be temporarily postponed.[2] Nothing has been heard of the Commission since then. The Chinese Government, on the other hand, has been hard at work in preparation for the long-promised investigation. In June, 1922, the Commission on Extraterritoriality, which had been organized in 1920, was entrusted with "the study of all problems relating to the eventual abolition of consular jurisdiction and other extraterritorial rights and privileges, and the formulation of plans to be laid before the International Commission of Inquiry." In addition to other work, the Commission on Extraterritoriality has undertaken the publication in English and French of the principal modern Chinese legislative enactments, including the Constitutional Laws, organic and political, the Codes, Commercial and Criminal and other Civil Laws, Laws and regulations of the Organization of the Judiciary, the principal Administrative Laws, a summary of the Cases decided in the Supreme Court and in other high judicial tribunals, the Codes of Civil and Criminal Procedure, and the Provisional Criminal Code.

One of the greatest abuses connected with the extraterritorial system in China as well as one of the most unjusti-

[1] *Ibid.*, p. 1010.
[2] New York *Times*, May 4, 1922.

fiable violations of Chinese treaty right is the usurpation by
the foreign Powers of the Shanghai International Mixed
Court. This Court was established in 1864, and though
designated as a mixed court, the latter is a misnomer, for
it was a purely Chinese court having jurisdiction over
Chinese defendants and administering Chinese law.[1] The
judges of the court were, moreover, appointed by the Chinese
Government.

With the outbreak of the Revolution, in 1911, Shanghai
declared its independence of the Manchu dynasty, and the
Taotai was unable to function in the " native city." He
was compelled to ask the permission of the foreign consuls
to exercise his official duties within the International Settlement. The consent of the Diplomatic Corps at Peking was
withheld from this proposition, and the Consular Body was
instructed to exercise such powers of control as might be
necessary to protect foreign life and property and to maintain the status of the International Settlement. Advantage
was taken of this authority to take a highly questionable
step, for which the Powers have not yet atoned. The Consular Body issued, on November 10, 1911, a public proclamation, taking over the International Mixed Court and con-
firming the appointments held by the three Chinese judges.[2]

Thus, the International Mixed Court, which should be,
and up to 1911 was, a purely Chinese court, was peremp-
torily subjected to foreign control by the action of a consular body, who had no diplomatic authority at all and with-

---

[1] According to the revised rules of 1869, "An official having the rank
of Sub-Prefect will be deputed to reside within the foreign Settlements.... He will decide all civil and commercial suits between Chinese
resident within the Settlements, and also between Chinese and foreign
residents, in cases where Chinese are defendants, by Chinese Law."
Hertslet, *China Treaties* (London, 1908), vol. ii, p. 662.

[2] Willoughby, *Foreign Rights and Interests in China* (Baltimore, 1920),
p. 60.

out the slightest legal justification. Though apparently demanded by the circumstances of the time, foreign control had absolutely no right to exist when a recognized government was established in China. And yet the Powers have been slow in restoring the Court to Chinese supervision, and they have repeatedly refused to consider the Chinese demand for its rendition. The Chinese have, however, never ceased to reiterate the demand. Even at this minute, a widespread movement is being sponsored in various centers, looking to the equitable settlement of the question by the Diplomatic Corps at Peking. The details of the correspondence have no place here, both because very little is as yet published [1] and because the Mixed Court issue in China is purely a violation of Chinese treaty right and should not be confused with the question of extraterritoriality, which, though anomalous, has a sound treaty basis.

It may be pointed out that the present policy of the Chinese Government is not to grant extraterritorial rights to any Powers, which have not entered into treaty relations with her and which may desire to do so in future. In October, 1919,

Prime Minister Chin . . . made it quite clear in reply to inquiries that all future treaties between China and the new or old nations would be based absolutely on equality, reciprocity, fairness and justice. This is the new policy of the Chinese Government which is endorsed by all its public servants. This policy was put to a test when the Greek Government in the course of negotiations of a commercial treaty requested that a clause be therein inserted providing for the enjoyment by Greek subjects in Chinese territory of the right of extraterritoriality as

---

[1] See Hollington K. Tong, "The Shanghai Mixed Court and the Settlement Extension," *Millard's Review*, vol. x, pp. 445-454; also *Lei Kuo Tsai Hua Ling Ssu Tsai Pan Chuan Chih Yao* (a résumé of the extraterritorial rights enjoyed by the Powers in China), published by the Commission on Extraterritoriality, appendix i, pp. 23 *et seq.*

enjoyed by subjects or citizens of the other treaty nations. In reply the Chinese Ministry of Foreign Affairs stated that while permitting Greece to have commercial relations with China, it could never grant to her subjects the privilege of extraterritoriality. The reason given was the adoption of a modern judicial system in China to supersede the ancient Oriental judicial system which prevailed in this country formerly when China first came into contact with the Western Powers. . . . [1]

[1] H. K. T., " Extraterritoriality and the New Nations," *Millard's Review*, vol. x (Oct. 25, 1919), p. 314. See also H. K. Tong's report of an interview with Dr. Philip Tyau, Councillor of the Ministry of Foreign Affairs, *ibid.*, vol. x (Dec. 13, 1919), pp. 56-60.

RECAPITULATION AND CONCLUSION

In the foregoing study the author has attempted to show that in its origin extraterritoriality was by no means a novel device contrived at any particular date to meet the special situation existing in any particular country. It was nothing but a legacy of the undefined or, at best, vaguely defined status of the alien in the ancient world, and a survival of the mediaeval theory of the personality of laws, which was once prevalent everywhere in Europe. The fact that there have existed in modern Europe countless vestiges of the latter principle is conclusive evidence of its abiding influence. Writers on international law in the seventeenth and eighteenth centuries, moreover, have not failed to bear testimony to the judicial competence of the foreign consul.

The Mohammedan religion coincided perfectly with the legal conceptions of ancient and mediaeval Europe. The *Koran* ordained the infidel to be outside the pale of Mussulman jurisdiction, and he was compelled to live under his own national laws. Long before the Europeans carried their crusading spirit into the Levant, Mohammed and his descendants had been in the habit of granting to foreigners the right to submit to their own jurisdiction. When the Crusades began, the conditions were favorable to the transplantation of the European system of " judge-consuls " to alien soil. Unwonted commercial opportunities were opened up, and numerous and important interests awaited protection against untoward mishaps. Furthermore, in order to induce the maritime States to keep up their indispensable assistance, the Christian conquerers were obliged to dole out exceptional privileges. These factors combined to establish in the territory conquered by the Crusaders the system of consular jurisdiction.

At the same time, the Mohammedan world was on the point of a steady expansion. Barred by their inborn disposition from seafaring adventure, the Mussulmans were compelled to invite external assistance. To the foreigners who flocked to their coasts they extended the privilege of judicial extraterritoriality, partly as an inducement to their enterprise, partly in deference to the commands of the *Koran,* and partly in accordance with established usage.

In 1453, the Turks conquered Constantinople. In the midst of transcendent glory, the sultans voluntarily perpetuated what is now regarded as the abnormal régime of the Capitulations. The motives responsible for this action were manifold. Influenced by the religious differences which divided Islam and Christendom, by the prospects of commercial development, and, above all, by the force of custom, the sultans left not only the foreign merchants, but also the non-Moslem subjects of the Porte, to follow their own persuasion and government. The grants to the foreigners were made in a series of public acts known as Capitulations. In essence, these Capitulations were gratuitous concessions on the part of the victorious sultans, who made them without the least intention of derogating from their sovereignty. In other countries of the Levant and of the African continent, privileges of the same nature were extended to foreigners.

In the Far East, the origin of extraterritoriality differed entirely from the rise of the Capitulations in the Levant. Neither differences of civilization, nor religious discrepancies, nor commercial considerations could have influenced the establishment of the extraterritorial régime in Eastern Asia. With the exception of Japan, the force of custom was rather against such a régime than in favor of it. The only plausible explanation is to be sought in the alleged imperfections of the native judicial systems. With the merits of the allegation we are not concerned here, but the fact is that in their intercourse with the Eastern Asiatic Powers, Western nations have not infrequently been led to voice their dissatisfaction with the local jurisdiction.

With the introduction of the territorial basis of sovereignty, to which the feudal system signally contributed, the theory of the personality of laws inevitably gave way to that of absolute territorial jurisdiction. In Europe, the system of " judge-consuls " began gradually to decline, and the incumbent of the consular office was forthwith converted into a mere commercial representative, although even there, as described in Chapter I, numerous survivals of the old régime have existed well into comparatively recent times.

Outside of Europe, the system of consular jurisdiction has likewise undergone a process of decline, the inception of which has, however, been late in coming. In the main, this process may be said to have dated from the middle of the nineteenth century. It was in the nineteenth century, as is well known, that the growth of nationalism reached its very climax in Europe. The contagion of national consciousness soon took hold of the entire world, and was destined sooner or later to exert an influence upon the progress of many an awakening race. Imbued with the spirit of nationalism, the peoples which have been burdened with extraterritoriality have realized its absolute incompatibility with their independence and sovereignty. In Turkey, Japan, China, Siam, and every other country where the system has prevailed, attempts have been made to put an end to it and to restore judicial autonomy.

The methods by means of which the abolition of extraterritoriality has been brought about or attempted are (1) annexation, (2) transfer of jurisdiction, (3) separation, (4) protection, (5) unilateral cancellation, and (6) diplomatic negotiation.

Of the reasons which have been responsible for the decline of extraterritoriality, the growth of national sovereignty has undoubtedly been an influential one. In the case of the territories annexed to countries which cede no rights of jurisdiction, the assertion of the principle of sovereignty as disallowing the continuance of the extraterritorial régime is, of course, implied. On the other hand, the independent Powers which have moaned under the yoke of consular jurisdiction have never failed to contend expressly for their sovereign rights in their fight for the restoration of judicial autonomy.

A second dominating reason for the decadence of extraterritoriality is to be found in the innumerable defects and abuses of the system itself. It is true that many efforts have been made by the Powers to remedy these disadvantages. The Mixed Court régime in Egypt and the International Court system in Siam represent conscientious endeavors to remedy some of the evils incident to the operation of conflicting jurisdictions. But there are many abuses inherent in the system, which are neither removable nor remediable. As an eminent authority says: " The actual organization of [consular] jurisdiction is very unsatisfactory in many respects, and it provokes the just complaints of the peoples and governments of the countries where it exists." [1] In elaboration of this statement, another writer makes this remark:

It is futile to find out . . . if a consul and, notably, if the assessors or judges who live so far from their country, in necessary and daily contact with their nationals, can always restrain

[1] Martens, *Traité de droit international* (Paris, 1883-87), vol. ii, p. 132.

themselves from the sometimes involuntary sentiment of weakness, partiality, and indulgence toward their compatriots. I repeat, all that is not indispensable to my subject. In my opinion, the evil is not with the persons; I even affirm, as a general thesis, their capacity and their conscience. It is the institution of consular jurisdiction which is defective and, from all points of view, inferior to the sole jursdiction of the territorial sovereign, from the moment the territorial sovereign possesses a complete judicial organization which responds to the exigencies of the general community of law.[1]

The third and most important reason is the general improvement of the judicial systems in the various countries concerned. Whatever may have been the original justification of extraterritoriality, in the course of time it has come to be adapted to meet the need of coping with a defective system of jurisprudence. As soon as reforms are introduced into the latter, however, it is evidently unjust and unnecessary to maintain an extraterritorial régime. In their claims for the restoration of judicial autonomy, all the governments concerned have invariably made use of this argument, calling the attention of the foreign governments to the reforms, if any, which have been inaugurated. Likewise, in their pledges for immediate or remote consent to the abolition of their extraterritorial rights, governments have been solicitous about conditioning their promises on the judicial guarantees that are offered to the life and property of their nationals. Indeed, even in the case of protectorates, the mere assumption of the power of protection does not necessarily transfer the rights of jurisdiction, which is usually dependent on the maintenance by the protecting Power of regularly constituted judicial authorities in the country over which it exercises protection.

[1] Paternostro, " *La Revision des traités avec le Japon au point de vue de droit international,*" R. D. I., vol. xxiii, p. 176.

Besides these reasons, there have doubtless been others peculiar to the different cases discussed. Sometimes, political as well as commercial considerations have entered into this complex situation. The abandonment of foreign jurisdiction in Japan, for instance, is in a large measure ascribable to the Japanese consent to open the entire country to foreign intercourse. At other times, widely varying conditions have been placed upon the ultimate surrender of extraterritorial jurisdiction. Great Britain gave up her jurisdiction in Madagascar only after France engaged to do likewise in the future in Zanzibar. The United States, in 1914, was unwilling to put an end to her extraterritoriality in Morocco, before certain pending issues regarding American interests in the Shereefian Empire were settled. Still other illustrations might be given, but they are not necessary. For such considerations as have just been pointed out are not essential to the present study, inasmuch as in the first place they are peculiar to each case individually, and in the second place they explain nothing in the continual development of extraterritoriality.

Such, then, is the story of extraterritoriality. It grew up at a time when the principle of territorial sovereignty was unknown. It has steered its course through centuries of legal transformation, and in its journey has kept abreast of the times. Now that the science of international law is developed to a point where territorial sovereignty has become the cornerstone of state existence, extraterritoriality is doomed to decay. For one reason or another, it has not completely disappeared from the structure of international intercourse. It is believed, however, that from an understanding of the salient facts connected with the rise and decline of consular jurisdiction, those countries whose judicial power is still impaired may take fresh impetus in their attempt to get rid of the yoke of extraterritoriality, and those countries which are still beneficiaries of this system may realize that it is a decadent institution and that reasonable demands for its progressive abrogation should at times be countenanced and granted. The interests of justice and fairness will best be served by the conscientious endeavor of the one side to improve the judicial system and of the other to refrain from introducing into what is primarily a legal question irrelevant considerations of a political nature.